Tortured

Tortured

When Good Soldiers
Do Bad Things

JUSTINE SHARROCK

WILEY

John Wiley & Sons, Inc.

7/10
wkf

Published by John Wiley & Sons, Inc., Hoboken, New Jersey
Published simultaneously in Canada

For general information about our other products and services, please contact our Customer Care Department within the United States at (800) 762-2974, outside the United States at (317) 572-3993 or fax (317) 572-4002.

Wiley also publishes its books in a variety of electronic formats. Some content that appears in print may not be available in electronic books. For more information about Wiley products, visit our web site at www.wiley.com.

Library of Congress Cataloging-in-Publication Data:
Sharrock, Justine, date.
  Tortured: when good soldiers do bad things
    p.   cm.
  Includes index.
  ISBN 978-0-470-45403-9 (cloth); ISBN 978-0-470-59281-6 (ebk);
  ISBN 978-0-470-59312-7 (ebk); ISBN 978-0-470-59313-4 (ebk)
    1. Torture–United States. 2. Iraq War, 2003—Prisoners and prisons, American. 3. Prisoners of war–Abuse of–Iraq. 4. Prisoners of war–Abuse of–Cuba–Guantánamo Bay Naval Base. 5. Guantánamo Bay Detention Camp. 6. Abu Ghraib Prison. I. Title.
  HV8599.U6S53 2010
  956.7044'3–dc22
                                                                    2009037588

Printed in the United States of America
10 9 8 7 6 5 4 3 2 1

Contents

Acknowledgments

This book could not have been possible without the help of my parents, Juliet and Nigel Sharrock; my sisters, Emily and Penelope; and my brother-in-law, Leo. Thank you for your constant support and encouragement.

It was Dale Maharidge who helped me with the initial vision of this project and saw its potential as a book. He pushed me to be a better writer and, as he put it, kept me climbing that ten-thousand-foot wall of ice. Without Dale's guidance and mentorship, I would not be where I am today.

My editor, Eric Nelson, was extraordinary with his feedback, insight, and encouragement. My agent, Amy Rennert, had faith in this project when others thought torture was a passing issue. My eternal gratitude to you both.

I want to thank everyone else at Wiley, including production editor Lisa Burstiner. My thanks also to Nikki Gloudeman and Taylor Wiles for their excellent fact-checking.

I am especially grateful to the soldiers themselves, particularly Chris Arendt, Joe Darby, Andy Duffy, and Brandon Neely, without whose candor, bravery, and answers to my endless questions there would be no book. This project was in many ways a collaborative effort. I am honored to have had the chance to help tell their stories.

I would also like to thank the many people who welcomed me into their homes and their lives, especially Kari and Tim Vivoda, Sarah Schulte, and Wendy Neely.

Introduction

On April 28, 2004, the infamous photos of the abuse at Abu Ghraib were broadcast to television sets around the world. We saw the now iconic image of the black-hooded detainee standing on the box with his arms outstretched, electrodes attached to his body. We saw naked men wearing women's underwear on their heads, chained in contorted positions to metal beds; naked prisoners stacked into pyramids; and prisoners on all fours wearing dog collars and leashes. For many, it was a moment of American shame, our moral standing now tarnished in the eyes of the world.

But for a large portion of Americans, especially those with military ties, the whole thing was blown out of proportion. In an ABC/*Washington Post* poll in the wake of the scandal, 60 percent of respondents classified what happened at Abu Ghraib as mere abuse, not torture. Keeping detainees naked and awake all night? That's no big deal. Making them stand for hours? Who cares? Even Secretary of Defense Donald Rumsfeld, in approving a 2002 list of "counter-resistance techniques," scribbled an addendum asking, "I stand for 8–10 hours a day. Why is standing limited to four hours?" As late as 2007, 68 percent of Americans told Pew Research pollsters that they sometimes consider torture an acceptable option when dealing with terrorists. While traveling across the country, speaking with ordinary Americans, I heard a common refrain: "At most, we are embarrassing them. What we did was nothing compared to what those terrorists did to us." Repeatedly I heard, "If we don't fight dirty, we will be fighting the war over here."

Particularly in the wake of the September 11 attacks, Americans' thirst for revenge knew no bounds. People argued that having to abide by the Geneva Conventions when the enemy wasn't doing so meant that we were tying our hands behind our backs. Chief Warrant Officer Lewis Welshofer, who used "harsh interrogation techniques," once told me, "Having played sports all my life, I apply the adage that if you are going to play, you better play to win. When you are at war and people are dying, there is no more appropriate time or place to apply that sentiment." It almost makes sense, until you find out that Welshofer killed an Iraqi insurgency leader by suffocating him in a sleeping bag during an interrogation.

When I first read the reports about the abuses, I wanted to hear the story from the perspectives of the men and the women involved, not from redacted documents and military representatives. My first inclination as a journalist was to seek out the soldiers who had committed the most heinous acts. I wanted to get the "good stuff"—the kinds of gruesome stories that make headlines. I interviewed Gary Pittman, who was charged with assault in connection with the death of a former Baath Party official. This official was found dead in an Iraqi prison, lying in the dirt, handcuffed, hooded, and covered in feces, with several ribs broken. I spoke with Damien Corsetti, who was dubbed "the King of Torture," for his role as the "bad cop" called in to rough up detainees during the notoriously abusive interrogations at the Bagram prison. I interviewed Alan Driver, who had been charged in relation to the deaths of two detainees at Bagram. They had been chained to the ceiling and beaten repeatedly, so it was hard to prove which individual was responsible for the fatal blow. I wrote letters to Charles Graner, who was serving a ten-year sentence for his role as the so-called ringleader in the infamous photographed Abu Ghraib abuse. I exchanged e-mails briefly with Chief Warrant Officer Lewis Welshofer, the officer convicted of suffocating that Iraqi insurgency leader. I traveled around the United States, visiting small college towns, suburbs, big cities, rural plains, the hills of Appalachia, and sprawling no-man's lands of strip malls. I spoke with dozens of soldiers who had worked in prisons in Iraq, Afghanistan, and Guantanamo Bay, Cuba.

Yet it wasn't the high-level officials making the policy decisions or the intelligence officers inside interrogation rooms who taught me the most about America's relationship to torture. It was the low-level soldiers working on the blocks, mostly using techniques that have been dismissed as so-called "torture lite."

There are CIA agents waterboarding al Qaeda suspects in black sites, but just as crucial are the regular low-ranking soldiers, the working stiffs, who are waking up detainees throughout the night, shackling them to the floor, and throwing sandbags over their heads.

It was strange to think that these young all-American men could be counted as our country's torturers. They were run-of-the-mill blue-collar folks—the guy next door, the kid in the back of your high school classroom, the teenager bagging your groceries. They seemed so ordinary, and what they described often sounded so banal—and they represented the most common experience of life inside the prisons.

Euphemisms like "torture lite," "harsh techniques," and "softening up" are used to describe the kinds of things these soldiers were doing to the detainees. But they are none of these; they are torture. Granted, putting someone in a small cage, making them miss one night of sleep or a couple of meals, might not seem particularly harsh. But when used in combination, as is often done in U.S. detention centers overseas, and over an extended period of time—sometimes daily over the course of years—these techniques are torture.

The torture debate centers on the permissibility of things such as waterboarding, yet it never even broaches the topics of solitary confinement, short-shackling, and sleep deprivation. The legal definition of torture is based on the level of intensity, a nuance that the administration, its lawyers, the military, the perpetrators, and even the general public have tried to turn into a loophole. How much pain is too much? How bad does something have to be in order to qualify as torture? Many of these techniques were purposely used because they didn't cause bloody injuries that could be easily documented by the Red Cross. The United States has admitted that it is violating the Geneva Conventions, but instead of recognizing that this implies committing war crimes, it has simply argued that those rules don't apply.

Part of the reason the United States has been able to pull off its torture regime is that it was hidden in plain sight. The process was normalized and sanitized, through rhetorical tricks, dubious legal arguments, and bureaucratic rigmarole, making it more palatable for the public and simpler for soldiers.

So-called torture lite has been proven to cause complete psychological breakdowns, permanent physical ailments, and sometimes death. Forced standing, for instance, causes ankles to swell to twice their size within twenty-four hours, which makes walking excruciating. Some prisoners faint and even suffer kidney failure. A 2007 study published in the *Archives of General Psychiatry* reported that treatments such as forced stress positions, blindfolding, threats against one's family, and sleep deprivation cause the same level of mental suffering, traumatic stress, and long-term psychological outcomes as physical torture. They have a long international history as proven effective torture techniques, used in regimes around the world and throughout time. No matter how you spin it, these techniques are torture.

Mostly, these soldiers described the work as boring. Leaving a detainee in a restraint chair out in the blazing sun for days with no food or water requires hardly any work from a soldier. But it is horrific in a way that was hard for them to explain to people who expected stories of bodies blown to bits. Seeing detainees be slowly destroyed, both physically and mentally, hearing them moaning like animals throughout the night and feeling the weight of their bodies was just a slower and more insidious way to fight an enemy.

These techniques broke down not only prisoners but also the U.S. soldiers who were, on a certain level, trapped inside those prisons. I interviewed a junior guard working at the same prison as Welshofer. Instead of suffocating people during interrogations, he was ordered to keep detainees standing and awake throughout the night in hot Conex containers. He was softening the detainees up for often-abusive interrogations but never even laid a hand on one himself—yet he came home a broken man, racked with guilt. Everyone has a different breaking point.

As Albert Camus explained, torture is a crime that attacks both the victim and the perpetrator. It has proved to be so insidious a machine that every cog—even those merely associated with it—is affected.

Drafting memos, writing signatures, and issuing orders happen at a safe distance. By contrast, low-level soldiers had to stare torture directly in the face. They signed up to serve and defend their country, only to find that it led them down a dark road, from which they are now struggling to return. They were sent off to war to be heroes, only to become torturers.

When I first set off to interview the rank-and-file guards and interrogators tasked with implementing the administration's torture guidelines, I thought they'd never talk openly. They would be embarrassed, guilt ridden, living in silent shame in communities that would ostracize them if they knew of their histories. What I found instead were young men hiding their regrets from neighbors who wanted to celebrate them as war heroes. They seemed relieved to talk with me about things no one else wanted to hear—not just about the acts themselves, but also about the guilt, pain, and anger they felt along with pride and righteousness about their service. They struggled with these things, wanted to make sense of them—even as the nation seemed determined to dismiss the whole matter and move on.

On September 15, 2003, twenty-seven-year-old Alyssa Peterson shot and killed herself with her service rifle while stationed at a prison in northwestern Iraq. After only two interrogation sessions, she said she could no longer withstand having to abuse the prisoners and refused her orders to continue. Although the military destroyed records of what techniques she used, her first sergeant, James D. Hamilton, told investigators that it was "hard for her to be aggressive to prisoners, as she felt that we were cruel to them." Unfortunately, Alyssa's story is not an anomaly.

Foreign policy scholars fear that the fallout from Abu Ghraib has already weakened the U.S. military's antiterrorism capabilities. Lawyers warn about war-crime tribunals and the implications of these legal precedents that dismiss the Geneva Conventions. Critics of the administration's interrogation policies warn that the ramifications will be felt across the globe, including by Americans unlucky enough to be imprisoned abroad. To anyone who is following this closely, the immense strategic risks of going from human rights advocate to human rights abuser are well understood. Yet no one is discussing the repercussions already being felt here at home. It's the soldiers tying the sandbags around Iraqis' necks and blaring the foghorns throughout the night who are reeling as a result. More than guilt or shame, the soldiers I interviewed described a deep-seated rage at having been betrayed. They thought they were nobly defending America, only to find themselves following orders that crossed moral lines. They were told that what they were doing was legal, yet they were committing war crimes. Even within war, there are certain lines that should not be crossed. In this war—and the next and the next—someone will always argue that there is a line, a moral line, that divides us from our enemies. People will argue that some techniques can be used, whereas we must leave certain strategies to the other side and their evil ways. But that line has a habit of being redrawn. In these military prisons, the unthinkable became thinkable.

Once the soldiers realized—sometimes years later—that their country had used them up and spat them out as disposable tools for implementing torture, this realization shattered their lives, and their very sense of who they are in the world. Betrayed, cast aside, they were left adrift to try to make sense of the horrors they had seen and to understand who they had become. That kind of suffering is not as immediately obvious as the death tolls, and is easier to dismiss.

Like many Americans, U.S. soldiers had agreed to the country's decision to torture without fully understanding its repercussions. Now, they understood at the most personal intimate level that yes, America is a country that tortures. Now the soldiers are left to grapple with this question: what is the point of fighting for your country if the way in which you fight means losing yourself and the ideals you are trying to defend?

PART ONE

Brandon Neely

1

Shoot First, Think Later

Brandon Neely was the first soldier to beat up a detainee at Guantanamo prison camp when it opened in 2002. In Iraq, he was on the battlefield the day the war began. He was an integral part in two of perhaps the most historic and infamous moments of his generation. In Iraq, it didn't take long for Brandon to become disillusioned with the military and conclude that what he was doing was neither noble nor heroic. But when it came to Guantanamo, that process took him four and a half years.

For Brandon, who was raised as an Army brat and moved from base to base throughout the South, the military had always been a major part of his life. When he was ten years old, his dad took him down to the shooting range and showed him how to assemble, disassemble, and fire an M16 rifle. Even then, he admired the power and authority his father, a high-ranking military officer, had. Soldiers had to complete any menial or difficult task his father ordered with a "Sir, yes, sir!" But on the whole, his dad left the military at work and didn't bring his job home.

He always told Brandon and his sister, "You can sign up, but college first." Brandon, more concerned with football and partying than discipline and drill, wasn't interested anyway.

If he had gone to college, Brandon says, he would have spent all of his time at frat keggers, not in class. So, instead of wasting his parents' money, he bagged groceries after graduating from high school. But one summer day a few days after his twentieth birthday, he woke up and realized he was wasting his life. He was still living the life of a teenager—even working the same job he'd had in high school. It dawned on him that instead of college, he could escape his hometown, get some training, and make something of himself by enlisting in the Army.

When Brandon gets an idea in his head, he becomes doggedly determined to follow through. His dad said that he had never seen Brandon run so fast as when he got out of the car to go to the recruiting station. The recruiter offered to show him a video, but Brandon said no. He already knew what he wanted. When he was a kid, he had met some military police officers on base, and they had made an impression on him. He had already done the research and was ready to sign the five-year contract as an MP.

Graduating from basic training was the proudest moment of Brandon's life. For the first time, he knew what people meant by a true sense of accomplishment and honor. He was no longer an ordinary guy. He was a warrior.

When people describe the gung ho soldier, they are thinking of someone like Brandon. Being a soldier was something that Brandon was good at. It fit his personality. He thrived under the discipline; he didn't have to make decisions about what to do but simply give his all when carrying out orders. He always kept his uniform freshly pressed and his boots shined. He liked the power he felt with a gun in his hand and knew how intimidating he could look. The more hours he dedicated to weight lifting, the more imposing his physique became.

On September 11, 2001, Brandon was stationed at Fort Hood, Texas. Immediately after he saw the towers fall on television, his officers ordered him to grab his M4 carbine and M9 pistol; they set up tight security on the base and searched every vehicle entering the gate. Brandon had never heard of al Qaeda, and he couldn't point out Afghanistan on a map. All he needed to know was that America had been attacked, and he was in a position to do something about it. His unit was already set to deploy to Egypt, and although it wasn't Afghanistan, it was a chance for Brandon to play a part in a large global emergency. His country needed him, and he was ready to make something of his life. He was ready for revenge and for war.

The few months' deployment in Egypt turned out to be a letdown—boring, in fact. So on January 5, 2002, when a squad leader came pounding on his door looking for volunteers for some missions with other units, Brandon jumped at the chance. He didn't even know where they would send him, but he wanted to get in on the action. Within forty-eight hours, he was told he was going to Cuba, to set up a prison to hold terrorist suspects. Brandon had no idea what to expect. He was disappointed not to be going to Afghanistan, but all the same, that night as he lay in bed, on the brink of embarking on the unknown, he had butterflies in his stomach.

The naval base at Guantanamo Bay, Cuba, has apartments, a school, swimming pools, movie theaters, and even bars. But when Brandon and his unit arrived, they drove past all that, to a group of makeshift military tents where they would be staying. Down the hill from their tents was a collection of three hundred cages spread over a large area covered with rocks, known as Camp X-Ray.

The cells were nothing more than dog kennels, completely exposed to the elements and the giant banana rats, lizards, and scorpions that roamed the camp. Civilian contractors were still constructing it out of old fencing and posts scavenged from around the island.

Looking around, Brandon simply thought, "Thank God I'm not staying down there." Beyond that, he didn't dwell much more on the detainees' situation.

Soldiers were given the rundown. First, never use the word *prisoner*. They were detainees in a detention center, not prisoners of war. Prisoners have rights; detainees have no rights. A whole new set of military laws would be replacing the Geneva Conventions. This was the first time anyone had ever run—or even conceived of—such an operation. This was a new kind of war, unlike any other that had been fought before. They were making history.

While the administration was publicly declaring that "we don't do torture," lawyers at the White House were concocting legal loopholes that exempted the United States from the Geneva Conventions and other laws outlawing torture. Al Qaeda was not a conventional army that represented a state; the terrorist organization did not abide by the same military rules, and therefore, the lawyers erroneously argued, the Geneva Conventions did not apply. Alberto Gonzales, then White House chief counsel, called the conventions "quaint" and "obsolete." In what are now known as the torture memos, White House lawyers explained that the United States could legally abandon its commitment to uphold military laws. Reversing a long tradition of American norms and laws, these memos laid down a path for the widespread, systematic use of torture.

January 11, 2002, was detainee arrival day. Brandon felt high with anticipation, waiting for his chance to finally meet the terrorists face-to-face. "I was ready to seek my own personal revenge on these people in whatever manner I could," he says. The World Trade Center attack was still fresh in his and the other soldiers' minds. They were ready to kick some hajji ass.

All the same, as the soldiers gathered around waiting, an intense silence enveloped the camp. The men who would be arriving were the "worst of the worst," capable of masterminding 9/11. Who knows what else they could be capable of? Brandon's escort partner told him that in case anything happened, he had Brandon's back.

Marines with .50 caliber guns escorted the first busload of detainees. When the doors opened, they threw the detainees down off the bus, yelling, "Shut the fuck up, sand nigger! You're property of the United States of America now."

The first detainee off the bus had only one leg. The MPs, who caught him, screamed at him to walk faster as they half-dragged him along. Eventually, a marine threw the man's prosthesis after him. The second detainee off the bus was handed off to Brandon and his partner.

The detainees were an odd sight in their orange jumpsuits. They wore hoods, black gloves, surgical masks, earmuffs, and gunner goggles blacked out with tape—in other words, they were in a state of complete and total sensory deprivation, which has been scientifically proven to cause mental breakdowns. They had been unable to see, hear, or move for the entire seventeen-hour journey from the Middle East. Most of them had urinated or defecated on themselves. Some had their handcuffs and leg shackles fastened so tightly that their wrists were bloody and their ankles swollen and turning colors. Soldiers had tied the waist chains that connected to the prisoners' legs too short, preventing them from being able to fully stand upright. MPs later bragged about punching and kicking the detainees throughout the trip. When the detainees' goggles were eventually removed, the collected sweat and tears poured out and ran off their faces, as they squinted to adjust to the light. They were a dirty, weak, bedraggled lot—not quite the hardened terrorists the soldiers had prepared themselves to face. Most of them were barely five foot five and maybe 120 pounds. It seemed unbelievable that this was what terrorists looked like close up.

The soldiers' orders were to force the detainees to walk head down so that they couldn't see where they were going, and to transport them as quickly as possible. Eventually, the soldiers made a game of it, competing to see who could move the detainees the fastest. In their leg irons, the detainees couldn't keep up and were dragged along the rocks. If they were lucky, they could pick up their feet and let the soldiers carry them.

First, the soldiers delivered the detainees to the holding pen, where they were made to kneel with their faces down in the gravel under the blazing sun. Some stayed that way for hours, until, one by one, they were escorted to the in-processing center and then to their cages. The detainees were made to sit in the middle of their cages and were forbidden to move, talk, or even look up. The detainees weren't allowed to know which country they were being held in. Brandon and the others would mess with them, telling them a different location every time they asked: Russia, Iran. "Your whole country has been nuked," the MPs told them. "It looks like a parking lot now. Your friends, family, house—everything is gone."

Each prisoner was given two buckets: one for water, one for a toilet, which the guards had to empty. (Eventually, the guards let certain detainees empty the buckets, an opportunity the detainees jumped at, if only to get some exercise.) Each was also given a sheet but wasn't allowed to use it to cover himself as he defecated into the bucket or tried to sleep. Bright stadium floodlights shone down on the detainees, day and night. In case that wasn't enough to deprive them of sleep, every hour Brandon and the other guards woke them up, forcing them to show their hands to ensure that they didn't have any weapons. For a while, blaring music was played over the PA system. Brandon could make out some of the songs, like Bruce Springsteen's "Born in the USA," but mostly it was so loud that he couldn't even figure out the song. Other times, though, the camp was dead silent.

• • •

That first day, as Brandon was putting an elderly man in his cage, he, as ordered, threw the man down on his knees inside the cage and began to remove his shackles. As an MP, he was well versed on handcuffing, but here the Army was using a complicated combination of leg and arm shackles attached together by a waist belt. An interpreter told the detainee to place his hands on top of his head and not to move. Brandon held the man by his shoulders, while his partner removed the leg shackles. The detainee tensed up and tried to get away. Brandon yelled at him to stop, but then as Brandon and his partner unlocked the first handcuff, the man jerked away. Acting on instinct, Brandon threw the detainee to the ground with all of his body weight. Each time the detainee tried to raise his head, Brandon bashed it back down on the cement floor, over and over.

Brandon's partner freaked out and ran out of the cage, leaving Brandon alone with the man. Later, the soldier was reprimanded for abandoning Brandon and making him do all of the work. Eventually, other soldiers arrived, hog-tied the detainee, and left him like that for hours, until the officer in charge delivered the release orders.

Brandon had the honor of being the first soldier to get to beat up a terrorist. That night, soldiers kept coming up to him to congratulate him. "Nice job, man, you really got some," they said, patting him on the back. It felt good to be getting so much praise, but Brandon says he was left oddly unsettled. For the first time, following the rules led him to do something he wasn't quite sure was right.

From day one, it was drilled into soldiers' heads that they would never be given an order that the higher-ups wouldn't do or that would compromise the integrity of the United States in any way. In order for operations to run smoothly, soldiers have to be able to automatically follow orders. There is no time to stop and question the strategy. As a gung ho soldier, Brandon had complete faith in the military. He trusted his commanders with his life. Why would they lead him astray by asking him to do anything that was less than honorable?

Brandon still has a hard time articulating exactly how he felt after this incident. People don't get it when he says that it was justified but that he still thought it was wrong. He had performed his duty well and hadn't broken any rules. War is war. But all the same, he had a nagging feeling that bashing the old man's head was wrong. The man might have been a terrorist, but he was old enough to be someone's grandfather. The next day when Brandon saw the bruises and the cuts covering the detainee's face, he felt worse.

A couple of days later, Brandon found out that the detainee had assumed that he was being placed on his knees for execution, as had happened to his friends and family back home. The news made the whole thing even harder to digest.

Even while Brandon had his doubts, every morning before the soldiers marched down to Camp X-Ray, they were reminded of the importance of their work in guarding these terrorists. "You are the front line of this war," their commanders said. "In terms of winning the war, everything will start and end with what happens at Guantanamo. You are saving your own families, your kids, your wives, your mothers. Keep the terrorists locked up and uncomfortable, do your job well, and the world will be safe." The soldiers headed down to the cells feeling pumped up and proud.

One morning when Brandon and the others entered the block, they heard some detainees talking. "What the hell?" the soldiers asked one another. The detainees weren't allowed to do that.

They found out that the International Red Cross had inspected the camp and called for changes. Detainees were allowed to talk and move about within their cages, and they were told they were in Cuba. What was next, the guards asked one another, issuing cigarettes?

Brandon said that having the Red Cross there made him think that what the soldiers were doing was okay. Otherwise, he figured, the Red Cross would intercede. However, the Red Cross only offers confidential suggestions to the country in question, which the country can implement or not in any way it chooses. Unbeknownst to Brandon and the other soldiers, there was much that the Red Cross did not approve of that was not changed. The detainees were given small concessions, but conditions were still harsh and interrogation methods brutal. Moreover, every time a new shipment of detainees was brought in, the soldiers reverted to the old rules: no talking, no moving, no praying.

Mostly the work was boring, and Brandon felt that his training was going to waste. Filled with 9/11 fervor and anger at Arabs, he was trained to kill, not babysit detainees. He was angry with the amorphous enemy for attacking his country and for his being stuck in a useless prison doing nothing about it. Soldiers were sent off to war with hopes and promises of being heroes—real men—seeing combat and helping America win. Brandon had imagined marching with his fellow soldiers onto the battlefield, risking his life to protect his comrades and his country and coming home with heroic tales of glory. At the prison he had even fewer opportunities to wage war than he had had in Egypt. Despite his superiors' rhetoric, he was just a cage kicker.

There was one assignment that seemed like it could be an opportunity for some real action: the Initial Reaction Force (IRF) teams, five-man riot squads that were brought in to deal with prisoners who had broken the rules. Brandon was selected to join the first of the squads. They received two days of training—more than on any other aspect of detainee handling. Dressed in full riot gear, with shields, batons, and kneepads, the IRF (pronounced "erf") team would enter the cage. The first man would use a shield almost as if it were a weapon, to throw the detainee to the ground, as the other four would grab a limb and hog-tie the detainee. During training, members of the IRF team revved one another up by drumming their batons across their shields. They were told to use as much force as possible and that this was their chance "to get some."

Calling in the IRFs, while not a daily affair, was common enough. Any time a detainee lost the privilege of using one of his comfort items—a blanket, a toothbrush, or a mat—the IRF team was called in to attack the detainee first. If a detainee exercised, cussed, or tried to talk to another detainee, he was attacked. A member of the medical team, unable to get a detainee to swallow a can of Ensure, called in an IRF. Detainees were IRFed if they refused medication and the officer in charge figured that technically this situation was similar enough. After the team hogtied the detainee, the medic entered the cage. Noticing Brandon looking on, the medic told him to stand a little to the left. Then the medic grabbed the detainee by the neck and tried to force the liquid down his throat, spilling it all over his face. The medic punched the detainee twice in the face and walked out as if nothing had happened. When Brandon turned around to leave, he realized that the medic had placed him in that position to block the line of sight from the watchtower.

This was the kind of thing that Brandon had hoped he would get to do at the prison. Finally, Brandon thought, something akin to being a tough soldier and not just a guard.

There was one IRF attack, though, that upset Brandon. Detainee Jumah al Dossari had been taunting a female guard, calling her a bitch. Even though male soldiers themselves are known to harass the women, they are extremely protective when detainees do the same. One soldier, Sergeant E-5 Starsky Smith, a giant 240-pound man who was infamous around the camps for abusing prisoners, felt pissed at Jumah's insolence. When the officer in charge called Smith and his IRF team in, Smith tossed his shield aside, took a running jump, and landed with his knee on Jumah's back. The female guard stood by, yelling, "Whip his ass!" Smith proceeded to grab the prisoner's head and slam it into the floor, over and over. Even after Jumah stopped moving, the team continued to rail on him, hitting, punching, and kicking him as he lay on the floor. Next, they gave the female guard a chance, holding the man down as she punched his head a couple of times.

The guards left the cell with their arms and uniforms covered in blood. Jumah was carried out on a stretcher and was hospitalized for two weeks for broken ribs and a broken wrist, not to mention bruising and lacerations. When soldiers tried to mop the floor of the cell, the soapy water turned bright with blood. They tried scrubbing and using hoses, but the cement remained tinged.

Brandon had watched the whole thing. It was quiet on his section of the block, and so, curious, he had walked over to get a closer look. Because you could see right through the metal cages, everyone could watch. Most of the soldiers were laughing and cheering, but Brandon says his reaction was one of disbelief. It was hard to process what was happening. These soldiers weren't bad people, and this guy—this terrorist—shouldn't have called that woman a bitch. But it seemed as if the soldiers were taking it too far. All the same, war is war.

That night the soldiers laughed about what had happened. According to Brandon, the officer in charge joked that he had never heard his name and "war crimes" mentioned so many times in one sentence. The whole incident had been filmed, as was the customary procedure, but afterward, the MPs said that the tape had been lost.

Even if Brandon had disagreed, there was no way that he would say anything. He was new to the unit, and besides, it wasn't his place. Who knew what kind of ostracism and repercussions he could face? In that kind of environment, you simply don't want to take that risk.

A week later, Brandon was assigned to work the block where Jumah was being held. When Smith showed up, Feroz Abbasi, another detainee, yelled, "Sergeant, have you come back to finish him off?"

Soldiers had a way of turning even seemingly routine tasks into opportunities for abuse. The soldiers mocked the detainees' language and played music during prayer calls. Detainees were allowed to take short showers, and some guards turned off the water while the detainees were still soaped up. Other guards took away the detainees' meals before they had a chance to finish.

Brandon saw a Navy physician perform violent rectal exams on new arrivals. Without lubrication, the doctor "just reached back and shoved his finger as hard as he could in their rectums." His fellow MPs told him that other doctors were doing the same, often while laughing. Brandon didn't see those, but they all heard the prisoners screaming. There was a physical therapist who, showing off for Brandon, stretched a detainee's arm straight, although the man could barely move it on his own because of a sustained injury. "You want to really watch him scream?" the medic asked, laughing, doing it again and again.

After work and on their days off, Brandon and his group of friends mostly hung out at the beach, snorkeling, fishing, and swimming, or at the outdoor bar, getting drunk on dollar beers. They played sports, went to the movies, and grabbed burgers at McDonald's. With so much to do, Brandon never felt homesick and rarely called home.

During downtime, no one talked about what happened on the block. It was the last thing anyone wanted to think about. Brandon says that maybe it was just because the work was so boring, but there was a certain understanding that whatever happens on the block stays on the block. "When your shift was up, you'd just leave the camp and go wake boarding," says Brandon. "We just blocked it out and did our own thing."

At times, it seemed like they weren't even deployed and certainly were not at war. It seemed unreal and jarring on those days off when they remembered that only two miles away from them, all hell was letting loose.

Every now and then, Brandon and a friend would ask each other, "Is this shit really going on?" This particular friend was a military history buff, who had spent some time at college and read up on all kinds of military regulations. Having been in the Army for two years, he had the most Army experience of all of Brandon's friends. He told Brandon that what they were doing was illegal, according to the Geneva Conventions, and despite what they were being told, the conventions always apply. Brandon didn't believe him. Technically, they had received training on the Geneva Conventions during basic, but Brandon said that it barely lasted twenty minutes, and the commander told them that they would never need to know any of it in the field. Like most soldiers, Brandon barely paid any attention. When Brandon looked it up on the Internet, he saw what the guy was talking about. Oh, shit, he thought.

All the same, Brandon figured that the high-ranking officials must have a greater grasp on the confusing legality of the issue than a low-ranking soldier like himself, who had never even gone to college. He was repeatedly told that he would never be given an illegal order. Even the unit's motto, inscribed on each man's patch under a skull with lightning bolts, read "Demonstrate Lawfulness Throughout the World." As a trained soldier, he knew right from wrong on the battlefield. But here, those rules didn't apply, and the lines were confusing. Camp Delta's Standard Operating Procedures Manual wasn't published until March 2003, nine months after Brandon left. Before that, they were making it up as they went along. The officers repeatedly told the MPs that it wasn't their jurisdiction to figure out what was legal or illegal. It was their job to follow orders and react, not question. "In the military, if you start thinking for yourself," says Brandon, "you become dangerous and they don't want you around."

When Brandon saw news reports about the camp, they were troublingly inaccurate. Why was the military trying to hide this from the public if it was legal? But on the other hand, he figured, maybe their operations were classified. That happens all the time during war—some soldiers weren't even allowed to tell their families where they were deploying next. Besides, he figured, so what if they had to bend the rules a little in order to get information to save American lives?

It's understandable that Brandon was confused about where to draw the line. The nation as a whole, after all, has been unable to reach such a conclusion, even with acts as extreme as partial drowning.

According to U.S. law, torture is an "act committed by a person acting under the color of law specifically intended to inflict severe physical or mental pain or suffering (other than pain or suffering incidental to lawful sanctions) upon another person within his custody or physical control." But the Department of Justice's Office of Legal Counsel parsed this definition, just as they did the label "prisoner of war." The lawyers seized on the meaning of *severe*, arguing that to count as torture, the pain had to be "equivalent in intensity to the pain accompanying serious physical injury, such as organ failure, impairment of bodily function, or even death." Moreover, that pain had to be "specifically intended." If there was any way to prove that it wasn't done on purpose—say, if a doctor were present or the perpetrator didn't realize how much it could hurt the detainee—then, legally, it wasn't torture.

Rumors escalated among the soldiers about who the prisoners really were. An E-7 told Brandon that some terrorists were of such high value that they were directly taken to a naval brig to be held in isolation. Other MPs who worked at the brig said that children were also being held, a fact that has since been confirmed.

Sometimes, when Brandon was bored on the blocks, he started up casual conversations with the English-speaking detainees. He often talked with a British detainee, Rhuhel Ahmed, who was only one year younger than he was. Ahmed had been captured while traveling in Afghanistan with two other UK detainees; this group is now known as the Tipton Three. Brandon was told that the detainees were the most dangerous in the world and not to interact with them or show any compassion. But Rhuhel seemed like an ordinary kid. Sometimes Rhuhel helped translate what other detainees were trying to say, which made Brandon's job that much easier. They talked about girls and going out on the town. "The kind of thing anyone their age would talk about," says Brandon. They discovered that they had the same taste in music, and occasionally Rhuhel rapped for Brandon. To Brandon, it sometimes seemed as if he and Rhuhel were just two regular guys, eating the same MRE bagels for breakfast and drinking tea together—except for the wire fencing that separated them. All the same, Brandon stood by as Rhuhel got IRFed, taken to interrogations, and later put in solitary.

Brandon was unsure whether following these orders was right or wrong. The only thing he knew for certain was that it was something that he had to do, so why even think about it? "After a while," he says, "it was just, keep your shit clean, go home, and forget about that place. Let's just get the hell out of here."

Brandon arrived home from Cuba on a Friday, got married that Monday to a girl he'd been e-mailing while deployed, and reported back to duty on Tuesday. There were no debriefings or exit forms beyond a nondisclosure statement in which Brandon and all the soldiers agreed not to share information about Guantanamo.

The welcome-home ceremony was rinky-dink in comparison to what soldiers would have had if they were coming home from the battlefield. Girlfriends and families gathered, but there was little fanfare. First the general cracked a joke that all they had done in Cuba was water ski, swim, and fish, which garnered a lot of laughs. But then, on a more serious note, he congratulated the men and thanked them for guarding the world's most dangerous detainees and stopping the terrorists from killing anyone else. Everyone cheered and clapped. Brandon felt good to have people shake his hand and thank him when they heard about his service. Any doubts he might have had were washed away.

Brandon didn't talk about the prison—not with his family, his friends, or even other soldiers—and no one asked him any questions. Within his unit, it was a nonissue, and the MPs were back to work with lots to do. Mostly, Brandon figured he would never see the camp again, and particularly since everyone who ever serves at Guantanamo has to sign that nondisclosure statement, he would probably never even hear another word about it.

Guantanamo was hardly in the news, so no one at home seemed to think much of it. Instead, there was talk about Saddam Hussein's connection to al Qaeda and the possible existence of weapons of mass destruction. Compared to that, a small jail in Cuba was hardly newsworthy.

Brandon told Wendy, his new wife, stories about jet skiing and snorkeling and described how beautiful the beaches and the sunsets were. It sounded like fun, and she was glad he hadn't been in any danger. "Just like any other normal person, I didn't think anything of it," she says.

When it came to explaining the prison work, Brandon told her that all in all, it didn't sound too different from being a prison guard anywhere else. Instead of cells, the detainees were kept in cages, and sometimes they refused their food or tried to fight back against the guards. He told her how some of them threw buckets of feces at the guards—something so disgusting and degrading that Brandon won't admit this to me later. But mainly, he told his new wife, it was just boring, and she didn't have any questions. She was proud of him for serving and keeping the terrorists locked up.

Wendy is quiet and soft-spoken, with a girlish nature. She looks so young that people jokingly asked Brandon whether she was of age. As newlyweds, they were wrapped up in honeymoon bliss. They drove around looking at houses, daydreaming about their future together. Brandon was sweet to her, buying her a card or flowers for no particular reason. When she said she was thinking about enlisting, he told her he'd help shine her boots. She was a welcome distraction. Between married life and work back at the base, he had little time to dwell on what had happened at the camp.

He just wanted to put the whole thing behind him and get on with his life, so he did. Time to move on to the next order of business: Iraq.

In Iraq Brandon finally got to be in the middle of the action. It was March 2003—the initial invasion—and he was on the front lines. As a military police officer, he patrolled the streets, providing convoys with protection as they drove through city neighborhoods that could turn into combat zones at any moment. He scanned buildings for snipers and streets for potential car bombs. At other times, the MPs raided houses, chosen at random, and arrested at gunpoint every man of fighting age.

Brandon craved the unique adrenaline rush of combat like a heroin addict searching for his next high. In Iraq, whenever there was a mission, he volunteered to go. If a door needed to be kicked in, everyone looked to him. He led from the front and experienced as much as he could. Brandon knew he was a good soldier and saw it as his responsibility to ensure that it was the Iraqis who were killed and not the Americans. He showed no fear, no hesitation. To this day, his commander tells new soldiers about Brandon's wartime feats.

If there is one phrase that could sum up Brandon's military experience, it's "Shoot first, think later." Soldiers never know whether they are going to have a fight-or-flight response until they are in the middle of the battle. For Brandon, when the pressure is on, he goes on adrenaline-fueled autopilot, running straight for the action and using full force. It was the same in Iraq as it had been when he had pounded the detainee's skull against the ground instead of fleeing the cage as his partner had. But when he came out of the haze of battle, he saw the path of destruction and the dead bodies left in his wake. It was only later, away from the enemy, that he realized what he had done.

2

You Can't Just Flip a Switch

When Brandon was growing up on bases, the military had helped soldiers out, whether it was with an injury or a problem at home with the wife or the kids. Now the military didn't seem to care. The message was, "If the military wanted you to have a family, we would've issued you one." As Brandon says, "They took the fun out of it."

Entering the battlefield in Iraq, a commander would announce the predicted casualty loss, as if those numbers didn't represent individual parents, sons, or siblings. If someone got hurt, he or she was considered useless and was thrown away. "When I realized that, I was like, my time is up and I am getting out," Brandon says.

In Brandon's first letter home to his father, he wrote that the war was "total bullshit." It was a gut reaction, but it was clear to him that the U.S. military wasn't helping people or spreading democracy. The Iraqis didn't even want them there. He still did what he was told, still ran head-on into gun battles, but only because he was ordered to, not because he believed in what he was doing.

Brandon was given two weeks of leave, but that was just enough time at home to remind him of everything he was missing—including his baby twins, who had been born just before he deployed. In some ways, after returning to Iraq, he wished he hadn't even visited Texas; it just made being deployed that much harder. "Over that year, it went from 'do what we have to do,' to 'I don't care what we do,' to 'when I get home I'm not going back.'"

A few days after he returned to Iraq, during a routine stop to buy ice at an Iraqi market, a mail truck driven by a private military contractor blew up barely ten feet from where Brandon was standing. It had been parked in the spot that one of the soldiers from his unit almost always used. By happenstance, the civilian, working for former Halliburton subsidiary KBR, had snagged the spot instead. The soldier had just stood there dumbstruck, unable to move, and Brandon, splattered in blood, had to slap her face to get her to help him so that they could sweep for bombs.

Afterward, it fully sank in for Brandon as well: that IED (improvised explosive device) was meant for them, not for an innocent postal worker. It could have been him—and as a soldier, maybe it should have been him. That night, no matter how hard he scrubbed his uniform, he couldn't get rid of the bloodstains and had to burn the clothes instead.

A few nights later, a call came in over the radio: an Iraqi semi had just rammed into the back of his friend's humvee on a three-vehicle convoy. As Brandon drove over, into an area infamous for constant gunfire, his mind raced, imagining the horrors of the scene he was heading toward.

When he arrived, soldiers were lying in contorted positions, covered in blood. The semi had hit the humvee with such force that the soldiers had been thrown from the vehicle, and the driver's seatbelt had ripped out from the bolts. The soldiers told Brandon that the semi had had its lights off at the time, and inside it was stacked with weapons.

Brandon says he will never forget the look of rage in his friend's eyes, as he lay on the ground drenched in blood, with one arm trying to cover up a female lieutenant who had suffered a massive head injury and his other clutching his M9 pistol. The soldier kept screaming, "That motherfucker did this, he ran right into us," pointing to an injured Iraqi man lying on a bench at the side of the road, who was moaning in pain.

"All the killing, all the bloodshed over my time there just ran through my head," says Brandon. "The war was just bullshit, and I didn't give a fuck anymore. Killing to me at that time was nothing." Brandon marched over to the man, pulled out his pistol, and aimed it straight at the man's head. Just as in Guantanamo, he was facing down a defenseless man and was hellbent on getting revenge. Another soldier, seeing that Brandon was about to shoot the man point-blank in the head, grabbed Brandon's arms and pulled him away. The Iraqi was taken to a hospital on a stretcher, most likely a first step toward being sent to Abu Ghraib or another prison, and Brandon headed back to his station.

That night, Brandon reached his breaking point; it was just too much violence, too many deaths. They were sacrificing their lives and those of their buddies, and all for nothing. Brandon had never dreamed that the military would put him in harm's way without a legitimate reason. An innocent mailman who had never hurt anyone had been killed, and Brandon, a killing machine, had been serendipitously saved. He was annihilating the area, destroying whole towns, killing people, and watching children die. Brandon couldn't handle seeing the type of person he had become and what he was capable of. "I couldn't take it anymore," he says. "I had become a monster." He still doesn't know whether things were getting worse in Iraq or whether he was just personally spiraling downward. That night, after a grim round of slugging on a bottle, he went out behind the barracks and put his 9 millimeter to his head.

Luckily, a friend, on his way to the latrine, saw Brandon and intervened. The guy told Brandon that he often felt the same way. "Fuck it, man," he told Brandon. "We just have to put our heads down, get through this shit, and get back to our families." Then, as Brandon says any good friend would, the guy never mentioned it again.

In fact, that night, while we were sitting together drinking Cokes at a Chili's restaurant, was the first time he has ever told anyone about that night. But that doesn't mean he doesn't think about it all the time. "Part of me died that night, and I know that," he says. "I wonder almost on a daily basis why I was put in those situations. Still, to this day, it's hard to handle."

When Brandon got home from Iraq in March 2004, he was determined to leave it all behind, even if that meant abandoning all of the things he still loved about the military and cutting off ties with men who had risked their lives for him. It was a complete one-eighty for Brandon. "I was Army for life. I would never talk bad about it. I was the most American guy you had ever met," he says.

When the officer pinned the medals on Brandon's uniform at the welcome home ceremony, Brandon just felt dirty. What he had done in the military wasn't honorable. He was no hero.

First and foremost, Brandon was a soldier, and without that identity, he didn't really know who he was. He had given everything to the military and to his country, and now he was left empty-handed. The military had tricked him into doing its dirty work, sacrificing everything, and it was all for nothing. He measured his self-worth by the value he brought as a soldier, and now the military was telling him that he and his fellow soldiers were disposable. He and everything he stood for was meaningless.

Other soldiers would have been shocked if they had known that underneath all of his bravado, Brandon had a hard time accepting who he had become in Iraq, or that he thought the war was a farce. One commander, Sergeant Starsky Smith, would have been particularly surprised and devastated.

Sergeant Smith was Brandon's mentor and close friend in Iraq—too close, perhaps, for people of different ranks. Every time Smith was assigned somewhere, he took Brandon with him. Smith said that Brandon reminded him of himself when he was first starting out: Army for life, gung ho, all-American. "He was totally by the book, never questioning his orders or superiors," says Brandon. "If you told him to run through a wall, he'd do it." And Brandon would be right there alongside him, doing the same. When they first got home and greeted their families, Sergeant Smith introduced Brandon to his wife as the man who was singly responsible for getting him home alive.

Smith was the soldier who had jumped on Jumah al Dossari's back and slammed his head against the floor in retaliation for Jumah calling the female guard a bitch. Brandon had vaguely known Sergeant Smith when they served together at Guantanamo Cuba. He'd played softball with Smith a few times and knew his reputation as being one of the harshest guards when it came to IRFing detainees. Brandon wouldn't tell me Smith's first name (which I only later figured out) but pointed me in the direction of the testimonies from Guantanamo detainees who were either victims of or witnesses to Smith's beatings. The reports were littered with his last name, describing that bloody IRF attack on Jumah al Dossari as well as others. David Hicks, for example, said in his affidavit to keep his British citizenship that Smith was a particularly brutal guard, "known to abuse detainees while they were being returned to their cells after showering and were defenseless at that time." Brandon says this doesn't surprise him. "That's Smith, all right," he says with a smile.

I ask Brandon how he could be so close with, and even look up to, someone who had violently abused so many detainees. Brandon explains, "Overall, Smith was a good guy." When detainee al Dossari asked Smith why Smith had beaten him, Smith replied, "Because I'm Christian." Brandon might not always agree with his tactics but says that Smith always believed that his actions were for all the right reasons.

Smith, who became the officer in charge of the unit's training, often gave the other soldiers a hard time, mocking them when they were weak, but Brandon knew that Smith wanted the best for the soldiers. As Brandon explains, Smith just had a funny way of showing it. Under Smith's macho front, Brandon saw a soft side. Smith bragged about razzing a young soldier who had thrown up all over his boots after seeing a soldier ripped in half. Brandon laughed along with Smith, but he tells me that he can remember when Smith puked, too.

During that same conversation at the restaurant, after Brandon describes his suicide attempt, he laughs as he tells me about preventing detainees from praying by pointing in different directions to Mecca. For Brandon, messing with detainees, even putting them in solitary, paled in comparison to the destruction in Iraq.

Brandon turned against the war when he saw how he and the other soldiers were used and sacrificed. It was harder for him to have sympathy for the enemy. The military was supposed to defend its own soldiers and annihilate those on the other side. He began criticizing the war while still overseas, but when it came to Guantanamo, it took him years to question what had happened. That's because the battles waged inside detention centers and the damage they do are far more subtle and covert than what happens in combat.

In 2005, while stationed at Fort Hood, Brandon saw Lynndie England, the infamous leash holder of the Abu Ghraib abuse scandal, on her way to the courtroom to face charges of abuse and conspiracy. It made him realize how lucky he was not to have been asked to do such extreme things to his detainees. If he had been one of the soldiers working Abu Ghraib's hard site, he knows he would have followed suit, and it would have been him in those handcuffs. He says that the thought that he could be charged for abuse at Guantanamo had never crossed his mind. Brandon hadn't been surprised when he saw the Abu Ghraib photos. All the same, he says, what he had been asked to do was completely different and unrelated to Abu Ghraib.

It's incredible to me that he doesn't see more similarities, particularly since the techniques used at Abu Ghraib originated in Cuba. Major General Geoffrey Miller, the commander of Guantanamo Bay, arrived in Iraq on August 31, 2003, for a ten-day assessment of the techniques that were being used, in order to determine why the quality of information was not on par with what they were collecting at Guantanamo. In his September 13, 2003, report, he advised, among other things, that interrogations should be stepped up a notch, that a "unified strategy to detain, interrogate, and report information from detainees/internees" should be instituted, and that the "detention operations function must act as an enabler for interrogation." Miller added, "It is essential that the guard force be actively engaged in setting the conditions for successful exploitation of the internees." The same day Miller released his report, Lieutenant General Ricardo Sanchez wrote the first of two memos officially authorizing a list of techniques that included stress positions, scaring detainees with dogs, and sleep management, but reaffirmed that unlike in Guantanamo, the Geneva Conventions applied in Iraq.

When everyone on television was calling the Abu Ghraib prison guards "the bad apples" and dropping the word *torture*, it's understandable that Brandon disassociated himself from these practices, even unconsciously.

It's not that Brandon never said no to a commander. In Iraq, he refused to go into combat with an inexperienced soldier, arguing that it would get them all killed. "Soldiers don't just follow these orders because they are mentally weak," Brandon says. "You do it because you are being asked by your country to do it, and it is the right thing to do."

To explain the Abu Ghraib abuse, many point to Stanley Milgram's 1963 Yale electric shock experiment and Philip Zimbardo's 1971 Stanford Prison Experiment. Zimbardo even testified on behalf of Chip Frederick, who was charged with abuse at Abu Ghraib.

In the Milgram study, middle- and working-class people were asked by a man in a lab coat to use electric shocks against other people as part of a learning exercise. The subjects were unaware that the other student was an actor, yet the majority was willing to administer a potentially fatal shock. The experiment illustrated that even ordinary people will inflict pain on others when ordered, particularly when reassured by seemingly more knowledgeable authorities that what they are doing is acceptable, even if they are doubtful.

In the Stanford Prison Experiment, Zimbardo placed college students in a mock prison, some acting as prisoners, some as guards. After six days, the study was terminated when the guards became excessively abusive. Even Zimbardo himself became inappropriately caught up and enthusiastic about the experiment. The experiment illustrated the powerful effects of one's environment. When cut off from reality, living under completely different rules and standards, whether it be in a university basement or a military compound, it is easy to lose sight of accepted morals.

An often overlooked yet important lesson from the research is the effect these experiments had on the participants. Ethical research guidelines were rewritten after the Milgram study to protect future subjects from psychological damage. During exit interviews after the experiments concluded, people described the psychological trauma of realizing that they could be so easily pushed to do such horrific things. Although Zimbardo denies that there were any repercussions for his subjects, some subsequent interviews have suggested otherwise.

The Stanford students' descriptions of the experience after the fact were eerily similar to those of soldiers such as Brandon. One guard said, "It's almost like a prison that you create yourself— you get into it, and it becomes almost the definition you make of yourself, it almost becomes like walls, and you want to break out, and you want just to be able to tell everyone that this isn't really me at all, and I'm not the person that's confined in there—I'm a person who wants to get out and show you that I'm free and

I do have my own will, and I'm not the sadistic type of person that enjoys this kind of thing."

Although there is something to say of Zimbardo's situationist perspective of the Stanford Prison Experiment, in explaining Brandon's and other soldiers' willingness to torture, it leaves out key elements. For one, the stakes were much higher for the soldiers than for the research subjects. People in the experiments wanted to participate to the fullest to aid academic research, but soldiers were pressured by believing that they were helping to protect their country, their families, and democracy from terrorists. They weren't dealing with fellow research volunteers; they were interacting with suspected members of al Qaeda. Moreover, if the soldiers had refused, they would be dishonorably discharged and even imprisoned. They would lose their benefits, hurt their ability to ever get a job, and lose the sense of respect, honor, and meaning that comes with being a soldier.

Most of all, the Stanford Prison Experiment and the Milgram study don't explain why Brandon Neely did what he did, because in Brandon's case it isn't a question of a good man doing evil things, but a good man doing what he thought was right. He wasn't shocking or abusing innocent research participants. He was saving his country from terrorists, serving the president, and fulfilling his patriotic duty to give back to his nation.

Brandon had joined the Army in part to escape Huntsville, but he found himself right back in the small town. As a teenager, he was bored by the place, but now that he is raising three young kids, the slow pace has its perks. He figures that as they get older, they'll have fewer opportunities to get into real trouble than they would in Houston, where kids bring guns to class. With the help of a VA loan, Brandon bought a manufactured home at the end of a winding dirt road for his family. It's spacious, with high ceilings and a sprawling floor plan, but sparsely decorated. The back bedroom has been converted into Brandon's den, with video

games hooked up to a flat-screen television in front of a large
couch. One gets the feeling that Brandon spends a lot of time in
this room alone.

Brandon came home from Iraq a broken man. His wife
and children barely recognized him. His oldest daughter was
scared of him, not wanting to get close lest he leave her again.
The twins, born just before he deployed, had learned to walk
while he was overseas. He either couldn't sleep or slept all the
time, tormented by nightmares. He lost all interest in working out or hanging out with his kids. Brandon was withdrawn
and emotionally numb, with no patience for his wife's questions about Iraq. All he wanted to do was to be alone, play video
games, and drink. He had left for the Army a party guy, and
these days he didn't even want to be around the crowds at his
son's Little League games.

After Brandon left the military, he was hard up finding work.
The options: Wal-Mart, the local university, or one of the eleven
prisons in the area. With only a high school diploma and a family
to support, Brandon made the obvious choice. Like so many of
his friends' parents when he was growing up, he reluctantly signed
up to work the blocks. He was assigned to the Ferguson prison,
maximum security, which housed young men ages eighteen to
twenty-four.

The Texas prison system is the largest in the nation, and
Huntsville, with thousands of prisoners and the oldest prison,
is considered its capital. The tourism bureau offers driving maps
of the units. At the local Texas Prison Museum, you can visit
the state's first electric chair and buy "Ole Sparky" shot glasses
and prisoner bobble-heads. There's the Estelle Unit for first-
time offenders and the mentally ill and the implausibly named
Holiday Unit for temporary prisoners, as well as separate facilities for juveniles and for women. Inmates awaiting execution stay
on death row in individual sixty-square-foot cells at the Polunsky
Unit. When it's time for the lethal injection, they are taken to
the state's oldest prison, colloquially called the "Walls Unit" for
its huge brick perimeter.

I ask Brandon whether it is depressing to have to drive by death row when crossing through town. He says it is no big deal, and he hardly thinks about it being there, except when all of the protesters and the television crews come on the days of executions. It is just part of the fabric of the town, a constant that is never questioned. More recent news about DNA exonerations is troubling to Brandon, but in Texas, it's an eye for an eye.

Brandon didn't enjoy working at Ferguson. Some guards smuggled in drugs and cell phones to sell to the inmates. It was hard to know whom to trust. Inmates sometimes tried to attack the guards. Brandon was assigned riot-control duty and was told how to ramp up force by first yelling, then pepper-spraying the prisoners, and then, only as a last resort, physically restraining them. He and the other guards had to watch themselves. Prisoners had the right to file charges and complaints against abusive guards. Once Brandon had a bucket of piss thrown on him, similar to what happens to guards at Guantanamo. But unlike the prison in Cuba, here Brandon was sent home to clean up and cool off.

Hearing Brandon describe this work, I want him to have some grand epiphany about the connections between domestic prison problems and the military detentions. I expect him to see how America's solution to so many problems is to lock them up and bury the key. With all the criticism of Halliburton's government contracts, I assume that he will recognize how this corporation has profited off its no-bid construction contract for buildings at Guantanamo, just as it has siphoned off state tax dollars to build maximum-security prisons. I figure that he'll realize that horrific prison abuse, though less egregious, happens right here at home. When Brandon tells me that many soldiers return home to work in prisons as he did, I think that he might worry about the drift of specific techniques, such as stress positions.

Yet Brandon sees no connections between the two situations. The scale and intensity of the treatment, he argues, are not comparable. Besides, he says, in the U.S. prisoners have recourse and rights. They've been tried and found guilty. They've brought this on themselves.

He maintains that working at the prison didn't bring back any memories of Guantanamo. All the same, sometimes he couldn't bring himself to go to work, and halfway there, he'd turn around, go back home, and get into bed. After two years, Brandon quit his job at the prison to work as a federal police officer in the Houston area, the kind of job he had always wanted.

During Brandon's hour-long commute to work in Houston, his mind usually turns back to Iraq. It's a monotonous drive, straight down Highway 45, past strip malls, fast-food joints, and car dealerships. Especially at dawn, it takes little concentration, so images of detonated trucks, bloody corpses, and detached limbs often flash through his mind. Unlike other vets suffering from post-traumatic stress disorder (PTSD), his memory has not been compromised. He remembers everything—too much, in fact. He wishes he remembered less.

Brandon berated himself for not being able to just get over Iraq, the way he did after returning from Guantanamo. He tried to suck it up, push it down, and move on. But when he couldn't, he only grew more frustrated with himself. Over and over, he tells me, "You can't just flip a switch."

Brandon's temper is still easily set off. Sometimes he enters an almost blacked-out haze where his rage takes the reins. It's a kind of autopilot that helped him run straight into gunfire while shooting rounds in Iraq, but here at home, that same kind of irrationality, especially out in public, only makes his children cry and his wife angry. The week before I visited, he had embarrassed his family by flying off the handle at his daughter's dance recital when the ticket taker asked him to pay an admission fee to watch his own kid. "Daddy got in trouble," his kids tell me. Brandon says he's never been physically violent, but he also mentions that a fellow veteran and an otherwise good guy beat up his wife during a similar blackout.

Brandon accepts that he is depressed, but his military pride prevents him from taking that extra step to go to a doctor. His wife printed out fact sheets about PTSD and left them in the bathroom for him to read. Yet he has heard too many horror stories about the VA to ever seek its help. He doesn't want to pump himself full of pills.

Brandon is now a firm believer that everyone who has been in combat has some form of PTSD. "Even people who support Iraq and Afghanistan have still seen shit that will affect them forever," he says. A Vietnam vet told Brandon that even if he hadn't committed any atrocities at war, he would be this way forever. It made him feel better to know he wasn't the only one. The hardest realization was coming to terms with the fact that he probably won't ever get over it.

When Brandon was stop-lossed in May 2007, he refused to go. He said he would rather go to jail than end up fighting in a war he didn't believe in. So when his orders to report came in the mail, he simply didn't sign for them. Despite the potential threat of prison time, he managed to hold out until his discharge date.

While searching the Internet for legal advice about refusing deployment, he was surprised to come across groups of antiwar soldiers. Even simply discovering that others like him were out there felt comforting to Brandon.

It's hard to believe that Brandon didn't realize how many people were morally opposed to the detainees' treatment at Guantanamo and the war. He says he didn't personally know anyone who was against it. Vice President Dick Cheney was on Fox News reassuring everyone that Guantanamo was keeping people safe from "the worst of a very bad lot . . . devoted to killing millions of Americans." Talking heads were justifying even waterboarding with the hypothetical ticking-time-bomb scenario. Even people who were outraged by the Abu Ghraib abuse scandal seemed to have no problem with the prison in Cuba that was run by the book. Military officials and politicians claimed that the detainees received better health care and food than they would back home. The cinema in Brandon's town refused to show the Hollywood blockbuster *Stop-Loss*, about a soldier who goes temporarily AWOL. He didn't even know that there had been thousands turning out at antiwar protests at the beginning of the invasion. If he had known, he would have been infuriated. But there had been no talk about that in Fort Hood, and by the time the war officially started, he was already in the Middle East. Deep in Texas's Bush country, being antiwar can earn you enemies. Brandon's antiwar stance was something that he just kept to himself.

The soldiers he read about online weren't simply against the war, they were publicly vocal about it, going to protests and speaking at events, even though some of them were still on active duty, and therefore breaking military law by voicing their criticism. One of the groups, Courage to Resist, asked Brandon to share online his story about avoiding redeployment. He knew it would feel good to help other soldiers evade redeployment, but what he didn't expect was how therapeutic it would be to finally voice his disillusionment with the war and the military. Finally, he had found a release.

Five months later, Brandon made the four-hour trip down to Austin to meet with soldiers from one of the antiwar groups he had found online. The activist soldiers were taken aback by Brandon's good-old-country-boy looks, Republican views, military buzz cut, and federal police officer job. Some of them thought that he must be a narc trying to infiltrate the group. But with time, they realized he was legit. Brandon might be a conservative, but when the group's members all made the trek to protest at the Republican National Convention, the police shadowed Brandon just as closely as they did the rest of the soldiers.

Brandon tried to reach out to other soldiers near Huntsville whom he suspected were just as fed up with how the military had treated them. But even if they disagreed with the mission, the antiwar groups seemed too radical to them. The soldiers were against the current war, but they didn't even want to be associated with anyone who was against war and the military in general.

Brandon told his wife not to talk to people about his association with antiwar activities. He is afraid that someone will talk badly about her and his kids or cause them problems. He won't wear his Iraq Veterans Against the War T-shirt in public when his family is with him. When he does wear it on his own, it garners disparaging looks. One day when Brandon was standing in line at Wal-Mart, a military recruiter started yelling at him that he was the reason no one was joining the military. People looked on, as Brandon walked right up in the man's face. Looking at his patches, Brandon could see that the recruiter had never even been to Iraq. Brandon ripped into him, saying, "At least one of us is doing our job," and walked off.

But even while protesting the Iraq war, Brandon never brought up Guantanamo. Few knew he had been there. Criticizing America's military detention policy and slinging around the word *torture* are much more serious than denouncing the war. Doing so would be challenging the mistreatment of "non-enemy combatants," rather than the misuse of U.S. soldiers. Even many people who wanted the troops to come home couldn't care less if terrorism suspects rotted away in jail cells on some island. Most people could accept that such acts as killing civilians were wrong—but those were aberrations, mistakes, and, in most cases, not even newsworthy. People didn't want to hear that war crimes were being committed on behalf of the whole country and had become the official military strategy. "It's hard for most people to accept these things," says Brandon. "People just can't believe this can happen in their name, with their tax dollars, so the first thing they do is get defensive and angry. It's like people with a drinking problem; they know it is true, but they don't want to admit there is anything wrong with them." As one of the culprits, Brandon himself definitely did not want to believe it at first.

3

Blowing the Whistle

In November 2008, a female soldier who had served with Brandon at Guantanamo contacted him on MySpace. She had seen Brandon's name on the "Courage to Resist" Web site and told him she was glad he was out of the army. She herself had gone back to living with her parents and had turned to fundamentalist Christianity for support. She had always been openhearted—too much so for the military, really, says Brandon. He had always felt sorry for her. Other soldiers had called her a whore when she had filed a case against one of them for rape. Brandon wrote back asking her what she really thought of Guantanamo. It was a question he himself had begun to toy with, and perhaps he was posing it more to himself than to her. Brandon never heard back from her. He figured that she just wanted to move on and put the whole thing behind her.

It had been almost five years since he had come home from Cuba, before it began to sink in that maybe what happened at the camp had been wrong. Maybe the justifications the soldiers had been given were lies.

The more he read about the war, the more he realized that his gut reaction against it had been correct. The hunt for weapons of mass destruction had been a sham. American death tolls were rising, but even when soldiers from Brandon's hometown were killed, they didn't make it into the news. Each news article or broadcast about the failures of the war was worse than the one before it. His country had sent him to war under false pretenses. If the Bush administration could lie about something as important as that, what else were they deceiving him about?

As Brandon puts it, the blinders came off, the curtain opened, and he started to question everything. He doubts that he ever would have questioned what happened at Guantanamo had he not gone to Iraq. "Things were bad at the prison, but no one was being blown up or shot like in Iraq," he says. "But mesh both of those places together, and it messes with you." Brandon's world was turned upside down. His deepest faith was shattered.

It wasn't only Brandon. Nationwide, there was a gradual shift. On the campaign trail, both Barack Obama and John McCain advocated for closing Guantanamo. More and more memos were being released proving that Abu Ghraib wasn't an aberration. Talking heads on MSNBC were discussing whether CIA agents who used waterboarding should be charged. The dialogue made it harder for Brandon to ignore the issue; the shifting sentiment made it easier to broach the troubling question of whether he had participated in torture.

"I bet there were some Nazis who thought they were doing a great thing," he explains. "I'm sure there was someone out there, some regular Nazi guard, who thought, I am doing the right thing, what I am being told to do, but he still felt like shit inside. Just because you are a Nazi at a concentration camp doesn't mean you are a bad person. It doesn't mean that you agree with the whole thing, or that when you look back at the whole picture, you aren't going to think it is messed up."

Now that Brandon is beginning to digest what he's done, the guilt and anger erupt and flood over him. "There has not been a day that goes by that I have not relived what I did or saw in Guantanamo or Iraq," he says. "It does not get any easier; it just eats you up inside, day by day."

It isn't only the gunfire and the bloody violence of combat that can cause PTSD; there is also the sense of betrayal and of being used or being tricked by your country to cross moral lines. Brandon doesn't hesitate to use the word *torture* to describe what he was a part of at Guantanamo. He says everyone who was there is guilty to some extent. Yes, he was forced into it and thought it was justified at the time, but that doesn't make it any less wrong.

Brandon began to hunt online for more information about Guantanamo. He found a professor at the University of California–Davis who was posting first-person testimonies of detainees and soldiers, along with a compilation of human rights groups' reports, government documents, books, and newspapers. Brandon was shocked when he started to read the testimonies. In some ways it was also a relief. Brandon wasn't the only one who had seen these things and was questioning them. Even the detainees' accounts matched his own memories. But seeing in print the things he had tried for so long to block out was difficult, and he began to realize the seriousness of just what he had done.

Perhaps most troubling were Jumah al Dossari's letters to his lawyer, interviews with reporters, and suicide notes.

"There were many times in Guantanamo when I felt as though I was falling apart, like a sandcastle being washed out by the tide," Jumah wrote to his lawyer. "I lost all hope and faith. The purpose of Guantanamo is to destroy people, and I was destroyed. I decided that I preferred death to life, and I attempted suicide several times." In one particularly gruesome attempt, his lawyer found him hanging from his neck, covered in blood from a gash in his arm.

Jumah al Dossari spent two years in solitary as punishment for one of his many suicide attempts. He said that solitary confinement was even more horrific than the physical assaults. Sergeant

Smith may have crushed Jumah's ribs during the IRF attack, and
an interrogator had slammed his head into a table, but being put
in the small metal cell alone with no end in sight was the worst.
Inside the cell, Jumah was stripped down to his shorts, with only
a prayer mat, and was subjected to freezing temperatures. Violent
beatings are relatively quick; so-called torture lite is seemingly
endless. With no faucet, Jumah was forced to drink from and
wash in the toilet. And it was Brandon who had done those kinds
of things to detainees.

On October 14, 2005, Jumah wrote a suicide note addressed
to a translator:

> Take some of my blood. . . . Take some of my remains . .
> . take pictures of my dead body when I am placed in my
> grave . . . send it to the world . . . to people with principles
> and values, "the fair-minded." . . . To make them carry
> this burden of guilt in front of history for this soul that
> was wasted with no reason. . . . After this soul has suffered
> the worst by the hands of "the protectors of peace and the
> callers for democracy, freedom, equality and justice."

A year and a half later, his lawyer received a letter from him:

> Death has become the ultimate hope to end my misery,
> my suffering, and my sad life. . . . What we have here now
> is what I call a cemetery for the living, and is a mark of
> disgrace and shame in the history of the United States . . .
> I am a human being—but a dead one, without rights,
> dignity, humanity or identity.

Many of the prisoners' claims of innocence turned out to be
true. It wasn't just alleged terrorists whom Brandon had shackled,
put in solitary, and dragged across the rocks, but ordinary people—
husbands, fathers, brothers. In July 2007, when the United States

released Jumah, they stamped his record with several allegations (but no charges), none of which related to terrorism, and all of which Jumah denies. Jumah was innocent, and Brandon had played a role in pushing him to the brink of suicide. For the first time, he saw that it wasn't only U.S. soldiers who were being senselessly sacrificed.

For a while, Brandon sat with the realization that Guantanamo had been wrong, but then he decided to simply focus his effort on trying to forget about it altogether. But just as with Iraq, the thoughts just wouldn't go away.

Brandon found himself slipping into another bout of serious depression. He isolated himself from friends and barely spoke to his wife. He realized that he had to try to do something; otherwise, he'd end up adding to the mounting statistics of veteran suicides.

Brandon e-mailed the UC–Davis professor and offered to provide his testimony for the Web site. For the next month or so, each morning Brandon found a message in his in-box that posed a question: Why did he sign up? How did the in-processing take place? Were the IRFings filmed? Brandon would then spend the whole day, at work, during his commute, and while having dinner with his family, thinking about his answer, and would type it up at night. Brandon is a slow typist, so the difficulty of baring all was only exacerbated.

After describing the detainee arrival day, he faltered. He knew he had to mention the story about slamming the elderly detainee's head against the cement floor over and over again. He felt ashamed to admit it even to himself, let alone to an academic who would find it abhorrent. If he decided to put it up on the Web, who knew who could read it, or what people would think?

Brandon didn't want to implicate himself. But he worried that if he didn't tell the story, someone else could come forward with the information about what Brandon had done. Then it would seem as if he was trying to shift the blame. He told himself it was time to fall in line. Finally, after all these years, to do the right thing. Including the story would also add more weight and veracity to his statement. Maybe if he admitted he was wrong, others would do the same.

After several days of deliberating, one evening, Brandon sat down at his computer and e-mailed the professor. "I am not a totally innocent person as far as what happened inside the wire," he wrote. "I am very ashamed to admit it and tell you that I was involved in the very first IRFing incident at Camp X-Ray. I left it out of what happened on Day 1, and I apologize for that. It's just something that I am very ashamed of. Here is what happened," and he proceeded to backtrack and tell the true story.

Even though such a first-person account is crucial in airing abuses, the professor said he understood if Brandon didn't want to go into detail about the incident. "Good people can do evil things in evil environments," replied the professor, echoing the Stanford Prison Project, paying no heed to the fact that Brandon, like so many Americans, had thought that what he was doing was noble. Seeing Brandon as a whistleblower and a witness is easier than acknowledging that the man you are talking to is a torturer. It is much more comfortable to encounter torture two steps removed.

Brandon said he would answer any questions, but still, he stumbled over the words, as he often does when describing the incident. He explained that he threw the detainee to the ground and held the man down. But without explaining how every time the detainee tried to lift his head Brandon slammed it back down into the concrete, it was confusing to imagine how the detainee had sustained so many injuries. At the professor's urging, Brandon tried to clarify the situation, but he also argued that he had never technically struck the prisoner.

In January 2009, the professor asked Brandon whether he would be willing to share the information with the press—it could, after all, show others that it's safe to come forward. Brandon agreed, not thinking much of it. It would be just one more soldier's story pushed aside by the media. In part, he was right—several national publications, including *Harper's*, *Newsweek*, and the *New York Times*, declined. Guantanamo was closing. The topic of torture was old news. It was time to move on. Only a lowly Associated Press reporter took the story, which was then reprinted in several newspapers on Valentine's Day 2009.

The AP article wasn't reprinted in the *Huntsville Item*, the local newspaper most of his friends read. But it did show up in the military newspaper *Stars and Stripes*, so Brandon assumes that many of his friends who are former servicemen, including Smith, must know. Even though the two men had stayed in touch, Brandon never heard anything from Smith about it.

Brandon received only one e-mail from a soldier he had served with. "I had forgot about a lot of the things about Gitmo, but some of it is coming back to me," the soldier wrote. "It was quite chaotic when we first got there as far as operational procedures went." But when Brandon e-mailed the soldier back, encouraging him to contact UC–Davis, he never heard from the man again.

The story caught the attention of MSNBC's liberal talk-show host Rachel Maddow. When the producers called to see whether Brandon would appear on the show, it seemed unbelievable: national television. Even though few people he knew watched the show, it was still a major risk.

With Brandon working for the federal police department, it could even cost him his job. He is legally allowed to speak publicly and to the press as long it is clear that he is not speaking on behalf of the federal police force. He made a point of never mentioning specifics about where he worked. He printed out the police department's regulations regarding free speech and carried them around in his pocket for a week after the Maddow show aired. If they try to fire him from his job, he will sue them; it will simply give him a larger stage from which to make noise.

I ask him whether he is concerned about more informal repercussions, because police are known to have a code of silence similar to the military's. Would they think that he would rat them out

if one of them broke a rule? Maybe let him catch a bullet instead
of them? Brandon told me that his coworkers had his back. They
knew he was a good cop.

Military retaliation was what he was really worried about. The
policemen's code of silence pales in comparison to that of the
military. In the public eye, cops are seen as individuals, not as
representations of their entire country as soldiers are. If Brandon
blew the whistle on a cop, people would say, "He was a good guy
for maintaining pride and peace in an American community,"
not "This guy just fucked his country." Brandon says that if the
military comes after him, he will start naming names—every
last one, from top to bottom. If what he did was illegal, then
everyone at Guantanamo has broken the law. Would they really
lock them all up?

Publicly unloading his memories about Guantanamo was therapeutic and absolving for Brandon. Speaking privately with
his family was another matter. "Strangers don't know you," he
explains, "and can't compare you to who you used to be. You
won't see yourself in their eyes every morning at breakfast." It's
a hard thing for his wife, Wendy, to understand. She's frustrated
and jealous that he will talk to strangers but not to her. He told
her she doesn't understand what he went through. She responds
that he doesn't let her. But he says he doesn't want her to understand or even know.

Wendy read part of his online UC–Davis testimony and
watched the Maddow segment, a fact that the two have still
never acknowledged. When I ask her about it, she says it just
seemed surreal to hear her husband describing people beating
up detainees. Like many Americans, she can see some justification for abandoning the Geneva Conventions and using torture
when dealing with alleged terrorists, but not for those who were
innocent. She had considered enlisting herself and wonders what
she would have done if she had been there. She doesn't think she

would be capable of that kind of abuse but also points out that Brandon said that he had no choice. When I ask her what she thinks of having her husband associated with the word *torture*, she says she has never thought of it that way.

Around his parents' house, Brandon's antiwar activities are taboo. His mother told him and his sister never to mention the Maddow segment around their dad. He had heard about it from a colleague and didn't need to be reminded of it. He had been supportive when Brandon resisted redeployment. He told his wife that he'd never seen the terrible things that Brandon has and knows that it must be a lot to deal with. "If this is how he wants to deal with it," his dad said, "that's his choice. Just leave me out of it."

When Brandon's sister, Melissa, saw Brandon's face appear on *Rachel Maddow* while she was flipping channels, it was after a late night of drinking, and she texted him ("OMG!"). But when I ask her what she thought about it, she claims that she never listened to any of what he said; it was just crazy to see her brother on national television.

I ask Melissa what she thinks more generally about the news of torture at Guantanamo. She says that she doesn't believe that the detainees' allegations of torture are true. She thinks they just made the stories up to make America look bad. "Proud American soldiers wouldn't do things like that," she says. She, Brandon, and I are sitting in the living room of her small apartment in Huntsville. It is a ballsy thing to say in front of him. "I know you have come out and said stuff has happened," she says to Brandon. "And I'm sure you are right. But I don't think all soldiers are like that. I think some soldiers go into the Army all idealistic and quickly realize stuff happens. But mostly they are good men and women there, following orders."

Brandon points out that the abuse was ordered, leading Melissa to get lost in a circular rationalization, trying to figure out what is right or wrong. She says the soldiers should follow their conscience and not their orders. But then she says she has no idea. "I guess if you are trained, you follow orders. Isn't that what you did, just follow orders? Even good people do bad stuff. I've done lots of bad stuff, and I'm a good person," she says, and changes the subject.

She explains that as a high school teacher, she has to be careful what she says. She's scared that she could lose her job if people knew that her brother was saying those things. A local gay teacher lost his job after he was seen kissing his boyfriend at a Walmart. The principal had already been angry when her classroom's debates over the war spilled out into the school corridors. Now, one of her students was asking her whether that was her brother on the show. Melissa had invited Brandon to speak to her eleventh grade U.S. history and politics class about the realities of going to war, but after he appeared on TV with Rachel Maddow, it was out of the question.

Later, Brandon tells me he doesn't believe for one minute that his sister, infamously nosy, didn't listen to him on the Maddow show. He says she just doesn't want to believe that it was her older brother who did those things.

Some people, even critics of Guantanamo, ask Brandon why he can't just let the issue go. They cleaned up Guantanamo, changed the policies, and are working to close the prison. It's a refrain coming from the media, talking heads, politicians, soldiers, and ordinary Americans. It's one of the arguments behind not having a national truth commission or pursuing prosecutions. It was so long ago; what's done is done. Case closed, let's move on.

There are others who thank him for sharing his experiences. He simply replies that he wishes he didn't have these stories to tell. Other people blame Brandon for not coming out sooner. Some surmise that Brandon merely wants to be on the side of the critics now that President Obama is talking about closing the prison and public opinion is starting to change.

Brandon also wishes he had spoken out sooner—maybe even while it was happening. He doesn't know why his guilt about Guantanamo arose when it did. The increased attention to the issue during the presidential debates did bring it to the forefront of his mind, but he insists that it wasn't because Bush left office. He says it just took him that many years to personally come to terms with the accusations of torture. In fact, Brandon is still trying to come to terms with what he did and make sense of it all.

He has searched unsuccessfully to find out whether that elderly detainee he beat up has been released. He hopes that the man isn't one of the thousands of former detainees who were innocent. That would make the whole thing even harder to bear.

Yet even today, Brandon still doesn't connect some of the dots. It was only while we were talking in the spring of 2009 that Brandon realized that making detainees at Guantanamo show their hands every hour during the night was a way to induce sleep deprivation. Without knowing, he was subjecting prisoners to psychological torture. Without the larger picture, Brandon says, there was no way for him to grasp the true horror of Guantanamo. He was an unwitting participant, which is ironic, given that at the time he would have been eager to break down the prisoners.

During house raids in Iraq, he ransacked houses at random. The soldiers held all of the men of fighting age at gunpoint, flexi-cuffed them, threw bags over their heads, and detained them for days before sending some of them to prisons. But it never occurred to him that the detainees at Guantanamo might have been captured in similar situations or that the people he arrested could have been sent to Guantanamo. Brandon maintains that it is totally different.

Jumah al Dossari's lawyer contacted Brandon when he saw that Brandon had publicly spoken about the camp. Jumah remembered Brandon from the camp. He said Brandon was not particularly nice to the detainees, but all the same, Jumah was impressed that Brandon was owning up to what he had done. He asked to speak with Brandon.

Brandon was nervous about what Jumah would say. But during the three-way conference call between Brandon in Texas, the lawyer in New York, and Jumah in Saudi Arabia, Jumah did not chastise him or get angry. They both started off seven years ago at Camp X-Ray, Jumah said, and now each had to find reconciliation in his own way.

Jumah had been suicidal and fiercely angry in Guantanamo, but on the plane ride to Saudi Arabia, he said he decided that if he was to be able to move on, he would have to forgive and, as he explained, would have to "open my heart to life again." He had lost too much time, suffered enough, as it was, and he wasn't going to let them rob him of anything more.

When Jumah first saw his daughter, who had been seven when he was captured, he thought she was his sister. His wife had divorced him, assuming she would never see him again, but they quickly remarried. His lawyer helped him find work, transition back into society, and reclaim his life. Seeing the kindness of his lawyer gave Jumah hope that not all Americans were bad.

On one of his first nights home, Jumah watched *United 93*, the Hollywood film reenacting the crash into a field of 9/11's fourth plane. It made him think about how the horrors of that day had pushed Americans to do "dark things." The hysteria and fear had unleashed a patriotism-fueled desire for revenge that could justify the horrors of Guantanamo in American minds. Americans didn't think they were fighting individuals like Jumah who were merely in the wrong place at the wrong time, but a larger force that was out to destroy the very essence of what their nation stood for.

Brandon couldn't believe that this man, who had been subjected to torture while locked up at Guantanamo for five and a half years, was coping better with the experience than he himself was. Jumah had been home just over a year and a half, compared to Brandon's six and a half. Jumah will forever have physical ailments from the abuse, and depression and anxiety will no doubt plague him. He has been robbed of years of his life. But guilt is also a heavy burden.

The so-called no-touch torture techniques were designed to disguise that level of suffering from the perpetrator and the observer. In Brandon's online testimony, he explained, "It's the detainees and the guards like myself who will have to live every day with what they went through, saw, and did while there."

It was hard to understand, but as a perpetrator of torture, Brandon was also a victim of the same crime.

PART TWO

Joe Darby

4

The Rat

Joe Darby hates the label "whistleblower," which is understandable, because it's earned him others, such as "rat" and "traitor." Joe is the soldier who reported the detainee abuse at Abu Ghraib. He is the one who turned in the photos of naked prisoners stacked in pyramids, the hooded detainee standing on a box with electrodes on his hands, and those leashed like dogs, with guards smiling and giving the thumbs-up. These were the photos that were shown around the world, igniting protests and outrage and raising the question for Americans of whether torture could be justified. Joe's actions triggered prosecutions of low-ranking soldiers, landing six of his unit's soldiers in jail, and, as his fellow guards are quick to point out, ruining the reputations and the careers of many more. He is the one, his critics say, who sold out his entire country.

I meet with Joe at a Starbucks in a strip mall along a busy four-lane route, in a quasi-rural area that could be anywhere in the

United States. Instead of being celebrated as an American hero, Joe has been forced into hiding because too many people want him dead. A security assessment of his hometown, Cumberland, Maryland, where most of his Army Reserve unit was from, deemed it too dangerous for him to return. "The overall threat of harassment or criminal activity to Darby is imminent," read the report. His house was too close to the road: people could easily shoot him. "Like with the Amish community, you do something wrong, you get shunned and thrown out," Linda Comer, one of the locals whom the Army Criminal Investigations Division (CID) interviewed for its security assessment, told me. "We do justice in our own way. No one would rent to him or sell him a house. If they did, someone would go destroy it. I'm not sure if it will ever be safe for him to come back." To some of his old neighbors, what Joe did was worse than the abuse.

Joe's still in hiding but in a sort of Where's Waldo? way: he's officially in an undisclosed location, but he's out in public working at a regular civilian job. He doesn't want me to describe his appearance, but it has changed somewhat from the recognizable round face that appeared in magazines and on television. He worked for the military as a mechanic for two years until his service contract was up. When he applied for his current federal contractor job with a medical equipment company, he had to tell human resources to Google his name because background checks came up as classified. There's no official record that he exists.

He says that being in hiding isn't so difficult. He's always kept to himself. In fact, it saved his rocky marriage. His wife had taken up with one of his friends while he was Iraq, and seclusion forced the couple back together. Whenever our conversation gets difficult, Joe fiddles with his wedding ring.

Some have celebrated Joe as a noble American, but he never received a thank-you from the president or a medal from the military. In 2005, Joe received the John F. Kennedy Profile in Courage Award, but for every handshake, he also got hate mail. He received a less-than-positive personal letter from Secretary of

Defense Donald Rumsfeld, sent to his unlisted home address, which Joe interpreted as a veiled threat.

Joe is an unlikely character to become a national hero. He insists that he's not a Goody Two-Shoes or a saint, by any stretch. He is not as morally upstanding as some paint him, nor is he the most dedicated or brightest soldier in his unit or even particularly idealistic. Friends and fellow soldiers describe Joe as a hothead with a bad temper, a gossip, and someone who caused turmoil and picked fights. He didn't seem to care what other people thought, and that rubbed a lot of people the wrong way. He was known more for his love of porn than for his moral character. "I'm as crooked as the next MP," he explains. "I've bent laws and I've broke laws." He recalls one incident in which he and a group of soldiers, frustrated by their lack of equipment, stole a fuel tank and two generators that Iraqis had left by the side of the road for a moment. "You can't ride the line the whole time. In war, we do what we have to," he says, "but we don't steal from our own." And you definitely don't turn one another in.

Growing up, Joe lived in a modest beige house with aluminum siding in western Appalachia outside the town of Cumberland. It's on a small road, down the hill from a church, halfway between what is now the 9/11 Flight 93 memorial and the Quecreek mining disaster memorial. His stepdad was a disabled truck driver, and the family was worse off than most other families living in the depressed area. In high school, Joe worked nights at a local hamburger joint, which left the smell of grease on his clothes. Former classmates say he got picked on, and the ritual hazing by fellow football players went way beyond the normal first year.

Joe joined the Army Reserve for college money but never ended up continuing his education. Instead, he married a local girl, and they moved to various small towns as Joe unsuccessfully looked for work. The small monthly wage from the military helped, but it wasn't enough. Eventually, they returned to the Cumberland area. Before he could settle in, he was called up for a deployment in Bosnia. When he came back in June 2002, he found construction work off the books with a fellow reservist, but eight months later, he was called up again, this time to go to Iraq.

The 130-degree heat in Iraq feels like constant blowing from the hot exhaust of a car. As a military policeman, Joe patrolled the streets of Al-Hillah, providing security and arresting Iraqis. But in October 2003, just when his unit was expecting to go home—in fact, half of the unit had already pulled back to Kuwait, and the soldiers had sent their bags home—they got a last-minute order that they were being sent to Abu Ghraib. Abu Ghraib, Saddam Hussein's former prison, now housed the thousands of Iraqis whom U.S. soldiers had arrested on the streets or picked up during house raids.

Assuming that they were going to provide security to the heavily mortared prison compound, the soldiers were confused—and pissed—when they were assigned the role of guards. They wanted to patrol streets, not babysit prisoners.

Joe asked for a job where he wouldn't have too much contact with the detainees; with his temper, he didn't trust himself around the Iraqis. He'd been known to exceed force sometimes as an MP.

"You don't beat somebody to death or anything, but stuff happens," he explains. So he became the guy you called to get a mop, garbage bags, or meals brought up to the cell block tiers. "I just went with the flow," he says. "I just wanted to do my time and leave."

At its peak, Abu Ghraib held seven thousand detainees. The burned-out buildings at the prison were full of rubble, sand had piled up in the corners of the bare cement cells with barred windows, and stray dogs roamed the compound. There were rooms that during Saddam's reign had been used as execution chambers, and murals of the former dictator that soldiers covered up with paint. The constant hum of the generators ceased only when the electricity cut out. Initially, soldiers slept in tents, but due to the relentless mortar attacks, they switched places with the detainees and slept in prison cells. Holes in the prison's ceiling were reminders that mortars could still rip through the four-foot-thick cement walls. Trips outside to the Port-o-lets or the wooden shacks with cold overhead showers left one in the line of fire. The interpreters and the Iraqi police who were hired by the military couldn't be trusted. Repeatedly, they smuggled in weapons, even guns, which the detainees used on guards. Without the proper manpower, cooks and mechanics manned the watchtower and served as guards, with everyone pulling twelve-hour shifts. As a result, 4 a.m. became confused with 4 p.m.

When members of the 372nd first arrived, they were given tours of the prison to acclimate themselves. Walking through Tier One, the cell's hard site, they saw naked detainees shackled into contorted positions with women's underwear on their heads. "That was weird," Joe said, "but the soldiers said it was in retribution for a mortar attack or something that had happened before we had gotten there." When Joe learned about soldiers being ordered by military intelligence to subject detainees to sleep deprivation, stress positions, and forced physical exercises, he, like many of the other soldiers, had no problem with it. "I've been up for thirty-six hours operating before," he says. "It limits your judgment, but it happens. Jumping jacks? I did that in basic training."

Months later, Corporal Charles Graner, who was later sentenced to ten years for his role as the so-called ringleader of the photographed abuse, showed Joe a photo of a handcuffed prisoner standing in a puddle of liquid. "The Christian in me thinks this is wrong," Graner told him, "but the correction officer in me loves to see a grown man piss himself." Joe was sitting on a woodpile, waiting for his ride back to his sleeping quarters. "I was crazy, half asleep," says Joe. "I just turned around and didn't give it a second thought."

The desert heat had warped Joe's snapshots, so he asked Graner, a perpetual photographer among the guards, for keepsake digital images, hoping for shots of camels, the Babylon palace, tanks—maybe even the shooting in the prison while he had been away on R&R—to show people back home.

Scrolling through the CD, Joe laughed when he saw the pyramid of naked Iraqis. It seemed like a fraternity prank—the kind of thing bored soldiers often got up to. Then he got to the simulated-fellatio pictures.

He shut down his computer, went outside, and smoked half a dozen cigarettes, trying to make sense of it. "I didn't want to be a stool pigeon or a rat," he says. "You are supposed to take care of your own." But some of these pictures seemed to cross the line.

Hearsay about the photos was already spreading throughout the camp. Joe asked his mentor and superior, Keith Comer, and his best friend, Jeremy McGuire, what they would do if, hypothetically, they came across those kinds of photographs. (Later, on February 9, 2004, Comer told the CID otherwise. "I knew the boy who [turned in the photos]," he said. "I don't blame him for doing it. I just wish he went to his chain of command. If it were brought to my attention, there is no doubt in my mind that those people would be relieved and facing charges, just like they are now.")

Joe heard that his friend Stephen Hubbard had told his squad leader, Robert Elliot, that there were photos of abuse but was informed that without the pictures in hand, there was no proof. Hubbard started asking around to see who had copies. "I sat down and thought, Why should I let Hubbard do it and put himself in harm's way when I should have the balls to do it myself?" Joe says. "Hubbard was a little mouthy guy. He probably would've told everybody that he did it, and Graner and them would've probably killed him."

Overall, it took Joe more than a month of deliberating whether he could be the group's conscience. When he finally turned in the photos, instead of going to his superior officer, he went straight to the CID, where soldiers can report everything from sexual harassment to theft. It was a major breach of the chain of command that many would later hold against him.

Four months later, Joe was enjoying his R&R at Camp Anaconda, a sprawling base with an Olympic-size swimming pool, movie theaters, and fast-food chain restaurants. Joe was eating in the mess hall, where CNN was on, showing Secretary of Defense Donald Rumsfeld's congressional testimony on prisoner abuse. Joe had no idea that his tip—which military investigators had assured him would remain anonymous—had led to a national scandal. He says he didn't want the photos to reach the public and had assumed it would be handled in-house. He says the acts were wrong, but there was no need for the public to know about it. In fact, he handed the photos in to CID, but it was Bill Lawson, the uncle of Chip Frederick, one of the accused soldiers, who had leaked the photos to the press, an almost universally overlooked fact.

Joe heard Rumsfeld name various people who'd provided information: "First the soldier, Specialist Joseph Darby, who alerted the appropriate authorities that abuses of detainees were occurring. My thanks and appreciation to him for his courage and his values." Joe dropped his fork mid-bite. Oh, shit. He felt four hundred pairs of eyes on him. He was sitting with four of his friends who already knew. One of them looked across at him and said, "Darby, we need to leave." Seymour Hersh had already published Joe's name, but, as Joe says, "Who reads the damn *New Yorker?*" Privately, some people told him he had done the right thing. But even his ardent supporters, including others who had reported the abuse to their superiors, were livid that he had gone outside the chain of command. "Everyone in the unit knew within four hours," says Joe. "And within seventy-two hours, everyone in my hometown also knew exactly who I was and that I had been the one to turn in the photos."

Joe's mother, Margaret Blank, was dying of cancer, had already lost an eye, and had difficulty walking because of her diabetes; now, the compassionate-leave request that Joe had filed earlier was rushed through, and he was sent home.

When Joe's plane touched down stateside at the Dover airport, he was surprised to find officers waiting on the tarmac with his wife. They escorted the couple to an undisclosed location, where they lived with around-the-clock security for the next six months. "All it takes is one person who has something against me, who gets on a drunken bender at the Big Claw bar and doesn't find me but finds my wife," Joe says.

Joe and his wife, Bernadette, had received death threats, ranging from phone calls and e-mails to whispers around town. Before Joe came home, Bernadette had overheard someone at the gas station calling Joe a dead man: "He's walking around with a bull's-eye on his head." Joe's uncle publicly denounced him, calling him a traitor. His family legally barred Joe from seeing his young stepbrother ever again. Those family members who stood by the couple faced retribution of their own. Bernadette's older sister, Maxine Carroll, woke up to find "Iraq" scrawled on the fence surrounding her house.

Reporters inundated Bernadette with phone calls. Her sister eventually took over as a sort of de facto spokesperson, offering up sound bites about their support for Joe's moral stand. If the questions even hinted at anything negative, she would simply hang up. But even as she complained about the media frenzy, she kept answering the phone, just in case, she said, President Bush was to finally call.

"I received a reality check from the people in my community where Joe and I lived," Bernadette told Diane Sawyer, who flew her and her sister up to New York City for *Good Morning America*. "I was an EMT. I was a firefighter. I mean, I helped these people every day, and then this happened, and it was like everybody turned."

When Sawyer asked Bernadette whether people were angry for the public admission that things like Abu Ghraib happened, she responded, "I think America is just angry about what happened September eleventh."

Joe blames the anger he's evoked on what he calls "America's notorious blind patriotism." "People aren't pissed because I turned someone in for abuse," he says. "People are pissed because I turned in an American soldier for abusing an Iraqi. They don't care about right and wrong. They care American, non-American."

That day at Starbucks, Joe told me this was his last interview before he put Abu Ghraib behind him forever. But in the summer of 2008, a *Washington Post* reporter started to call Cumberland residents, asking whether they knew of his whereabouts. Every time a new mainstream news article or television segment comes out about Abu Ghraib, the issue is raised yet again.

These days, Joe has Graner's proposed release date marked on his calendar: January 14, 2015. Joe figures that when Graner gets out, he's coming for him. During the trial, Graner had kept Joe locked in a cold stare. Joe has no faith in a restraining order, so instead, he says, he has his own plan. He's going to fly to Kansas and stand outside the gates of the prison and confront Graner head on.

"If he has a problem, fine, if not, not," Joe reasons. "But I would rather go out to Leavenworth and get him than have him come after me and my family."

5

Torture Town, USA

In early 2004, soldiers from the 372nd National Guard unit began to make vague telephone calls to their families back home in Western Maryland's Appalachia. "Something bad is going on," they warned. "I can't tell you more. But there's going to be trouble."

There were rumors that Lynndie England, home on temporary leave in November, had told her mother about "strange stuff" going on in Iraq. Her mom said that she honestly didn't even want to hear about it and had told Lynndie to just talk to her dad about it instead. Still, her mother worried, and she asked the military whether she could keep Lynndie home through Christmas. The request was denied.

Some families had already received snapshots of abused detainees, which were sent home as trophies of war. Bill Crawford, the executive director of the local Red Cross chapter, got calls from his two stepsons, Jeremy and Mickey McGuire, who were in the unit. Jeremy, Joe Darby's roommate, was nervous about questions the CID investigators were asking him. They wanted to know whether the image of the back of one man's head was his brother Mickey. Such an accusation alone could tarnish a reputation. Jeremy Sivits wrote a letter to his parents, Sissy and Daniel, explaining that he was being investigated for witnessing "some shit that happened in the prison." His father, a Vietnam vet, had warned Jeremy when he first enlisted that he'd disown him if he was ever dishonorably discharged. Now Jeremy wrote, begging his father not to abandon him and saying how scared he was. Chip Frederick had been writing home to his family, telling them about "softening up" prisoners for the interrogators. He said it was difficult seeing the detainees being made to stay kneeling on the floor with their noses to the wall. "A lot end up crying," he wrote. "Sometimes I feel sorry for them, but then I realize that they are the reason I am here, and the feeling goes away." Mostly, though, the accounts were vague.

On April 28, 2004, when the photos of the naked pyramids and the hooded prisoners were splashed on television sets around the nation, the picture became all too clear for everyone. Suddenly, they knew far more than they wanted to. They used to scour the newspapers for any mention of Abu Ghraib, in hopes of details about their soldiers' deployment. Now the phrase was an inescapable household word. Parents and spouses watched, hoping their loved ones weren't directly involved. Others weren't as lucky.

Lynndie's father, Kenneth, saw images of his daughter giving the thumbs-up and leading a prisoner by a leash, as did the welders and the machinists who worked with him at the CSX railroad in town. They continued to pledge allegiance to the flag before each shift, as they have since 9/11, and support him as best they knew how: by not mentioning it.

Meanwhile, a group of public relations experts convened at the Pentagon to advise on how to handle the scandal. To deflect attention from the higher ranks, the administration propagated the "bad apple" spin, stressing that it was the work of a few "recycled hillbillies from Appalachia." As a National Guard unit, most of the soldiers were from the same rural area, so the scandal quickly became a community issue. The families barely had time to process the news when they were called on by the media and the nation at large to explain how their town had birthed such "sick rednecks." Newspapers and television commentators started to debate whether the acts in the photos were examples of torture. Letters from around the country filled the mailboxes of the local newspaper, the city council, and the mayor's office. Cumberland became known as a breeding ground for torturers and was suddenly under siege.

Linda Comer kept hearing the words *Abu Ghraib* on television as she flipped through the channels. At first, she tried to ignore it. Her husband, sixteen years her junior, was working at the prison. But he was having an affair with another soldier, and his and his unit's well-being was low on her list of concerns. Plus, she rationalized, it could be any one of a number of units stationed at the prison. That night a reporter woke her up with a call about the scandal, and she realized that her husband's unit had been directly involved—and by proxy she was as well.

Linda runs the local Army Family Readiness Group (FRG), which is like a PTA for the military, and provides a support network for military families, with meetings once a month. Particularly for the families of members of the National Guard and the Reserves, who don't live on military bases and have never prepared for deployment, FRGs can be a crucial lifeline while soldiers are deployed. Sometimes it is practical things that families need, such as help navigating health insurance paperwork or finding emergency funds when single mothers can't cover child care, but just as often people need emotional support from someone who is going through the same difficulties. FRGs are also the key source for information about the units' deployments when soldiers aren't able to call home. Before long, families were calling Linda, frantic to know what was happening.

Linda loves the attention that her position with the FRG brings her. She calls herself "proactive"; others use words like "busybody," "attention hungry," and "cliqueish." Linda likes to be at the center of things and tends to get overly involved. She dishes out unit gossip about who is sleeping with whom and who is neglecting his or her parental duties, as she dramatically rolls her eyes. But when it came to the scandal, she says that she didn't want to know the details—in fact, she asked people not to tell her. If she knew more, she says, she wouldn't be able to resist telling everyone about things she thought no one should know. "We're trained not to talk about the war," explains Linda. "What happens in Iraq stays in Iraq."

Linda also admits that when she finally sat down and looked at the images, she wasn't ruffled. "The photos were pretty vivid," she says, "but honestly, I didn't feel anything at all. That might sound weird, but war is war." After the scandal broke, she told me, the recruiting center filled with high school seniors, who "were just fascinated by that kind of thing. They liked that you could do that in the military, and they wanted to be a part of it, part of that unit."

The soldiers' gear was already back stateside, and welcome-home plans had been made, but with the scandal, the soldiers were kept in the Middle East, away from public scrutiny. Linda and the other families went into high gear to make sure all the soldiers in the unit, accused or not, knew that the town was behind them. Families stapled yellow ribbons to utility poles and hung posters that read "Support the Troops" and "Jeremy Sivits our hometown hero" around town. They wrote letters of sympathy to families and complaints to congressmen about how unfair it was to prosecute low-level soldiers for following orders. A petition to "Free Lynndie" was set up at the counter of the local dollar store. Bumper stickers and T-shirts emblazoned with "Free Chip Frederick," one of the soldiers facing charges, were distributed by his family.

Linda called the families of the accused to let them know she was there for them. But Linda and the other families did not call Joe Darby's wife, Bernadette. If she were to come to an FRG meeting, Linda says they would have talked to her. But Becky McClarran, an active member of the FRG, says it would have been "embarrassing and uncomfortable, to say the least."

On the rainy eve of the arraignments for Sergeant Javal Davis, Staff Sergeant Ivan "Chip" Frederick, and Specialist Charles Graner, and the sentencing of Jeremy Sivits, supporters organized candlelight vigils throughout the area. The plan was to hold them every Saturday afternoon until the troops came home.

In Hyndman, a small community north of Cumberland, more than two hundred people showed up at the open chapel on a campground—impressive for a town of less than one thousand. They lit candles and prayed for support. The Boy Scouts sang "America Gives Me Liberty, but Jesus Gives Me Love," and the crowd waved small American flags. Jeremy's father, Daniel, wearing a black MIA bandanna, told the crowd, "I want to make explicitly clear that Jeremy, no matter what, is still my son. . . . He is always a vet in my heart and in my mind." Thomas Cunningham, Hyndman's former mayor, created an informal committee, misguidedly hoping that if its members made enough noise to keep the incident in the public eye, they could help get Sivits exonerated.

That same evening in downtown Cumberland, more than fifty people gathered in the rain for a candlelight vigil. People stubbornly relit their candles every time they were extinguished by the drizzling rain. High school student Becca Graham sang "God Bless America," and a church choir member did a solo of "The Star Spangled Banner." "For those accused of abuse or crimes, let them know that they are still your children, no matter what they have done or allegedly have done," Lutheran Reverend Stephen Yelovich recited during a prayer. As a team of reporters looked on, Tom Landaker, the pastor of the First Baptist Church and the chaplain for the local Vietnam Veterans of America, led a prayer at one of the vigils, asking God to give everyone the strength to withstand the liberal media's "poisonous views of our community."

"It was probably the best summer the Holiday Inn has ever had. The reporters were just like locusts swooping down," said Becky McClarran, laughing. Becky became the self-appointed unofficial spokesperson for families with soldiers in the 372nd, a natural role given her maternal protectiveness and her small public relations company in town. Reporters showed up on people's porches with cameras and microphones. They telephoned soldiers' families, knocked on their doors, and harassed her son, the one soldier who had returned early. "The families were horrified," reports Linda Comer. "They felt like they were being prosecuted, and they were, in their own way. Let the court-martial do it, not the media." Cameramen trailed families of the accused like paparazzi. Nowhere was safe. They descended on the IGA supermarket where Lynndie had worked; the Big Claw, where members of the 372nd often drink on drill weekends; and the local VFWs. Reporters sat on top of the roof of the Tasti-Freeze, hoping to catch a glimpse of Lynndie's family, knocked on doors of any house with yellow ribbons, and camped out on the side of the road.

Only a month earlier, hundreds of locals had lined that road, flags in hand, saluting and crying, at the funeral procession for local boy Brandon Davis, who was killed by an IED near Fallujah. Now, a CNN helicopter hovered over the trailer park where the Englands lived. The owner of that trailer park banned any and all reporters, and the Army put up a fence around the unit's headquarters. Other helicopters circled one of the local high schools. Scared students frantically called home. Jeremy's mother, Holly Sivits, had to leave her job at the local dollar store after her boss got upset about reporters following her to work. She and her husband dropped out of their social circles for a while and had someone park a tractor trailer, decorated with miniature flags and yellow ribbons, in front of their house to shield them from the public.

Lynndie's older sister, Jessica Klinestiver, and her best friend, Destiny Goin, held a press conference at the volunteer fire department to try to counter the negative press coverage. As cameras flashed in their faces, they held up photos of Lynndie before the scandal—on vacation with Graner, hugging her brother Josh, and dressed up for her high school prom. Klinestiver defended her sister. "Certain people in the Army told her to do what she did. She follows orders. I don't believe my sister did what she did in those photos. I believe they were posed," she said. "I'm very proud of my sister."

Locals were angry that the press was trying to perpetuate an image of the soldiers as "recycled hillbillies" and their towns as backwoods, straight out of the movie *Deliverance*. "The reporters came in here and went into the corner bar, probably the most run-down place around here, and interviewed the guy with no teeth who is there from one p.m. until midnight," says Renee, who played softball with Lynndie back in high school and returned to the area after college to work at an espresso bar.

"Just because someone is from here and lived in a trailer park doesn't mean that they are going to do those things," says Renee. "People got very defensive of their town, and that, in turn, helped people defend Lynndie, too." That defensiveness was everywhere. Ask people in town what they think of Lynndie, and they will respond that she is local, and that is all they need to know. One of the local recreation boards hired Lynndie to run the annual Strawberry Festival. A woman answering the phone at one of the VFWs told me, "We one hundred percent support Lynndie. The child got a wrong deal. She was a very nice, gullible person." Most people refused to say anything more. When I asked a bricklayer hanging out in the bar next door to the trailer park where Lynndie grew up whether what she had done was wrong, he said, "No. She was a local resident; I knew her dad. She was a young kid who used to work at the supermarket. She was just doing her job." He was angry that I was down there asking questions, and, like others, he wondered out loud why he was even talking to me.

I traveled to Cumberland, in the western panhandle of Maryland, to understand this town that the media dubbed Torture Town, USA. I wanted to understand the perspectives of those who blame the whistleblower, not the abusers or even the higher-ups in the administration, who had ordered and authorized the detaince treatment. "It started with one action: Darby," says Linda. "One soldier embarrassed the whole country, from the president on down. Because of him, the president had to come out and talk about this."

Cumberland is a veteran's town more than it is a military town. Sixteen percent of the county's population are veterans, meaning there is military blood in most families. A giant "Let's Roll" sign hangs on one house; trucks are covered with Support the Troops magnets and miniflags on the antennas. Flags have always blanketed the town, long before 9/11.

The expanded veteran outpatient clinic now offers tele-psychiatry sessions, basically a shrink via TV, to deal with all of the cases of post-traumatic stress disorder. Military recruiters working out of a storefront in a Cumberland strip mall have always had it easy. They offer more than a hard-to-come-by paycheck and a ticket out: they offer honor, responsibility, and meaning, things that are rare in Appalachia. Even when asked, local soldiers and veterans don't complain that the military often doesn't follow through with its promises of benefits. They see that they are taking the brunt of the cost of the war, but that there is also an honor in being the ones to lead Iraqis to freedom.

The area is a union stronghold but without enough factories left to make that meaningful. In 1964, Lyndon B. Johnson stood

on the steps of Cumberland's city hall to address the very people
he was trying to save through his War on Poverty. "Poverty not
only strikes at the needs of the body. It attacks the spirit and it
undermines human dignity," he told the crowd. But neither the
coal-mining industry nor the later manufacturing boom, now
bust, has been enough to win that battle. Of "the big four" factories in the area, only the paper mill is left, which is mentioned
more in conversations about the toxic smell in the air and the
unfishable branch of the Potomac than in discussions about
jobs. The world stopped needing bias-ply tires, and upgrad-
ing the machinery to make radials was expensive, so in 1986 on
Thanksgiving weekend, 1,675 workers at the Kelly-Springfield
tire plant lost their jobs, something that is still mentioned with
disbelief. The plant had been in operation sixty-six years. "It is
like a sonic boom," Kelly's president, Clifford Johnson, told the
local paper at the time. The company's motto, "Quality Not
Quantity," became obsolete.

Four years earlier, the Celanese synthetic fiber factory, which
in the 1940s employed more than 10,000 people, laid off its
final 310 workers, and those at the Pittsburgh Plate Glass factory
dwindled from 500 to 50 to none. The local breweries that produced beers with names like "Sweetlife" and "American" survived
Prohibition and the Depression, only to be put under by larger
consolidated companies in the seventies. A one-step counseling
center for recently laid-off workers was set up in an abandoned
storefront. Politicians called for relaxed environmental laws to
attract industry; others courted the federal government for a
prison or looked to tourism to boost the local economy.

Now the 161-acre property that used to house the Celanese
factory, whose public swimming pool charged only twenty-five
cents per person, has been turned into a prison complex. It is a
sweeping expanse of glimmering barbed wire, corrugated-metal
buildings, and the jammed parking lot for the hundreds of
employees who work at the complex. The prison is infamous
for prisoner abuse. In 2008, four guards were convicted for

brutally beating inmates; another two were fired and charged for the same. In 2004 inmate Ifeanyi Iko, a Nigerian immigrant, died there under circumstances that are still disputed. Next door to the Western Correctional Institution is the brand-new $24.8 million Panopticon prison, built by out-of-state contractors and lauded as a state-of-the-art maximum-security facility.

Four miles from the prisons, barely across the West Virginia state line, sits another of the area's major employers, Alliant Tech. Between 1985 and 2006, the plant won $250 million in earmarks, thanks to Senator Robert Byrd, known as the "pork king." As the nation's largest military ammunition plant, it made $4.2 billion in 2008, largely from military contracts. While most of the economy is dying, the "Rocket Center" plant had been adding hundreds of new employees each year. To meet the demand for missile defense systems, it is partnering with colleges and high schools to prepare kids as young as the eighth grade for entry-level jobs. The EPA classifies it as a Superfund site because of its high levels of depleted uranium. Even local activists, angry over the links between depleted uranium and Gulf War syndrome, are hesitant to complain, realizing that without those twelve-dollar-an-hour paychecks, many of their neighbors couldn't survive.

With nearly 14 percent of the population living below poverty and 8 percent unemployment, the county is losing people who have lived there for generations. In 2005, the most common jobs were in food service and bars, flipping burgers and pouring beers, which paid an average of $218 a week. Most people shop at the local Walmart, but taxis line up outside the Pay 'N Sav downtown to shuttle people home with their bags of white-labeled generic cans of food. A food bank operates out of a former bread factory. For the first time, homeless people camp out in public doorways downtown, refusing to enter the shelters. The newspaper reported that a high school football player shot himself during a game of Russian roulette; another article described the arrest of a man who stole $90,000 worth of cemetery vases to sell for scrap. And this was all before the national recession.

While in Cumberland, I asked people what they thought about the war, and they responded with information about how few jobs there were. Supporting the troops was akin to union solidarity—a pact among the people doing the country's grunt work. As one local ex-Marine told me, "Sometimes you just have to do what you can to get by. And you have to be able to believe in the validity of what you're doing." Like so many working-class towns, everyone believes there's honor in doing a hard day's work if you can find it, no matter what it is.

The Abu Ghraib detainees were humiliated, but as Jimmy Linaburg, who runs C&J Cycles on Warrior Drive, told a *Washington Post* reporter, "Every stinking day I'm humiliated."

Like a quarterback obsessed with his high school glory days, Cumberland tends to prove its worth by pointing to its past. The old trains and canal barges have been turned into historic attractions in a feeble attempt to draw tourism, but, as one local put it, who is going to go visit an old barge they pulled out of the mud? A downtown bank has been transformed into a history museum that largely chronicles yesterday's commerce. Next door, on a shuttered storefront, hangs a small black-and-white photo depicting the store back when business was booming.

In 1806, America's first highway started in Cumberland, but in the 1990s, when the state built a new freeway, it bypassed the town, depriving the citizens of the strip malls and the chain stores that freeways bring. "It put us at a standstill," says Ed Mullaney, who is in charge of downtown development. "We are a throwback in time in many ways, but I mean that in a positive way."

Trains still cut through the downtown area, reminders of a time when being a railroad hub put the town on the map. No one mans the train station where the one daily Amtrak train comes through. "Standing there," one local said, "you don't know if it is coming or not." After 9/11, the small commercial airport, which had mainly catered to Kelly executives back in the day, closed down for good.

When the modern world has literally passed you by, it's easier to hold on to an idealized version of America. In that bubble, insulated against harsh realities, where the local paper reports on church events and not on secret CIA black sites, the myth can survive. America can still stand for apple pie, and war can be pictured as a heroic battle straight out of a John Wayne film. If that is all you have to hold on to, you have to fight to protect it any way you can.

When I first visited Cumberland two and a half years after the Abu Ghraib scandal, the anger around town toward Joe Darby was still palpable. That December, the local paper's poll found that 30 percent called Darby a traitor, the rest a hero. But when the paper sent a reporter to follow up, no one would speak on the record in Darby's support. Even when I last returned there in 2008 it was the same. Ask people what they think of Abu Ghraib and you are met with a blank look. Ask them about the Darby issue and they are filled with opinions.

When the scandal broke, there were no holds barred for locals when they denounced Darby to the press: "If I were [Darby], I'd be sneaking in through the back door at midnight," Janette Jones, a local mom, told a *Washington Post* reporter. "They can call him what they want," Mike Simico, a veteran visiting relatives in Cresaptown, said to the same reporter. "I call him a rat." Even the old school bus driver Barb Lehman told a reporter from the *Toronto Star* that she "wouldn't want to be in his shoes. We don't believe in ratting people out like that."

All the same, people tell me that the threat against Joe was exaggerated. The university's chaplain had been harassed for hosting an antiwar event. The newspaper's columnist advocating gun control and the county planning commissioner proposing new development both received death threats. A black student who protested classmates wearing Confederate flag T-shirts to school had to go into hiding after being threatened. But no harm had come to any of them. Besides, people say, a few isolated threats against Joe don't represent the community as a whole.

Colin Engelbach, the commander of the local VFW post, explains to me that by "get him," people just meant they would make Joe's life hell. Colin called Joe a "borderline traitor" on national television. "Do you put the enemy above your buddies? I wouldn't," he had added. The segment propelled him into the national spotlight as a symbol for the hatred against Joe. Once again, letters from around the country filled the mailboxes of the local newspaper, the city council, and the mayor's office, denouncing Cumberland as a town of torture lovers, a casualty of the scandal. The VFW made a public statement distancing itself from Colin. Even if most VFW members were angry with Joe, it was something they said privately. Colin's statement was no good for PR. Colin was asked not to run for another term of office during the VFW's next election.

Colin is a small man whose eyes had trouble meeting mine. He spent ten years in the National Guard and four on active duty. Now he works double shifts making depleted-uranium weapons at Alliant Tech. Colin says he doesn't worry about the health effects of working with uranium, but he also explains that he had to sign a confidentiality agreement with the company and can't really talk about it. For six months after our interview, he called me with "dirt" on Joe; his overall message was that Joe had put himself before his comrades, that he was not a real American.

"His motivations aren't pure," Colin tells me, a sentiment repeatedly echoed by others. "The issue isn't so black and white," people say. "He wanted attention, fame, to go home, to avoid having to do his duty." "It was a way to get promoted without having to pass the physical test requirements." Some speculate that his snitching was in retaliation against the soldiers who picked on him, just as the kids in high school had. The soldiers in his unit frequently called him "fat bastard" because he was too obese to pass the physical tests. Even Joe admits that it was partly personal. He calls Sabrina Harman, a guard who was charged in the abuse scandal, "a piece of shit," and while he admits that Charles Graner has a charismatic hold over people, he describes Graner as a manipulative guy with an evil, dark, morbid side. And Chip Frederick, he just plain didn't like.

Joe has been criticized for speaking about issues he didn't know the first thing about. Which in many ways is true. He didn't witness those acts of abuse firsthand and never saw the logbook in which soldiers carefully documented every order they received to carry out abuse and torture. Joe holds steadfast to the "bad apples" account, denying the fact that the orders came from above, despite reams of memos, investigations, and testimonies proving otherwise. He thought it was just photos of a few bad apples playing what would later be called Animal House on the night shift. Perhaps if he had realized that the orders went as high up as Donald Rumsfeld and Dick Cheney, Joe wouldn't have reported the abuse.

Even Joe's supporters in Cumberland are quick to distance themselves from him. They explain that Joe and many of the soldiers don't even come from there. The mayor wrote a letter in response to the hate mail, saying that the town's support of the "brave men and women of our armed forces" includes Sergeant Joe Darby, and that the "misguided statements of a few local citizens do not represent the views of the residents of the city." But the mayor concluded by saying that while Joe was always welcome, he was "not a resident of our city."

It is true. Joe comes from Corriganville, five miles from downtown Cumberland, little more than a gas station, a bar, and a firehouse. As with all Army Reserve units, the members hail from communities within a hundred-mile radius of the unit headquarters, which is located six miles from Cumberland in Cresaptown. Most are little more than clusters of dollar stores, bars, and gas stations scattered among the rolling farmland, the forested mountains, and the cement strip malls. They seem more like neighborhoods than proper towns.

Cresaptown itself lies at the junction of U.S. Highway 220 and State Route 53. There's no town hall, the civic improvement center is shuttered, and old toys sit forgotten on the front porches of houses behind low wire fences. It's stumbling distance from Pete's Tavern to the Big Claw bar and the Eagles Club, which a few years back launched a minor scandal by admitting a black man. ("He may be a nigger, but he's also a cop," one of Pete's regulars told me, "so they had to let him in.") There's the Liberty Christian Fellowship, the Boy Scout building, and the technical college (whose sign declares "teamwork" the word of the month).

Then there is Hyndman, a half–square mile of houses and a smattering of businesses—a gas station, a dollar store, a pizzeria— off Route 96 north of town. South of Cumberland, over the West Virginia border, is Ft. Ashby, population 1,350, a strip of low-budget shops, a diner, a gas station, and a run-down bar interrupting the rural landscape, where Lynndie grew up in a trailer park. Keyser is a city proper further south, where Lynndie now works for her former trial lawyer. It is half strip mall and half just broken. Most of the storefronts lining what used to be Keyser's main street are empty and abandoned. Among the survivors are a fake-flower shop, several taverns, a parole officer's office, a library, and a hair salon. A bookstore sells only paperback Harlequin romances, mysteries, and religious books. The other small fluorescent-lit stores sell a mishmash of used or discarded items: broken baskets, unused bottles of deodorant, well-worn children's shoes. Flags adorn most houses and mobile homes: American flags, American flags with yellow ribbons on them, flags of eagles, and flags depicting flags.

But most of the soldiers travel to the same Walmart to do their shopping, wind up in the same bars in the evenings, and know one another from high school. Some of their children might be on different soccer teams, but they all share the stadium seating when cheering for their kids. While some soldiers have to commute, many work together at the local ammunition plant, the hospital, or one of the many prisons. And each month, the 125 unit members travel to the same inconspicuous small brick building headquarters of the 372nd in Cresaptown for training.

Cumberland, relatively progressive and well off in comparison to the surrounding areas, tends to attract people who don't quite fit into the rest of Appalachia. Like most places in the world, it has contradictory layers of subcultures, immigrants, and newcomers. Dejected Hot Topic–clad Goth kids loiter in the downtown outdoor mall, and young punk rockers drink forties in alleys. The college in nearby Frostburg attracts hippies and jam bands. There is even a vibrant gay scene slightly below the radar, which draws homosexuals who range from married tourists to confused teenagers seeking refuge from the surrounding towns. In the late hours, certain sports bars look like a scene in San Francisco's Castro district, with queens on the dance floor, meth in the bathroom, and Blondie on the jukebox. Gays are welcomed as entertaining oddities at the local Eagles Club, but they also know not to stick around for long. And there is no way, they say, that gays would survive any of the bars on the outskirts of town.

There is even a peace group in Cumberland. It's spearheaded by Larry Neumark, the Protestant chaplain at local Frostburg State University, whose sweaters and soft voice conjure up Mr. Rogers. Early on in the war, the group—mostly consisting of faculty from Frostburg and nearby community colleges who clung to one another as "lifelines"—struggled to find open ears. "You'll be accused of being unpatriotic and un-American if you speak up," said Neumark. Local schools have rejected courses with "peace" in the title as unpatriotic. The members have been lambasted in letters to the newspaper and harshly criticized on air by the local talk radio host, but mostly they are simply referred to as "polite nuisances." Mainly it's a "subtle nonverbal opposition" that they contend with. "People give you the cold shoulder, people you once thought were friends," said Neumark. "But in the last six to seven months, people have been more willing to talk."

In the fall of 2006, Neumark nearly lost his job for inviting Ray McGovern, a retired CIA officer, to speak on campus against the war. By the spring of 2007, Neumark was having a hard time filling the *pro*-war slot on a panel discussion he was setting up.

Torture, though, was another story. Neumark had proposed a panel discussion on the topic. But people were "very on edge" about the issue, as Daniel Hull, the sole student member of the group, told me. Even the activists were split on whether they should "go in that direction."

Eventually, Neumark did pull together his panel, with speakers who included a man who had been tortured in the Philippines during the regime of President Ferdinand Marcos. About a hundred students, many of them earning extra class credit by attending, listened to the man recall the mock executions, the solitary confinement, and the interrogations he'd endured. In response, one student argued that the Geneva Conventions were outdated. "Has fear been used to effectively deaden our critical senses?" Neumark asked. An audience member stomped out. In the back someone snoozed. "Torture is a form of terrorism," offered Neumark. "Why do you think people aren't speaking out about this?" No one had an answer.

The next year, Neumark retired, and the sustainability of the peace movement looked grim. Craig Etchinson, one of the core members, still planned protests, but now, with few remaining members, he had little hope.

"People here feel more hurt by this whole thing than anything," John Kershner, a member of the 372nd, whispered into my ear. "I just wish Darby would shut his mouth and let the rest of us move on." It was early Friday evening, and I was sitting in the Big Claw bar, about twenty yards from the National Guard headquarters, when "Sarge," as the regulars call him, motioned for me to come over.

The Big Claw is where some of the reservists party after their weekend drills, where locals go on benders, and a spot that African Americans, gays, and any kind of outsiders avoid at all costs. The bar used to serve ribs and steamed crab before prices shot way up. Now it serves Miller Light and shots of Jaeger, and the pizza shop next door occasionally sends over pies. People line up their change and dollar bills on the wooden bar to buy dollar-fifty beers and lottery tickets. If anyone gets too drunk—which happens often—there's always someone around to take the person home.

On most nights and afternoons, you'll find Sarge sitting quietly at the bar, smoking his USA brand menthols (only three dollars a pack, he boasts) and drinking beer, but tonight he decided to talk to me—talk more than he has in a while, he admitted. He was polite in an old-time kind of way, making a point of ordering me a drink and taking off his well-worn Eagles Club hat indoors to reveal his balding, closely shaved head. His light blue eyes were hidden behind thick glasses with smudged lenses. Sarge knows Joe personally. He was the man who hired Joe as a foreman off the books at his self-storage construction company, after the two served together during a deployment to Bosnia. But I learned about this connection later from Joe, not from Sarge. Knowing Joe isn't something to bring up at the Big Claw.

Sarge had to sell his construction business when he deployed to Iraq. Now employers tell him he's either overqualified or, at a weathered, war-broken, booze-worn fifty-six, too old. His story is a common one. Even though, legally, reservists are supposed to be able to pick up at their old jobs where they left off, things aren't always so simple. Economies move on, people become redundant. Sarge has been filing for his veterans' benefits for two years now, trying to straighten out his record to qualify for retirement, but he continues to get the runaround.

Going around the bar, Sarge pointed out the locals: "That guy puts up self-storage units. He works at the weapons plant.

She's a beautician, and he's out of work." That night I heard echoes of what I've heard throughout the area. "I'm not saying that the photos were correct. But our people had their heads cut off," remarked one guy with muddy work boots. "We weren't murdering people, just slightly humiliating them," argued one woman in her early thirties who was drinking beers after her shift.

"Those gentlemen can still talk, walk, and see. Look what they did to the bodies of our men. It felt like retaliation," added her boyfriend.

"Other countries can torture our men to death and it's okay, but if we drop one decimal dip below our higher standards, you have guys paying the price," complained Sarge. "Now you need permission to even shoot back when you're under attack. You let them win there, and we'll be fighting here next."

Over and over, in bars and diners and living rooms, with policemen, firemen, contractors, factory workers, retirees, and parents, I heard these refrains. What we did wasn't as bad as what they do. They beheaded our guys, and all we did was embarrass them. We didn't rape or kill them. We just made their lives a little uncomfortable. If we don't fight dirty over there, we'll be fighting them on our soil with another 9/11.

America is a country that prides itself on its military might. Particularly in the wake of the 9/11 attacks, people wanted to get revenge American-style, which meant using large guns, tanks, and bombs. The incidents at Abu Ghraib seemed like gutless, minor acts, and yet the country and our soldiers were being lambasted. Having to abide by the Geneva Conventions when the enemy didn't meant that we were tying our hands behind our back. If we didn't fight dirty as the terrorists do, we would lose. And the thought of America being anything less than a superpower is worse than imagining us losing our supposed moral high ground.

•   •   •

The global war on terror was sold as retaliation not against a specific group of people, but against "enemies of freedom" and the Axis of Evil. It was a crusade to defend all that America stood for and, as President Bush put it, "all that is good and just in our world." Lives and oil were at stake, but mostly the war was sold as a worldwide battle of almost mythical proportions, representing good versus evil. The evening of 9/11, Bush announced, "our way of life, our very freedom came under attack. America was targeted for attack because we're the brightest beacon for freedom and opportunity in the world. And no one will keep that light from shining."

On 9/11, when Flight 93 crashed into a field only twenty-five miles away from downtown Cumberland, the threat of terrorism felt real. Locals say they felt the ground reverberating from the crash. At the makeshift memorial on the site, Boy Scouts to bikers to tourists brought in on buses have left mementos: a Jesus license plate, Confederate flags, Beanie Babies, a Sunoco gas sign with "Never forget" scrawled across it in black marker, and union stickers.

The smoke was still rising when U.S. citizens first called for torture in retaliation. The hysteria, patriotism, and fear that swelled after 9/11 can lead people to think in extremes. Questioning the policies put forward by President George W. Bush and Vice President Dick Cheney became unpatriotic. Being "un-American" became the ultimate accusation.

All over the country, hate crimes that targeted Arabs and Muslims—and those perceived to be Arab or Muslim—skyrocketed after 9/11. On September 19, 2001, on Route 15 near Cumberland, a white man in his blue Ford pickup truck shot his rifle at Satpreet Singh, a young turbaned Sikh, who was driving home. Singh filed a report with the police, but nothing came of it. The cops said the case was on the back burner.

Jobs usually distract people from these kinds of angry ruminations, but in Cumberland, jobs are hard to come by. Epithets such as "sand-niggers," which were used freely among soldiers in Iraq, were echoed on the barstools in western Maryland. This amorphous combination of anger, fear, religion, racism, and patriotism manifested in violence against prisoners in Iraq and a support for torture among people back home.

People in Maryland's Appalachia sounded both angry and embarrassed when they talked about an America too weak to win the war or even provide jobs for hardworking citizens. They idealistically believed in their country, yet it was failing them so badly.

Becky McClarran, whose son Danny Mizak served at Abu Ghraib with the 372nd, argues that people made too big a deal about what had happened, considering the context. "We didn't kill anyone," she says. "Does that make it any less wrong? No. But 9/11 changed the way we felt. We were violated. The culture in the Middle East is something most of us don't understand. We're fighting people way different from us."

When I met with McClarran at the antiques cooperative where she works on weekends, she took on the tired tone of someone who has been through this too many times. Throughout the interview, she repeated the refrain about the unit being unfairly blamed for the actions of a few. "Not every soldier comes from a nice family," she explained. She hinted that the war is a failure, but when I asked her point-blank, she replied that with a son who had just been stationed there, she couldn't tell me what she really thinks. "We are a tight-knit community. We stick together," she said.

Despite talking extensively with reporters, she said she has never talked to her son Danny about his time working at Abu Ghraib. They discuss how he finds the local Frostburg State University stiflingly liberal and how he can't relate to other students who haven't been to war. But "like most soldiers, Iraq isn't something he talks about," she said. She doubts that any of the reservists will speak with me.

Danny clearly has issues about the war that he needs to unload. He has lashed out several times during antiwar discussions on campus. He adamantly believes in the war and has reenlisted, this time in the full-time military instead of the National Guard. It's his job, so, of course, he will go back if called. The military is almost an oasis for him, where people understand what he's been through. But he refused to go to the ceremony to accept his Purple Heart.

6

The Black Mark

After the scandal broke, Major General Karol Kennedy flew into Cumberland on a helicopter to meet with families at the unit headquarters to answer their questions about the fate of their soldiers. Mostly they weren't concerned about the scandal, but about when the unit was coming home. She gave strict orders that when the troops did return home, there were to be no local celebrations, no parades or restaurant dinners, no publicity-drawing fanfare.

When that day finally arrived, on August 3, 2004, families made the five-hour drive to Fort Lee Army Base in Virginia, to greet the soldiers as they got off the plane. Holding signs, balloons, and flags, the families stomped on the bleachers, chanted, cheered, and cried. "Heroes deserve a hero's welcome, and that is exactly what we are giving them," yelled one Army dad from the bleachers.

But back home, things were quiet. Some people hung signs, "Well Done 372," "Welcome Home," "We Missed You," but others were scared that this would only attract the attention of reporters.

In lieu of a ticker-tape parade, an announcement in the local paper urged people to hang yellow ribbons. Bill Crawford, one of the parents to spearhead the effort, explained that the idea was "to literally saturate the region with yellow, so that no matter where the soldiers go when they return, they will see visual reinforcements of the love and thanks we feel for them."

Normally, soldiers have a huge welcome-home event and are honored at a ceremony. But this time, it was different. "They kept it on the down low," explains Mickey Comer, who was with the 372nd at the time. "We busted into Cumberland, got to the unit, and everyone left. When we came home from Bosnia, we had more of a celebration than this."

Studies have shown that "homecoming stress"—the shame, the negative interpersonal interactions, the social withdrawal, and the resentment that soldiers can experience when they first come home—is the most significant predictor of PTSD, more so than even the wartime events themselves or the social services the soldiers receive after that. Others have shown that National Guard and Reserve soldiers in the war on terror report substantially higher PTSD rates than full-time military soldiers do, making the toll on communities like Cumberland even more pronounced. Part of this is because they don't have the resources to deal with the traumas of war that the full-time military do. The soldiers of the 372nd faced a double whammy.

Two months after the soldiers returned, the town threw them a homecoming party, under the guise of one of the town's Friday After Five weekly summertime street parties. In the downtown pedestrian mall, shops placed signs that read "Welcome Home 372nd" in their windows and hung flags and yellow ribbons on poles. Families drove from nearby towns to join the locals and crowded the mall to drink Budweiser and cheap wine from plastic cups. The Lady Birds barbershop quartet sang "God Bless America," cheerleaders performed a routine, and the Vietnam veterans group displayed the color guard. Even House representative Roscoe Bartlett and Mayor Lee N. Fiedler gave speeches.

The unit's company commander, Donald Reese, received a standing ovation when he spoke onstage to the crowd.

Arguably, the celebration was more for the benefit of the town than for the soldiers. Many residents had felt robbed when they were asked not to hold a homecoming parade and wanted a chance to restore the town's reputation. As the downtown mall manager Ed Maloney says, it was a way to show the world that "we aren't secondhand citizens. We weren't going to be victimized a second time."

The fifty-some unit members who showed up downtown didn't wear their uniforms. They simply wanted to blend in and dodge any questioning reporters. Many even eschewed the event altogether, opting only for an after-party dinner at the local armory. Eighteen different restaurants and fast-food joints, from the Burger King to the local baker, donated the food. Another thirteen companies and stores, including an auto shop, a supermarket, and the Walmart, donated door prizes. The YMCA set up a game area for kids, and the Rent-a-Center lent televisions and a game station for the teenagers. "I always tell people, the soldiers and their families got a lot more support than we would have if we didn't have a scandal," explains Linda Comer. "Instead of hamburger, we got filet mignon."

The event was limited to veterans and members of the military and their immediate families. "The event is to be a celebration, not a circus," read the official announcement in the newspaper, explaining why the event was closed to the public. "We would prefer a parade or similar recognition. Unfortunately, that simply is not possible."

The members of the local VFW chapter were particularly defensive of the unit, fearing that this homecoming might be controversial, akin to some of the painful Vietnam War homecomings. That night, they stood guard outside the doors, chain-smoking cigarettes and making sure no media came near. "We wanted to let them know we were behind them, no matter what was said," says president Roger Krueger. "They got a very raw deal." The VFW opened up its beer nights to the 372nd families and generally made it known around town that supporting the unit was mandatory.

"Locals knew the soldiers needed to be able to walk down the street and go to church and the mall and not be recognized, not be singled out or associated with any of the things that went on over there that were especially negative," Crawford told me. "Do we just want to continue to spit on them because they went through hell? That's not the way people work in this area. War changes everybody in big ways, obviously, but to us they were the same people as the ones who had left, and we treated them the same."

Quietly slipping back into civilian life unnoticed proved impossible. The very first day that Mickey McGuire, Crawford's stepson, came home from Abu Ghraib, three hungry reporters, drawn by the Welcome Home sign, knocked on his front door. He told them to go away; he just wanted to be with his family. Neighbors and coworkers were not much better. Whenever Mickey grabbed a beer at the local bar, people inevitably asked, "Oh, come on, you must have known the abuse was happening. Did you see the pictures? Did you get in on the action?" He didn't even talk about it with his family. "I just kind of swept it under the rug or joked about it," says Mickey.

It's been four years since then, but this is the first time he is really speaking about the prison. I'm sitting with him at his kitchen table, drinking juice out of McDonald's souvenir glasses. His small raised-ranch house with a cluttered porch in Cresaptown is surrounded by similar homes, separated by narrow yards that are filled with lawn ornaments—frog statues, mini-windmills, and girls in bonnets. Inside, his house is crammed with evidence of dedicated parenting—cheerleading uniforms draped on hangers, children's toys piled up in the corners of the living room, and the fridge plastered with photos of beaming kids. Most of the lights are off, the television is tuned to the game but with the sound off, and Mickey's wife has taken the kids to the mall for the day so that they won't overhear what he has to say.

Mickey had been one of the soldiers ordered to take over guard duty on Tier One when Graner and his pals left. In lieu of proper training, he shadowed the guards who worked the day shift on the tier to get a sense of how things were done. Mickey was being watched closely: officers were ordered to check the blocks on a routine basis. It was clear that there were to be no naked pyramids or women's underwear on prisoners' heads. But the guards showed the soldiers how to implement the scheduled sleep deprivation, the stress positions, and the fully enclosed isolation cells with bright twenty-four-hour lighting. They were still ordered to put hoods on prisoners' heads and take away their pillows and blankets from time to time.

"I thought we were fairly decent to the prisoners," Mickey says of all this. "Obviously, they were prisoners, they were Iraqis, the people who we were fighting, so you have ill feelings toward them from the start." He thinks that Graner took things too far, especially when he sucker-punched a prisoner, but Mickey also says he is not one to judge and that some of the "naked stuff," like the stacked pyramids, merely seemed like a sick joke gone wrong. "That's what kills me with the whole media thing; the detainees are there because they are a threat or attacked the U.S. military. As far as treating them humanely, do people think about how the circumstances would be different if we were in those cells and the Iraqis were guarding us? They would probably treat us like crap, and the world wouldn't care."

Mickey is understandably cagey when he talks about how he treated detainees while in Tier One. "I don't want to even be associated with it," he says. "There might be that shadow, like when a girl cries rape, and even if they prove the guy innocent, it is always there in the back of people's minds for the rest of his life."

Yet in the Cumberland area, having Abu Ghraib on your résumé doesn't hurt your reputation or hinder your chances of getting a job. Mickey went back to working in the food service department at the local hospital, a job his father had held before him. He considered applying the skills he'd learned as an MP at a position in one of the many prisons that have opened, as his brother Jeremy and several other members of his unit have done. Mickey says the rotating shifts would be too much while he is trying to raise kids, but one can't help but wonder whether time at Abu Ghraib has been enough prison work for one lifetime.

His wife has been "more or less supportive," but it's hard to talk to someone who can't relate. "You kind of push it away as best you can." Occasionally, he gets "drunk and stupid" and tells his wife things he "probably shouldn't," but usually he doesn't even remember it the next morning. "Honestly, she gets more upset that I was drinking than about what I told her," he says, laughing. A year later, on the Fourth of July, Mickey texts me at three a.m. to tell me that he has left his wife and three kids.

At first, Mickey says he thought about Iraq and Abu Ghraib constantly. He was physically back home, but his mind was still in the war zone. He still has nightmares but is no longer rattled by sudden loud noises like cars backfiring. Now that he no longer has to show up for training, he's let his beer gut grow out but still keeps his head closely shaved. Besides his brother, Mickey's not really in touch with anyone from the unit. Occasionally, he'll text message with some of them or see them around town. One of his squad members has a daughter on the same cheerleading team as his daughter, so they run into each other at football games. Sometimes he sees Lynndie England in the aisles of Walmart but doesn't know her well enough to say hi.

Unlike his brother, who is fiercely loyal to Joe Darby, Mickey blames Joe for the unit's tarnished reputation. "Everyone has a little ill feeling toward him for blowing the whistle. Which I guess I have to say I do a little bit, too," admits Mickey. "You've heard it your whole life: nobody likes a snitch." When his brother Jeremy invited Joe to be a groomsman in his wedding, Mickey was taken aback. "I didn't protest going to my brother's wedding because

Darby was there, but I didn't make it a point to talk to him either." According to Mickey and the other soldiers, the whole unit has a "black eye" now, and always will.

As of 2009, the 372nd still hadn't been redeployed. The military became so desperate for soldiers that it is now accepting people with criminal records, even child molesters, but members of the 372nd who volunteer to go have to join up with other units. If they were to go, the scrutiny would just be too much, say the soldiers.

The unit has such little presence now that many people around town assume that it has been dismantled. In February 2007, the local paper announced that it was being relocated to another state as part of a larger military reorganization plan. There would be another local unit here but with a different name, thereby removing the Cumberland–372nd connection. The move never happened. Soldiers still meet once a month for training, but around town the unit has become part of a dark past.

Larry Bennett, who has been with the unit for twenty years, is one of the few soldiers who served at Abu Ghraib who hasn't left the 372nd. Larry was Lynndie England's supervisor at Abu Ghraib. He wishes she had listened more when he counseled her and hadn't wandered off so often. He says she wasn't the brightest, but wasn't a bad kid.

Larry always braces himself for the moment when soldiers in other units ask him what company he is with, because it always elicits the inevitable, "Oh, you're the guys from Abu Ghraib." It's easier, he says, just not to mention it. "Sometimes they ask questions, but even if they don't say anything, you know they know."

"What the army did to that unit is the most shameful thing they can do to a unit," said a soldier from another National Guard unit. "They rolled their colors up. That is an awful, terrible thing. That is a stigma you have forever."

"I think it's something that will always be an issue for as long as I am around," says Larry. "It still is a touchy subject." The guys at the local sheriff's station where he works threw him a welcome-home party, but his wife left him and their infant son shortly after he came home. He faced the inevitable questions around town about whether he had been involved. His friend told him to check out an HBO special about the scandal, which had footage of him at the prison. "They say time heals all wounds," says Larry. "That's true, but that was an event that will take a long time to become a faded memory in people's minds."

Getting kicked out of the military takes a serious toll on soldiers that civilians may not understand. When Jeremy Sivits was demoted, sentenced to a year in prison, and expelled from the Army, it was the last action that was the biggest slap in the face for him and his family. "I love the Army," Jeremy had said from the witness stand. "I love the flag. All I ever wanted was to be an American soldier. I want to stay in. I think I can teach other soldiers the difference between right and wrong. I am truly sorry. I am truly sorry for what I did." He and several others of the accused got bad-apple tattoos, a permanent visual mark of their status as throwaways.

"These soldiers returned with a cloud hanging over them and a deep uncertainty as to how they will be treated and what the future holds for them," explains Vietnam veteran Bob Adams. Adams is an adviser at Re-Entry, Cumberland's private veterans' counseling center, which most veterans seem to prefer to the impersonal VA hospital an hour away. Adams has an intimate understanding of the toll that war can take and has already begun to see the effects Abu Ghraib has had on these soldiers.

Adams is also the owner of the impossibly named Adams Family Funeral Home, which hosts many military wakes, including that of Jason Bolinger, who at age thirty-two shot himself in the head a few months after returning from his third deployment to Iraq.

While he was overseas, Jason and his wife, Melissa, regularly wrote to the local newspaper, unintentionally chronicling their desperation as the war progressed. A month after 9/11, Melissa wrote angrily that even if there were no weapons of mass destruction to be found, the soldiers should still be considered heroes, not pawns. A year and a half later came a war dispatch from Jason describing young soldiers trying to salute with hands that had been burned to the bone, others whom he rocked like babies. With "so many busted-up kids," he wrote, "it is hard to stay on track." The letter was accompanied by a diatribe from Melissa against people who said they supported the troops but not the war. She said her husband insists that the troops feel that what they're doing is right, but she also described how he cries a lot, how he is seeing things that will traumatize him for the rest of his life, and how she worries about him.

In October, Jason wrote an op-ed piece, saying that the war was worth all of the sacrifices. Then came his obituary, on March 4, 2006. Eagle Scout, father of two, husband, son, brother, and friend. He'd committed suicide. The paper's last reference to Bolinger was a letter from his former teacher Craig Etchison, a Vietnam vet and member of the town's peace group. "He didn't have 'personal problems,'" wrote Etchison. "What he had was a continuous loop tape of blood, death, and destruction in his head that he couldn't turn off."

"Everybody needs his time over there to mean or count for something," says Sergeant Ken Davis, a teetotaler who had been nicknamed Preacher Man by the other MPs at Abu Ghraib. "It has to be right in the greater scheme of things. But if the U.S. government was truly at the helm, ordering the abuse, then it actually means nothing. And now we live with ghosts and demons that will haunt us for the rest of our lives."

Ken, who has a clean, bleachy smell to him and says "dang" a lot, was in some of the photos, and he says he reported the abuse to his superior. For that, people at the police department where he worked call him a narc. He's become an Abu Ghraib junkie, attending the trials, testifying at some, collecting photos and evidence, corresponding with the accused. It's a way, he says, to get closure. "A lot of soldiers, when we come back, are lost. You don't belong anymore. It's especially true for a unit accused of abuse, when you hear lies about what happened, and people deny what you saw." He's particularly worried about the younger soldiers he served with. "They were put in situations where they had to do things they didn't agree with just to survive," he says. "All they know about being an adult is the military. We've got a lost generation on our hands."

But what none of them talk about is how the country as a whole now also faces a deep uncertainty. It isn't only these soldiers and the town of Cumberland that are tainted. It's us as a nation. We have laid down a new precedent that has redrawn the lines of who we are as a people and what we are capable of. Bob Adams focuses on the grim realities for the individual soldiers, just as many Americans place the blame on them as rogue soldiers. The rush to answer the question of what kind of person would do this belies the fact that we know the answer: Americans would do this.

PART THREE

Andrew Duffy

7

A Lot of Gray Area

The twenty-mile drive from Baghdad to Abu Ghraib is notoriously one of the most dangerous rides in Iraq. One night in October 2005, twenty-one-year-old Sergeant Andrew Duffy and the other medics with the 134th medical company of the Iowa National Guard made that trip, driving down the wrong side of the road through mainly Sunni neighborhoods, shooting flares at oncoming traffic and warning shots into the air. The weather was warm and the air was clear—the kind of night that if Andy were home, he would be outside barbecuing on the grill. Yet here he was, this kid from small-town Iowa, scared as shit, looking around for any person who could kill him.

After about twenty minutes, the convoy turned the corner and there it was. The huge metal gates of the twelve-foot-high blast walls surrounding the 280-acre Abu Ghraib prison compound. There were fields of outdoor tents and burned-out buildings, surrounded by four kilometers of looped concertina wire. Jesus Christ, Andy thought. This isn't a prison, it's a concentration camp.

Straight out of Nazi Germany. "It just slapped me in the face," he says.

The prisons in Iraq stink. Ask any guards or interrogators who have worked in one, and they'll tell you it's a smell they'll never forget: unwashed soldiers and detainees, sweat, fear, and rot. The decibel level inside Abu Ghraib was deafening. Thousands of detainees yelling back and forth to one another, guards screaming, diesel engines roaring, and the constant hum of the giant generator. Then there were the mortar attacks, which no one could tell whether they were outgoing or incoming. The electricity kept shorting out. Soldiers sprayed water on the massive, overburdened generators to try to stop them from overheating, but it rarely worked.

Andy had heard the stories about the Abu Ghraib abuse and had seen the infamous photos, but he still wasn't prepared for what he found at the camps. "Turns out, I was totally naive," he says. The detainees were subjected to stress positions, sleep deprivation, prolonged segregation, and worse. Andy saw detainees in "human restraint chairs," their chests, wrists, and ankles strapped down and their heads thrown back, left out in the scorching sun for hours. Others were caged in segregation cells too small for them to lie down in, for up to twenty-four hours at a time.

If a high-level detainee pissed off the guards, they would wake all of the detainees in the tent every five or ten minutes during the night. As punishment, food was served for up to a week without the flatbread that most Iraqis need to eat meals, to essentially starve them. Guards placed blacked-out goggles and duct tape over some detainees' eyes to make them feel scared, vulnerable, and disoriented. The military police officers bragged about tasering, pepper-spraying, and shooting detainees with nonlethal rounds. "It was always, 'Oh, man! You should've seen what I did to those guys,'" says Andy.

It wasn't only Andy who had been in the dark. The public perception was that Abu Ghraib had been cleaned up after the infamous abuse scandal. The Pentagon vowed that the detainees were no longer being abused.

"We didn't have naked pyramids," explains Andy. "But there was still a lot of gray area."

Back home, Andy had been the type of kid whose popularity among his friends far surpassed his appeal with their parents or his teachers. He was a laid-back, friendly guy, the joker, the partyer, and had friends in various cliques, but he was also a slacker and a prankster. He was elected to the student council but got kicked out because he never showed up at the meetings. He got good grades but didn't play sports or join any clubs. Despite his endless antics, a couple of suspensions, and his nonstop scheming to get around the system, he was a genuinely good kid. So when it came down to it, even the teachers and the parents would let him off the hook.

At Andy's high school, the military had always been presented as a good alternative to college. Military recruiters were a constant presence. They set up a table that every student had to walk past each day to get to the school cafeteria. Marines sometimes made guest appearances at gym class, impressing students with their inflatable obstacle courses and rock-climbing walls. Students clamored to work out with the soldiers. And the military's efforts paid off: Andy estimates that around twenty kids in his class signed up before graduation.

It had always been in the back of Andy's mind that if there were a war, he'd go. His grandfather, with whom he'd spent summers and weekends on the family farm, had served in World War II. He didn't tell Andy much about the war, but Andy knew enough from movies, books, and history class to be certain that his grandfather had been a brave and noble soldier, fighting the good fight.

Watching the Gulf war on television as a kid, Andy had been fascinated and impressed. At the time he had thought, We bombed and decimated them. Saddam was an evil dictator and we kicked his ass. America won and we helped these people out.

And now there were weapons of mass destruction, and even
if there was no connection between Iraq and 9/11, it would be
a quick and noble mission. Another victory for America. Andy
wanted in.

Even though his parents could pay for college, the idea of
enlisting and not having to depend on them financially appealed
to Andy. He'd be truly independent, a real adult, without having to
answer to anyone. The military, he also figured, would keep him
out of trouble and steer him onto a better path. Andy had had a
few potentially serious scrapes with the law. His dad, a local cop,
pulled some strings, but Andy knew that he could test his luck
only so many times. He'd grown up around guns, so it wasn't a
far cry to become a soldier. He figured he was in good shape, so
how hard could the nine or ten weeks of basic really be?

On March 19, 2003, the same day that the Iraq war began
and Andy turned seventeen, he enlisted with the Army National
Guard. He had already completed all of the paperwork and got
his parents to sign the permission slip to allow their only son
to enlist.

Andy, in turn, convinced his buddies to join. Soldiers and veterans now get $2,000 for everyone they recruit. But in Andy's
case, he got a coffee cup for one recruit and a pen for another.

In retrospect, Andy thinks there is something unethical about
recruiting kids as young as sixteen. He tells me that if he were to
write a book about his time in Iraq, he'd call it *363 Days in the
Life of a Child Soldier*. But all the same, he takes full responsibility for his decision. "Don't feel sorry for me," he says, "because
ultimately I got myself into this."

He scored a 95 percent on the Armed Services Vocational
Aptitude Battery test, which qualified him for pretty much any
job in the Army. At first, he figured he would just do something
easy, like be a mechanic, but the recruiter told him that he was too
smart for that job and it would be a waste. There was a medical
unit in Iowa City, and the recruiter pointed out that as a medic,
he could work part-time as an EMT while he finished college.

The idea appealed to Andy, plus, he figured he'd actually be helping people and accomplishing something—rescuing people hit by floods and tornadoes at home in Iowa or saving soldiers on the battlefield—instead of just destroying stuff and shooting people.

On April 9, Saddam Hussein's statue was toppled. Newspapers reported that "jubilant Iraqis" were celebrating in the streets. On May 1, Bush announced the end of major combat operations in Iraq in front of a banner reading "Mission Accomplished" aboard the USS *Abraham Lincoln*. A month later, in the summer between Andy's junior and senior years, he hopped a plane for basic training in Fort Benning, Georgia.

Andy had a relatively easy time at basic. Sure, he hated the running, but by keeping his nose down, he avoided the punishment and harassment that some soldiers get when they can't keep up.

During predeployment, Andy went through a basic three-week EMT course, but most of the training focused on infantry practice. The recruits spent two weeks at a mock Iraqi village, practicing house raids and probing for mines. They had an hour, maybe an hour and a half, of training on detainee handling. A former guard showed them how to search prisoners and herd them into pens. If they ever felt uncomfortable, the recruits were told, just hit the prisoners in the testicles and get away. Andy thought it was ridiculous: as a medic, when would he ever use these skills?

There was a soldier who had picked up some Arabic while serving in the Gulf war. He taught them a "word of the day," things like "thank you," "please," and "you're welcome," but never words that might be more useful for guards and medics, like "pain," "innocent," or "blood."

Beyond that, the main message regarding Muslim culture was no pornography. "It was just hearsay stuff, nothing formal," says Andy. The enemy was repeatedly dehumanized. The officers referred to every Iraqi as "hajji," a derogatory catchall name for any Muslim. They hyped the soldiers up to hate and fear the enemy.

"All the hajjis want to kill you," they were told. "They'll be hiding AK-47s under their 'man dresses.' Even the women and children probably have suicide vests under their clothing."

But what troubled Andy most was the talk about the war among the drill sergeants. They kept describing it as a second Vietnam: unconventional guerrilla warfare with no battlefront, wildly unpopular, and with no successful end in sight.

The following summer at the military technical school, it was clear to Andy that he had made a mistake. The year he'd spent back at high school had only highlighted the freedom that he was giving up. The authoritative, regimented military environment wasn't right for him. He thought about trying to get out but knew it would hurt his ability to ever get a job. At that point, you can't bail out. There's no quitting.

"By the time I left for Iraq, I wasn't exactly a fan of the war," says Andy. "I took the perspective that even if I don't agree with this, I need to do whatever I can to survive. I didn't want to die for a cause that I didn't even believe in."

The sign above the in-processing desk at Abu Ghraib read, "Winning the hearts and minds of the Iraqi people, one detainee at a time." The center, really just a tent, was so packed that the approximately three hundred detainees had to take turns sitting down so they could sleep. Some had been there for a few hours, others for up to a week. Entering the tent was like opening an oven, with the heat literally radiating out. Inside, people passed out from heat exhaustion and dehydration on the litter-strewn floor, which flooded during the rainy season. Without bathroom access, the room smelled of feces, urine, and vomit, combined with an unbearably intense body odor.

Andy and the other medics waited at the in-processing center for arriving detainees who needed medical treatment. Many had any variety of diseases found in a war-torn country that lacked proper health care, such as tuberculosis. Others arrived with injuries and gunshot wounds inflicted during capture, particularly if the U.S. soldiers had turned them over to the Iraqi forces before bringing them to the prison. According to a Department of Defense survey, most of the abuse and injuries sustained by the average detainee are during capture, as well as in processing.

It seems counterintuitive that a medic would be involved in anything that resembles detainee abuse, but Andy and the others were called on to "soften up" the detainees on arrival. Hitting his fists together, the soldier in charge told Andy, "Get them in here fast, and get them scared." So Andy yelled at them until he lost his voice. He screamed profanities, got up in their faces, and did whatever he could to intimidate them. Guards pointed non-lethal weapons at detainees' heads and taser sights at their bodies, grabbed them, and pushed them around. And then there were the massive, snarling German shepherds that guards held close to detainees' faces. Even Andy was too scared to go near these dogs.

One day at the center, Andy had a particularly hard time with a certain belligerent detainee who he suspected was showing symptoms of diabetic shock. The military police officers stepped in to help Andy hold the prisoner down so that he could check the man's vitals. One guard pulled out his taser and turned it on, letting it crackle, but then changed his mind. "Fuck this," Andy recounts him saying as he put his taser back in his pocket. "Let's get him." As Andy held the prisoner's head down on the ground, the guards pulled his hands behind his back, crossed his legs, pushed them up to the middle of his back, and cuffed him in a hog-tie. "I thought it was excessive, wrenching him up in that position," says Andy, "but we needed to restrain him, and they reassured me that once he calmed down, they would let him out." Andy checked his vitals, which were fine, recommended that the psychiatrist examine him, and left.

Later, when he ran into the MPs, they bragged that they had left the man like that for twelve hours. "That definitely counts as torture," says Andy. "I don't want to portray myself as some kind of good guy to these detainees because I wasn't," he admits. "Being at Abu Ghraib turns people into something other than themselves. You look back, and you're almost like, 'Man, I was a monster.'"

When Andy first qualified to be a medic with the National Guard, he had thought, What could be more noble? When he was deployed, he imagined that he would be saving soldiers who were risking their lives. But now, here he was, breaking down detainees and helping others do even worse.

Flouting the Geneva Conventions, Andy's platoon leader, Sergeant First Class Eric McArtor, gave the soldiers specific instructions that if anyone from the Red Cross should show up to see the prison to tell him or her nothing and send the person away. McArtor even ordered the medics to strip their uniforms and ambulances of the Red Cross emblems that denoted them as noncombatants. Andy protested but was shot down. New policy, he was told. Removing the patches, his superiors contradictorily argued, would protect Andy and the others from insurgents. "It was such a bullshit answer," says Andy. Besides, "just because some general officer wrote it in a memo doesn't mean they can just amend the Geneva Conventions."

Andy says McArtor always seemed paranoid about winding up in prison. It was usually about small stuff—soldiers who drank on base, reckless driving, or entering the encampment to treat a detainee who was too ill to walk, instead of making him come out to you. "We don't want to get arrested," seemed to be his answer to everything, even hypothetical situations. When it came to the egregious acts of abuse, however, he seemed less than concerned. All the same, it was a constant reminder of the ramifications of always teetering on the edge of the law. There was this sense that potentially anything could quickly turn into an illegal situation without forewarning.

Some things clearly violated the law. One day Andy was called in to help with a semiconscious Iraqi man in the back of a five-ton track. He was blindfolded, with his hands and feet tightly bound. The sergeant in charge asked Andy whether he thought the detainee would be able to walk the approximately fifteen feet to the doorway. Andy revived the prisoner and told the sergeant that it would probably work if the guard assisted the prisoner. The soldier then picked the man up by the flexi-cuffs and threw him off the truck, facedown in the gravel. "You can't spell abuse without Abu," the soldier said, grinning. Andy and his partner didn't laugh. Instead, they just turned around and headed to the chow hall to grab some food.

Beyond the Geneva Conventions, military health-care professionals, like all doctors, are beholden to higher medical standards, such as the Hippocratic Oath: "First, do no harm." Various international and national medical associations and human rights groups have issued specific ethical guidelines requiring the same standards within military health care. In fact, for more than five decades, starting with the prosecution of Nazi doctors during the Nuremberg trials, in which seven were sentenced to death, the Pentagon made a point of ordering its physicians to abide by international norms. The 1975 World Medical Association's Tokyo Declaration specifically prohibits medical involvement in torture and abuse, whether directly or indirectly. The World Medical Association, which counts the American Medical Association as a member, had issued clear directives: Doctors could not assist in torture or cruelty of any kind and were duty bound to report abuses they witnessed. The United Nations later clarified that the rules apply to all medical personnel—from surgeon to nurse, to psychologist, to medic. Even now, the Army's *Military Medical Ethics* textbook echoes the Geneva Conventions, noting that a doctor-warrior's priority is always "physician first." But Andy was being told the opposite.

Andy faced a conflict of loyalty in his two roles. "To be a military physician is to be subject to potential moral conflict between commitment to the healing of individual people, on the one hand, and responsibility to the military hierarchy and the command structure, on the other," wrote Robert Jay Lifton, a psychiatrist and a former military medic, in a July 2004 issue of the *New England Journal of Medicine.* Although traditionally the military rule, as dictated by the Geneva Conventions, is that medical responsibilities are primary, Andy says that the ethos that is always repeated within the military is "Warrior First."

If he went back, Andy says, he wouldn't be a medic. "You have all these codes you follow as a health-care worker, but then it's 'Now we're in Iraq, forget those,'" he says. "You have to go against what you believe in, what you are in it for. It'd be so much easier just to be a gunner, because then you aren't violating your principles, just following orders."

Some medical personnel used every opportunity they could to mess with detainees. One medic gave laxatives to a detainee with diarrhea. Others were purely sloppy and caused unnecessary risks. Medics didn't change gloves between patients or sanitize equipment. Andy says one nurse used scissors instead of forceps to pull the gauze out of a detainee's abdominal wound, essentially digging around with the blades in his stomach.

Yet most medics, including Andy, tried to do what they could to help the Iraqis. Andy even attempted to spearhead a program in which medics would accompany convoys to give out TB shots to villagers and actually win some Iraqi hearts and minds—but he was shot down by his superiors.

Despite the medics' best efforts, there was only so much they could do. Medics were forbidden to enter the detainees' encampments, even if the prisoner they wanted to see was too weak or injured to walk. To avoid taking prisoners to the hospital, yet still be able to treat the detainees' festering wounds, the medics set up medical tents, which were hardly more sanitary than the detainees' living quarters. The available medicine was often past its expiration date, sometimes by years, and the equipment was frequently broken or inadequate. They'd have the tube for the needle system, for example, but not the port valve; other needles were too old to work with the locking mechanisms. Andy still has nightmares about not being able to save people. "There was a constant feeling of 'That guy made it through, but what if the next guy doesn't?'" says Andy. "'What if I don't have the proper equipment?'"

Doctors are ethically supposed to treat anyone: the wounded cop as well as the gang-banger who shot him. But at Abu Ghraib, refusing care was not uncommon and was often ordered. Andy can understand why people wouldn't want to help the detainees. Caring for the enemy in a war zone when he and other soldiers were constantly being mortared was extremely conflicting. One day Andy found himself trying to care for a Marine who'd had his legs blown off; later, he was treating a detainee, who could have easily been the one who had detonated the bomb, for a headache. Some detainees refused to be treated by a woman, leaving female health-care workers no choice but to walk away. Andy's female partner faced repeated harassment from detainees, infuriating not just her but Andy as well. Fed up and protective of his partner, Andy would then refuse them any care, and at times did even worse. At times, though, it bothered him.

Once when Andy was rushing an unconscious elderly detainee suffering from a heart attack to the hospital in an ambulance, the AED defibrillator pads didn't work and the oxygen mask, too old and warped by the heat, was useless. Andy resorted to mouth-to-mouth for the ride to the emergency room, but without his being able to shock the patient, the man died. When the hospital staff members heard about this, they balked. "Why did you make out with that hajji?" they asked Andy. "Why didn't you just let him die?" When Andy told his commander, the man said, "That's too bad, but he was only a hajji." For the next month, Andy kept hearing it around the chow hall: "That fucking medic gave that hajji CPR."

Andy was never asked to provide a sworn statement about the death. He had filled out a regular run sheet but felt that it was unfair, not to mention medically unethical, not to be able to include any more details than simply death by natural causes. Even weeks later, Andy's platoon sergeant McArtor still hadn't ordered new AED pads, despite Andy's repeated complaints.

Treating prisoners often meant getting them healthy enough to be mistreated once again. Andy was asked to attend to the detainees who were being abused. He'd find them dehydrated, wrists bleeding from too-tight handcuffs, ankles severely swollen from forced standing, and with joints dislocated from stress positions. Some had been pepper-sprayed and hit with nonlethal rounds. Andy and the other medics used their ambulances and litters to transport detainees who were too injured to walk to and from the interrogation rooms. The orders were explicit: transport only. No medical care. No paper trail. As a medic, Andy was even more cognizant than the guards of the damage the interrogators were doing to detainees. Health care workers are also uniquely positioned to help. As Steven H. Miles, a bioethics professor at the University of Minnesota Medical School, explains, medical personnel "are on the front line as human rights workers in prisons, with a duty to prisoner welfare. They have the skills to see signs of abuse. They can see prisoners who may be hidden from ordinary human rights monitors. They have the ability to act where others don't." Yet Andy and the other medics knew they had to keep their written evaluations vague, never mentioning the cause of injury as a standard medical report should. At times, Andy injected the recalcitrant prisoners with anesthetics and sedatives, but mostly he gave them only ibuprofen or saline IVs. "There was not much to do beyond that," says Andy defensively, "because ultimately they were just going to do it again."

Andy never saw any interrogations, but not for lack of trying. He was allowed to step inside the rooms when delivering and picking up prisoners, but his welcome was short. Medics weren't allowed into the hard site where the highest-level detainees were kept—military intelligence had its own soldiers for medical procedures. He tried asking whether he could sit in on an interrogation but was denied. "Who wouldn't want to see what one looks like, after all this controversy?" he asks.

This kind of morbid curiosity was common among soldiers. Some asked Andy whether they could accompany him to the in-processing center to see what it was like when the Iraqis arrived fresh off the trucks. They had heard stories about some of the abuse that went on there, and figured it was worth checking out.

Soldiers elsewhere in Iraq described similar attitudes. Tony Lagouranis, an Army interrogator, worked at the Mosul airport detention center in early 2004, using harsh tactics such as hypothermia, sleep deprivation, isolation, and dietary manipulation. He intimidated blindfolded detainees with snarling dogs, kept them up with loud music, and forced them into stress positions. He was working in a shipping container just outside the prison, and the loud music and yelling attracted soldiers who were walking by. They often stopped to see what was going on and asked Tony whether they could get in on the action. According to Tony, "Every single person who would come by was fascinated with what we were doing. They wanted to go into the shipping container and beat the person up or electrocute them. It was pretty astonishing." It got to the point where Tony had to forcibly keep people out. They weren't even soldiers working with intelligence but merely, as Tony puts it, "soldiers who wanted to fuck people up."

Although Andy never described anything that extreme, it didn't sound too far off. "The military is in the business of death," he explains. "People are rewarded for their violence, for being a hero, kicking ass, and killing the bad guys. It's an ingrained attitude that the military fosters. There were people who got off on it." Andy admits that even he was drawn in by the power of aggression and is still shocked by the level of blood thirst it triggered. Violence and the authority it brings can be intoxicating, especially that first whiff.

· · ·

On some level, Andy bought into the way detainees were being mistreated. "It's hard not to get hyped up when they are scaring the shit of you," Andy says. "It was still a shock to be there. The best you know, you are surrounded by these people who are out to get you. You can justify abusing them."

Most of the detainees, Andy had found, were fairly docile and just plain scared. "After a while, their spirit was broken, and you could get them to do whatever you wanted," he says. That level of domination can go to soldiers' heads. "You have the ultimate power over people. You control every aspect of their lives. They say 'absolute power corrupts absolutely,' and I think to some extent that is true. I can't say that there were never times that I really wanted to lay into some guy, but I controlled myself."

There were times when he was less controlled, such as the day that he repeatedly lashed a detainee's back, which was covered with third-degree burns. Even a soldier who signs up with the most noble of intentions can be seduced into abusing detainees.

All of this was fueled by his overwhelming rage. "I don't know how you could live at Abu Ghraib—as a guard, prisoner, chow hall worker—and not be pissed off every day," he explains. Andy was angry with his commanders and the situation in general—the living conditions were appalling, the war was a joke, they didn't have the proper medical equipment to do their job. They were constantly putting themselves at risk for no legitimate reason: the ambulances weren't armored, and the prison was always being mortared. Repeatedly, I heard guards and interrogators describe their anger, as their patriotism and idealism slammed up against reality. Their sacrifice for the nation seemed worthless, yet it continued. The soldiers set up a professional-looking boxing ring at Abu Ghraib, where they could unleash their aggression on one another. But that provided only so much of a release. Detainees became easy targets.

"I hate to say it," says Andy, "but when I got up in the detainees' faces, when I felt myself really worked up, I don't know if I could say that it felt good, but it was kind of like, 'I just shut this guy down!'"

• • •

When Andy first deployed, he had hoped to get a job working as a medic with the Iraqi police teams patrolling the streets. That way, he figured, he'd learn about the Iraqi culture, maybe even pick up some of the language. But in retrospect, he says that he probably learned way more about the Iraqi people by working at the jail. He spent hours with them, one on one, over long periods of time. He talked with them, examined their bodies, and even built up relationships with some of them. But all the same, while he was working, he tried hard to mentally disassociate himself and develop a thick skin. "Ultimately, you have to do it anyway, so it is easier to just not think about it," he says. "Farmers don't view every cow as a pet. If you looked at every prisoner as a human being, how could you stick him in a cage?"

Yet after the fact, Andy says, it started to sink in. Sometimes Andy would pray. He prayed to God to get him through this, to keep his family safe, and he prayed for God to forgive him for the things he was doing to those detainees.

Over time, Andy thought a lot about what it would be like to be in the prisoners' position. He figured that he would either try to escape—which was futile—or take his own life, for sure. "Free myself somehow," he says. "But we even took away their right to kill themselves if they wanted to."

Most people have heard about the hunger strikes only at Guantanamo, but in other military prisons, including Abu Ghraib, detainees protested their confinement through refusing food as well. Andy tended to prisoners on hunger strikes, administering IVs to keep them alive, even though it is recognized as a violation of international medical ethics codes. He managed to convince most of the prisoners to accept IVs by arguing that the IVs didn't count as food, and that he was just there to help them. Unlike the doctors in the hospitals, Andy didn't violate medical regulations by force-feeding the detainees, but still, he says, it felt morally shady. He compared it to doctors working on death row who have to keep inmates alive until they administer the drugs to kill them.

It wasn't only Andy and the medics in his unit who were being asked to do these things. At Abu Ghraib and other U.S. facilities around the world, the direct and indirect involvement of military physicians, nurses, and medics in torture has been widespread, systematic, ordered, and condoned. Whereas military doctors have traditionally upheld the highest medical and human rights ethics, in the global war on terror some of them have helped design, monitor, and assist in torture, including that which occurred inside interrogation rooms.

Army Major General Geoffrey Miller authorized Guantanamo's first Behavioral Science Consultation Teams—colloquially called "biscuits." These interrogation teams employed psychiatrists and psychologists to prepare prisoner profiles and advise interrogators on the most effective use of environmental manipulation, sleep deprivation, exploitation of individual fears, and other coercive methods. The doctors would sit in on sessions or watch through a one-way mirror and provide direct feedback. As outlined in 2003 Department of Defense memos and information from the International Red Cross, other medical doctors also handed over information about detainees' past and current physical weaknesses, prescriptions, and family histories, all of which were invaluable fodder for harsh interrogations.

The leaked interrogation log detailed fifty days of the eight-month interrogation of Mohammed al-Qahtani at Guantanamo in 2002 through 2003, evidence that medical personnel repeatedly checked his vital signs and evaluated whether he was physically able to continue the harsh interrogation. Doctors helped develop the interrogation plan, which involved stress positions, shackling, monthlong sleep deprivation, sexual harassment, military dogs, extreme cold temperatures—even leashing him and making him perform like a dog. One doctor advised the soldiers to put the detainee on a swivel chair so that he couldn't fix his eyes on one spot, in order to keep him awake. They forced an IV on al-Qahtani, injecting three and a half bags of liquid, when the norm is a single bag. The interrogator subsequently refused to let him use the toilet unless he confessed.

In the *2004 Taguba Report*, Thomas Pappas, the chief of military intelligence at Abu Ghraib, said that doctors typically had the final say on what was mandated, including sleep deprivation, dietary restrictions, stress positions, and environmental and sensory manipulation. In a 2004 report of detainee abuse at Camp Nama, Iraq, an interrogator explained that every harsh interrogation used against the detainee was approved by medical personnel.

A 2007 Red Cross report indicates that CIA medical personnel presided over hundreds of waterboarding sessions, including those of Abu Zubaydah and Khalid Sheikh Mohammed. One health-care worker used a pulse oximeter to make sure Khalid Sheikh Mohammed had enough oxygen in his blood while being waterboarded at a CIA detention center. One al Qaeda associate, an amputee named Walid bin Attash, told the Red Cross that health-care workers periodically measured the swelling in his remaining leg as he was shackled in a stress position at a CIA black site. Gitmo military doctors twice sent alleged 9/11 planner Mohammed al-Qahtani to the hospital after his heart rate fell to dangerously low levels, only to send him back to the torture chamber when he improved.

All this was condoned and codified. The DOD was officially arguing that medical ethics and the Hippocratic Oath didn't apply to medical health-care professionals in certain military settings.

In December 2002, Defense Secretary Donald Rumsfeld issued a directive allowing interrogators to withhold care in "non-emergency" situations—men with injuries, even with gunshot wounds, were denied treatment as a way to make them talk. (The directive was soon revoked, but the practice continued.) Four months later, Rumsfeld ordered that doctors certify prisoners "medically and operationally" suitable for torture and be present for the sessions.

The CIA received similar advice in 2002 and 2005 from the Justice Department, whose torture memos recommended that physicians and psychologists be present for the interrogation of "high-value al Qaeda detainees." Having doctors on hand, the lawyers argued, would show that no harm was intended— thereby preempting any legal torture claims. Doctors weren't just involved, they were fundamental to the entire operation.

But it was in June 2005 that the Pentagon delivered its biggest ethical bombshell. It issued a directive that allowed doctors to participate in torture and share medical records with interrogators as long as the detainee in question wasn't officially their patient. Even medical records of U.S. citizens were fair game.

The Defense Department even argued that detainees don't have the same medical rights as ordinary citizens. In 2005, then deputy assistant secretary of defense for clinical and program policy David Tornberg issued a directive explaining that "physicians assigned to military intelligence have no doctor-patient relationship with detainees and, in the absence of [a] life-threatening emergency, have no obligation to offer medical aid. A medical degree is not a sacramental vow, it is a certification of skill."

Realistically, according to Andy, "you can't pick and choose when you are a medic. I tried to avoid situations where I was the aggressor. As a medic, you want to be separate and have people trust you." Particularly when he was asked to use medical procedures to keep detainees in line or when complicitly hiding and enabling the abuse, the separation is moot.

The legality of what they were doing was confusing. Rules changed on a daily basis, if not more often, according to Andy. No one was stopping the abuse, so it seemed that it was allowed. "There is no black and white, just this huge gray area of, you can do this, and maybe this, and you probably won't get in trouble if you do this," he says. "They made things intentionally hazy."

As much as Andy was into the abuse at times, he resented the fact that the medics were constantly being put in morally and maybe even legally compromising positions, without having any way to say no. His commander seemed to care only about his own ass, and Andy wouldn't be surprised if he made the low-level guys take the fall if something went down.

8

The Cycle of Rage and Resentment

When I ask Andy why he didn't try to report the torture and abuse while in Iraq, he responds, "It was standard operating procedure. What would be the point? You don't want to participate in it, but when it comes down to it, no one is going to listen to me if I say, 'Hey, I think these camps are inhumane.'"

Andy's not alone. A 2008 military report on soldiers' ethics found that less than half of the Army soldiers and the Marines surveyed from the current operation in Iraq would report a team member for unethical behavior. Only 32 percent of Army soldiers and 46 percent of Marines would report the mistreatment of a noncombatant. Considering that most people tend to present an idealized self in surveys, these numbers are a staggering testament to the code of silence.

Among low-level soldiers, there is the recognition that it could easily be you crossing the line. Andy doesn't even blame the man who hurled the detainee off the back of the truck, even though he used that anecdote as an example of an egregious act of abuse.

"In ordinary everyday life, that soldier is probably a good person," defends Andy, who points out that the guy always made sure the medics got enough water and Gatorade when they were working together. "I think he had kids and stuff. What if his wife had told him that day that she was leaving him? He was just put in a horrible situation and made some really bad decisions."

The secret to surviving the military is to not stand out. As Andy had learned in basic, just lie low and get home alive. Don't be the highest achiever, the squeaky wheel, or the slacker. So although he was upset with what was going on, he just tried to get along with everyone, avoid offending anyone, and joke around whenever possible.

Reporting abuse came with significant risk—as we have seen with Joe Darby, who served as an example for every soldier after him who was grappling with whether to blow the whistle. "If you complained about someone in that type of environment, they would kick your ass, and there's no way to be protected over there," Andy explains. "You would be fucked. And nothing would even come of it."

Soldiers who have tried to blow the whistle on abuse particularly while still overseas have faced serious repercussions and retaliation. Some have been given work assignments such as searching dead Iraqi bodies for identification or have been put in dangerous situations without their weapons. Others have lost their security clearances, been physically threatened, and even ended up in psychiatric hospitals and jail. There is fear of being "suicided" or "accidentally" killed by friendly fire. As of mid-2008, almost three thousand soldiers have filed complaints with the Inspector General's office for retaliation against them when they tried to blow the whistle. That number, though, does not include the multitudes who were too intimidated— or simply too despondent—to make reports. The situation is especially dire for lower-ranking soldiers. "If you are deemed a whistleblower in the Army, there is a very good chance of it ruining not only your career but your life," says David Debatto, a U.S. Army counterintelligence special agent who saw several such instances while serving in Iraq in 2003. "You are looking at going to a prison like Leavenworth or being put in a psych ward."

In June 2003, Sergeant Frank Ford, working as a counterintelligence agent in the California National Guard 223rd Military Intelligence battalion, reported five instances of torture and detainee abuse that he witnessed. They included asphyxiation, mock executions, lit cigarettes being forced into a detainee's ears, and arms being pulled out of sockets. Hearing the complaint, his commanding officer, Captain Victor Artiga, said he was delusional and ordered a psychiatric examination. When the psychiatrist assessed Ford as mentally healthy, Artiga stormed down there and told her it was a military intelligence issue and that the form had to be changed immediately. Thirty-six hours later, Ford was on a gurney getting shipped out on a flight to a military mental ward in Germany. The psychiatrist, who ended up accompanying him, apologized and explained that she thought it was safer for him to get off the base. All of the evaluations at the various military psychiatric wards Ford was sent to during the next several months deemed him mentally stable. Eight months after blowing the whistle, he was honorably discharged. Although this is not a common occurrence, by any means, there are numerous accounts of soldiers being sent for psychological assessments for combat stress after they blew the whistle. Some have spent months in mental wards and years trying to clear their records.

Sergeant Samuel Provance, who worked at Abu Ghraib in 2003 through 2004, repeatedly heard about ongoing problems of detainee abuse and torture, often by his fellow military intelligence officers. He was scared that if he reported it, his complaints would go nowhere, because he had only hearsay evidence. Moreover, he'd be ostracized and maybe even put in danger. But when the Criminal Investigations Division (CID) saw the infamous photos and opened its inquiry, its officials asked all of the soldiers to share what they knew. Sam took the opportunity to answer the CID's questions truthfully. But his frankness earned him a demotion, threats of jail time, and endless humiliation and harassment. During briefings, officers made an example of him, telling soldiers that he was a liar and a traitor. He lost his security clearance because, as they said, his "reliability and trustworthiness" had been "brought into question."

For most high-ranking officials, the risk is usually limited to transfer or demotion and a decrease in pay. But even Lieutenant Commander Matthew Diaz, a Navy JAG officer, was imprisoned for leaking the names of the Guantanamo detainees. Despite the Supreme Court ruling that granted detainees habeas corpus rights, the military was still denying lawyers' requests for the names that were needed to actually file cases. So, in 2005, on the last night of his tour, Matt anonymously mailed a list of the names in a Valentine's Day card to a lawyer at the Center for Constitutional Rights. The lawyer, however, handed them in to the judge's clerk who was working on her case, who in turn handed them over to the Justice Department, thus initiating an FBI investigation. Matt was court-martialed, convicted on four felony counts, and sentenced to six months in a naval brig. He lost his law license and, with a felony conviction on his record, faced a litany of problems, including being blocked from housing, loans, employment, and, in some states, even voting. When he was accepted to teach at a New York City public school, the board of education denied him the job at the last minute when he failed the background check.

The memory of detainee number 173379 still haunts Andy. When the twenty-three-year-old prisoner showed up in March 2006 among a truckload of captives, he stood out. He was belligerent, yelling gibberish, and staggering like a drunk. Having witnessed this kind of behavior before with detainees in diabetic shock, Andy measured the man's blood sugar level. From 80 to

120 milligrams per deciliter is normal; his read 431. The prisoner explained that the Iraqi soldiers had held him for five days without his insulin. Andy immediately called the compound's hospital to request a transfer but was ordered, twice, over the phone by his captain to give the man only water. "He's just a hajji," Andy reports her telling him. "He probably won't die, but if he does, it wouldn't matter." Andy was used to this. The prison's medical officers routinely rejected medics' requests to hospitalize sick and wounded detainees; the general sentiment, Andy says, was "screw these guys."

Early the next morning Andy and his partner, Andrew Nissen, checked back on the detainee. He still was not well, but once again their transfer request was denied. This time the captain in charge told them to administer saline through a fourteen-gauge needle.

A fourteen-gauge needle is huge, about the size of a fork prong. On the rare occasion that civilian doctors use it, it's for extreme trauma situations, usually when the patient is unconscious. Otherwise, it's used in conjunction with a local anesthetic to numb the pain, without which the needle feels like a scalpel cutting through the skin. But at Abu Ghraib this was a routine order to discourage detainees from asking for care and to punish them.

The next morning Andy and his partner were summoned by the CID: detainee 173379 had died. Interpreting the detainee's symptoms as insubordination, MPs had pepper-sprayed him and put him out in a segregation cell, in the blazing heat. Andy filed a five-page sworn statement explaining the events, but the captain denied that Andy had ever called her, and the case was dropped. Everyone involved was told not to discuss it, for fear of charges. Andy's platoon sergeant said to just let sleeping dogs lie. It was difficult for Andy to work with the captain after that: she kept making snide remarks and giving Andy and his partner a hard time. A few months later, the *Stars and Stripes* reported that the twenty-three-year-old detainee had died of natural causes.

Several days after the incident, Andy and his partner found out that the detainee had been a close associate of Abu Musab al-Zarqawi, a high level terrorist leader, whom Colin Powell falsely used as evidence connecting Iraq and al Qaeda. Other soldiers came up to congratulate them. Andy's partner told me that he was upset that his superiors had tried to blame them for the death, but as for the detainee, "I didn't lose any sleep over that one."

Being so impotent in the face of authority enraged Andy, and he had a hard time keeping it bottled up inside. Unable to address his commanding officer, he unleashed his fury on the only targets available: the detainees. The anger and resentment cycled and fed off itself. The effects of torturing became the cause for torturing.

Pro-torture voices in ivory towers and the halls of government point to the hypothetical ticking-time-bomb scenario to justify abuse. There is also a ticking time bomb inside the soldiers who are so angry at the military and stressed out by their situation that they are ready to explode. The military amps them up, dehumanizes the prisoners, and then sets the soldiers loose with orders to "soften up" the detainees. It's a recipe for abuse.

In June 2006, orders came down to close Abu Ghraib. Detainees were released or transferred elsewhere, and the building was abandoned. But instead of having private contract companies transport everything, the military simply buried what it could and burned the rest. Underneath the sand at Abu Ghraib, there is now an archaeological record of the U.S. occupation and abuse: five-ton trucks, hundreds of miles of razor wire, and segregation cells. "It was one of the most messed-up things we did," says Andy. Toxic smoke rose from the burning cases of permethrin insecticide–treated clothing. "There's no EPA over here," said his superior. That same platoon sergeant argued that donating medical supplies to the locals would land them in the hands of the terrorists, so the supplies were destroyed and buried. Medics were ordered to burn the medical records of both detainees and soldiers. As Andy threw them into the flames, he saw reports of soldiers who had been placed on suicide watch and recommendations to hospitalize abused detainees. If the soldiers applied for future benefits based on claims that they had reported problems overseas, they would be denied in the absence of a record. If a report of detainee abuse were filed, there would be no paper trail or evidence.

When Andy's time at Abu Ghraib was over, he was sent to Camp Cropper prison near Baghdad International Airport. It had been a month and a half since he had had to work with detainees, and if Andy was assigned to another prison, he didn't know what he would do. So he told his colonel that if he had to work with detainees again, he was afraid he would try to kill one of them. It was something that the colonel had heard before from other soldiers, so he let Andy off the hook. "It was kind of like, 'Congrats, since you said you would kill someone, you won't have to do the work,'" says Andy.

At his last stop, at Camp Victory, Andy filed an online complaint about his commander's behavior and medical negligence with the Inspector General's office. Since he was on his way out, there was a relative level of safety—by the time anyone discovered what he'd done, he would be back home. There might be other repercussions, but at least his physical well-being wouldn't be at risk.

Yet he never received a response. Instead of retaliation, there was only silence. Andy didn't know which was worse.

Andy received a classic war hero's welcome, complete with flags and yellow ribbons. As the charter bus pulled into Washington, Iowa, people came out on their porches to wave. The cheering crowds lined the roads along the soldiers' route downtown. Every soldier wants to be a hero and to be thanked for what he or she has done. It's part of the nostalgic image we all have from World War II: a parade down Main Street, families flying flags, children saluting, the national anthem playing in the background.

A whole community brought together by the hardships of war and the glory of its heroes. But we don't live in that world anymore.

As the bus circled the town square, which was surrounded by small shops left over from a bygone era, all Andy could think was how naive the well-wishers were. "It was just more of this blind patriotism that I resent," says Andy angrily. "People like that are the ones who allow this war to continue."

Families had waited for the troops inside the high school gymnasium, where the welcome-home ceremony was being held. The soldiers were delayed twenty minutes by a news van blocking the driveway. The anticipation was too much for the crowds, and they wildly stomped on the bleachers, cheering and chanting.

During the ceremonial speeches, as the brass talked about honor, duty, and pride, Andy felt like a hypocrite for accepting their thanks. We hadn't done a great service for the country, he thought. We aren't heroes. We shouldn't even have gone there. All Andy wanted was to get the hell out of the ceremony. Yet at the same time, he was angry that the mayor hadn't appreciated their sacrifices enough to show up. (A few years later, when the mayor died, Andy called his friends to celebrate.)

At first, when random strangers approached Andy to thank him for his service, he felt uncomfortable. Now he curtly replies, "Don't thank me." People are usually taken aback. Some mistakenly interpret it as modesty, but there are also those who get it.

Back home, Andy was still pumped on the adrenaline he had needed in the war zone. He was on automatic attack mode, jumpy and easily set off. Whenever a car backfired, he'd duck. He drove erratically, instinctively avoiding potholes, which in Iraq could contain IEDs. Every time a helicopter flew overhead, he was mentally on a tarmac dealing with a medevac situation. His intrusive thoughts about detainees and mortars made it hard for him to concentrate. At night, if it wasn't insomnia, it was nightmares.

Although he'd physically flown back from Iraq on a plane, a major part of him was still over there.

Only twenty years old, Andy was still too young to drink legally, but if he showed bartenders his veteran's card, they'd forget how young you could be to enlist. Instead of getting carded, he'd get free beer. He had always been a drinker, but it had been in a celebratory "Let's go out to the clubs, pick up girls, and have a blast" kind of a way, whereas now it was Andy sitting on a couch or a barstool trying to get obliterated. "You are thinking about this stuff all the time, and it is too heavy," he says. "So it's 'I'm going to drink a bottle of tequila. I'm going to drink a bottle of vodka. I'm going to try to get as drunk as I can to just get away from this stuff.'"

But he couldn't escape, so instead he ended up breaking things and getting into fights. One night, he punched out all of the car windows along the block, leaving his fists bloody. In crowded bars, he'd decide that the next guy to look at him was going to get his ass kicked. In general, Andy is a laid-back, friendly guy, and it is difficult to imagine this side of him. But he's still the enraged man he was in Iraq, without any real way to address that anger bottled up inside.

On other nights, his benders turned into sobbing sessions, which made everyone uncomfortable. His friends let these things slide. They were always up for grabbing a drink with him, and when he got out of control, they tiptoed around him, knowing they couldn't fathom what he had gone through, and not really wanting to.

Having lived the Iraq war every day, Andy found it inconceivable that the war was such a nonissue for people at home. At Kirkwood Community College, where he signed up for classes, students were more concerned about what bar they were going to and whose birthday would translate into a free pitcher of beer. There had been protests during the lead-up to the war, but now there was nothing. Andy felt disconnected and isolated, but at the same time, he could understand why people would want to block it out.

Andrew Nissen, Andy's medic partner in Iraq, who now lives one town over, understood exactly what Andy was going through. The two spent nights getting dangerously drunk, ruminating in disbelief about their military service, infuriated with how they had been treated and the brutality of what they had seen. Nissen's ability to relate was a relief for Andy, but it also brought back too many memories.

People of Andy's parents' generation who grew up around World War II veterans were trained never to ask about the war. Andy's grandfather had served overseas but had only referred to his time in the war a few times. Andy's mother was particularly reluctant to ask about Andy's service, in part because she was naturally standoffish and had an uneasy relationship with her son, but also because she couldn't handle knowing what had happened. While overseas, Andy had sugarcoated what he told her. They had talked about life at home in Iowa, not about the fact that Abu Ghraib was the most heavily mortared base in Iraq or that he was roughing up detainees. He shared some of these details with his father, a no-bullshit career cop, who had seen his share of blood and suffering on the force. But their conversations were short and limited to the war, not focused on the emotional difficulties Andy was having in response.

How does one even begin to broach the subject of what your friend, son, nephew, or grandson did in the war zone? Andy hadn't even served in traditional combat, so it wasn't even clear what kinds of questions to ask. If Abu Ghraib had really been cleaned up, as the president was saying, then all that Andy would have were boring tales of being little more than a nurse. It would be humiliating for him to have to admit to having no heroic war stories. But if the abuse had been perpetrated by more than a few bad apples, did anyone really want to know whether Andy was just like those soldiers who had been court-martialed?

Andy worried what his childhood friend Kyle would think about him. They had grown up together, riding bikes, fishing, and sharing the secrets children share. Now here Andy was, back from Iraq, having committed all of these abuses. Andy didn't want to be this new person to Kyle, and he found himself determined to keep the secrets that soldiers keep.

Andy sometimes tried to raise the topic of war with his friends from high school, but they didn't want to listen, especially the die-hard Republicans, with Bush '04 stickers still on their SUVs and sports cars. Even though they could see what the war was doing to their friends who had fought, they refused to criticize or even question it. They didn't want their faith in George W. Bush shaken.

When people did broach the issue, the results were no better. Some people are drawn to the pornographic gore of war. At the bar or the mall, acquaintances would laugh while asking, "So, did you stack naked Iraqis into pyramids?" or "Did you kill anyone over there?"

"They want to hear about the dead body: what it looked like, smelled like, felt like," says Andy. "I don't want to talk or even think about that. I want to talk about why the war is wrong."

Whenever professors at the community college found out that Andy had been at Abu Ghraib, they always wanted him to relate his experiences to the class. Essays on the topic were easy A's. What professor would fail a soldier's account of war? Instead of being academically challenged, Andy only thought more about the war. During class discussions, classmates clearly preferred the Fox News version of the war but were still reluctant to engage Andy, lest it seem like they were attacking a soldier.

Even the "Support the Troops" movement was off-putting. The yellow-ribbon decals infuriated him, and he sometimes tore them off cars. He often refers to a quote from another veteran that he posted on his Facebook page: "When I was hauling around Baghdad, I never looked over to my nervous friend and said, 'Don't worry, buddy, I hear back home they've got little yellow ribbons on almost every car. We're going to be fine.'"

People hide behind the Support the Troops message, not realizing that for soldiers like Andy, real support would mean actually questioning why we are sending them to war in the first place. The yellow ribbon decal on Andy's SUV reads, "Support the Truth."

In the midst of the drinking, crying, and fighting, there was Sarah Schulte. It may have been her big brown eyes, her understated beauty, or her slightly shy, yet approachable, demeanor that made Sarah so appealing to Andy. Andy knew Sarah from high school parties, but they were never close. Sarah had been on the fast track academically, exhausting all of the available math classes by her junior year. So, she graduated early, moved into her own apartment, and enrolled in college. After high school, she sometimes hung out at the nonstop-party house that Andy rented with another enlistee, trying to cram in good times before leaving for Iraq.

Now Sarah emerged as the one friend who seemed genuinely concerned about Andy. Instead of acting scared of him, she actually listened. She quickly became the one who walked him home when he was stumbling drunk and took his 4 a.m. phone calls when no one else could talk him down. Sarah worried: an emotional drunk shouldn't be left alone in a house with a rack of hunting rifles. Having suffered from depression herself, she felt some empathy for Andy. But still, "It's weird to see someone absolutely break down in front of you," she explains. Yet without her understanding what had happened in Iraq, it was hard to help. So she flat-out demanded that he tell her everything.

For Andy, it felt like a risk to open up to a stranger. He wanted to flirt with this cute girl, but instead he ended up telling her stories that made him look like a damaged monster.

Two weeks into hanging out, they started dating. Four and a half months later, they were engaged. It seems rushed until you realize the intensity of that time. With Andy unloading his experiences in Iraq, they became honest, "painfully" honest, as

Sarah says. She, in turn, told him about her past problems with depression, her ex-boyfriends, everything.

Most soldiers hide their war experiences from their wives and girlfriends. With Sarah sitting next to us on the sofa, doing her economics homework, I was afraid that Andy wouldn't open up about the war. But he became even more honest and open, not only about what happened, but about his feelings of anxiety and guilt. Without Sarah in his life, it is easy to imagine that Andy wouldn't have made it through. Now and then Andy will get a mass-mailed postcard about suicide prevention, a "Thinking of killing yourself? Call this 1-800 number" kind of thing. One arrived a few weeks before a National Guardsman, Don Bartly, shot himself in the head. Bartly, whom Andy knew from high school and drill, had found out that he was being stop-lossed, and, coincidentally, his girlfriend dumped him.

"It doesn't take a doctor to put two and two together," says Andy.

The military gave the unit a suicide-prevention class afterward, but it was about as useless as the telemarketer-style calls that soldiers received about their health-care needs after the Walter Reed scandal.

You didn't have to look at a pamphlet or a poster at the VA to realize that Andy had severe post-traumatic stress disorder: irritability, anger, hypervigilance, a sense of doom, insomnia, and difficulty concentrating. Sarah, realizing that there was only so much she could do, encouraged Andy to go to a doctor. But at the understaffed and underfunded VA, it was weeks of waiting and filing forms before he could get an appointment. Then there were rounds of testing to rule out whether his problems were due to preexisting conditions—even undiagnosed autism—or whether he was simply faking it. Eventually, the doctors gave him antidepressants, but these caused negative side effects, which were countered with even more medication. Suddenly, Andy was taking a pile of drugs each day and building up a tolerance.

The VA often acts like nothing more than a pill factory, doling out antidepressants, sleeping pills, and other medications without proper follow-up or therapy. There is no easy fix for PTSD. But drugs commonly prescribed to vets with PTSD can have side effects. Going off them cold turkey can cause psychotic attacks with hallucinations, dysphoric manifestation, aggressiveness, and anxiety. The drugs also shouldn't be mixed with alcohol or other medications. It's not exactly an ideal solution for a vet fresh from the battlefield.

Many military doctors, pressured by the Department of Defense to get soldiers back on the battlefield, are hesitant to deem soldiers with PTSD unfit for duty. But Andy lucked out and found a very skilled and sympathetic psychiatrist, one with an impressive Harvard pedigree and a practical approach. He argued that sending Andy back into the situation that had caused his problem in the first place would be medically and ethically unsound. He diagnosed Andy with 50 percent disability on the sole basis of his PTSD. Andy was still waiting for a medical discharge, but in the meantime, he wouldn't have to drill and still could collect a monthly check.

Admitting to having PTSD is still taboo for soldiers; having a medical diagnosis seems to make it easier for vets to acknowledge that they haven't made it through the war unscathed. Pointing to an official document is easier than trying to articulate what the war has done to them. More important, it legitimizes their condition to others and provides a basis for soldiers to get support and disability status.

Some of his peers give him a hard time about his PTSD, especially since his diagnosis qualifies him for financial support. He hadn't even seen combat, and now he was complaining that he was too depressed to get a job? They think Andy is simply trying to scam the system. He's young. He isn't missing a leg or anything. Why can't he just get over it? When people think "disability," most think "wheelchair," not a psychological condition. It looks as if Andy is living a normal life, and it is hard for many people to realize how much the disease has debilitated him.

9

The Price of Speaking Out

It's hard to reconcile Andy's description of himself as a belligerent soldier in Iraq with the twenty-three-year-old I met in Iowa. Without his military uniform on, Andy still looks seventeen, the age when he enlisted. He is polite and friendly, and with his short stature and unassuming manner, he looks like the antithesis of a warrior. When I first saw him in his black flip-flops, low-slung jeans fraying at the bottom, baseball cap, and "Veterans for Peace" T-shirt, I thought, How could this guy have any experience in detainee abuse? I worried that coming out to interview him was going to be a waste of time.

Andy complains about living in Iowa but admits that he loves to hate it. He's always lived in the area around Iowa City, although back when he went to elementary school, the road by his house was still gravel. Andy spent weekends and summers at his grandparents' farm south of town. As the only son of his grandfather's only son, the fact that Andy was the favorite grandchild was no secret. When Andy was a boy, he caught frogs in the bordering river, helped feed the animals, and learned how to shoot guns.

Iowa City is a college town with a progressive bookstore and an organic co-op; but some neighborhoods were also a sea of red "Vote for John McCain" signs. He and Sarah go downtown near the University of Iowa's campus most days, but they are also looking at houses farther out in the country, where Andy can hunt and fish and where the ethos of small-town life still exists. For now, he and Sarah live in a two-bedroom condo fifteen minutes from downtown. Photos from their wedding and honeymoon adorn the light green–painted walls. The head from a deer that Andy shot on his grandfather's land is mounted over the mantel, placed to the side to allow space for the next hunting season's trophy. Their fridge is filled with deer meat he has butchered himself, as well as twelve-packs of Mountain Dew. His dachshund, Violet, who drinks out of a regular water glass, skittles around the room playing with toys or burrows into Andy on the couch. The television is usually on, tuned in to the National Geographic channel or CNN.

When Andy first came home from the war, he followed information about Iraq religiously. These days, he still reads the news online for a few hours each morning but tends to skip the stories about Iraq. It's just too depressing. From time to time, he will look at the hundreds of photos and video clips from Iraq that he keeps on his computer. There are shots of vineyards, sheepherders, children on their way to school, and interpreters in black ski masks at markets; others of him and his friends at the Swords of Victory statue and in front of palaces. He and his friends posed for each other as tough hot-shit soldiers with huge guns and goofed around in sexual poses. There are images taken illegally inside the compound: a crude "Dirka Dirka Blvd." sign, bloodstained ambulances, holes in the prison walls from mortar attacks, soldiers' racist graffiti, and massive snarling German shepherds. Most eerie, though, are those pictures taken at the infamous hard-site cells after the detainees left, complete with the recognizable bare overhead lightbulbs but without the pyramids of naked detainees.

In his kitchen drawer Andy keeps other mementos from Iraq. There are the amulets he took with him to Iraq: the rosary from his first catechism teacher, a medallion engraved "Faith," and a Celtic cross from his mother that is just like the one tattooed across his back. Most prized is the St. Joseph's medal that his grandfather had carried during World War II, which Andy kept in his breast pocket every day in Iraq.

There is also a plastic ziplock bag containing pieces of shrapnel from the mortar that hit him at Abu Ghraib. It wasn't heroic, admits Andy. He was coming out of the port-o-potty when a mortar attack knocked him unconscious. Andy got up to make sure no one was seriously injured, a fact that the military later used to argue that he hadn't been injured enough to qualify for a Purple Heart. A Purple Heart is supposed to be automatically awarded to any soldier wounded in the battlefield, and although Andy lets his dog wear his other medals, he can't let go of the injustice of this one denial.

One night while I was visiting, Andy, unable to sleep, started to think about the question I had posed earlier that day: what exactly constitutes torture? For Andy, it mostly comes down to a question of duration. Yes, waterboarding or the restraint chair, when used at all, constitutes torture, but when it comes to forced standing, sleep deprivation, segregation, and restricting water and food, a few hours or even a day seems harsh, but not torture. Giving someone time out in a segregation box might help him calm down; leaving him there for days crossed the line. Twisting someone's wrist to get him under your control is reasonable force; leaving him twisted up and hanging by his wrists in a stress position is torture.

Andy admits that under that definition, the detainee whom he hog-tied and left for twenty-four hours was tortured. But when I ask him upfront whether he would call himself a torturer, he candidly says, "Of course not. Who would want to incriminate themselves or think of themselves in that way?"

I ask him which has had a greater effect on him: working with detainees or as a gunner on convoys. In both situations, he says, he was getting mortared, but "I felt more free on the convoys. It felt better, depression-wise, than when I was around the detainees.

"If someone tells you it isn't a rush to be going sixty miles an hour, holding this heavy weapon, in one of the biggest cities in the world, knowing you could kill or be killed at any second, they are lying," says Andy. "You will never attain that same feeling again." That adrenaline of war is also addictive, and there is nothing in the civilian world that can match it. There were days after he first got back that he wished he were back in the war zone, where at least people understood why he was acting the way he does. He even considered signing up as a contractor for Blackwater or AEGIS, so that he could go back yet actually make some real money in the process.

At Abu Ghraib, watching people, over time, up close, in those deplorable conditions was too much. "You are sucked into this black hole that you can't get out of. I never felt as depressed in my life," he explains. "I thought my life sucked at the time. I can only imagine how those guys felt."

Several times I try to broach the ethics of medical complicity in abuse. I showed him the article by Steven H. Miles that condemns doctors for their direct and indirect involvement in torture. Andy's response is always, "Yeah, that's the whole thing," and "It's messed up," but he would never elaborate or even tell me if he has looked at the article. At Abu Ghraib, he and his medical partners would discuss the problems with the camp's medical care, problems with their commanders, and lack of supplies, but they never mentioned their own roles in physically enabling abuse and injecting detainees with the oversize needles.

When I ask Sarah where she draws the line in terms of acceptable force, she is more condemning. Sitting next to Andy on the couch, she says, "You are no better than them if you are beating them up." Sarah is hesitant to let me interview her one on one, partly because of pure shyness, but during casual conversations at the mall or the bar and while I'm interviewing Andy, she will chime in with her own opinions. She thinks Abu Ghraib was a disgrace and the Iraq war a mistake.

She's always been a math whiz, who sees the world as a series of numerical patterns, but when it comes to the issue of Andy's abuse, answers aren't as straightforward as her calculus theorems. The fourteen-gauge needles? It's "sad" and "not okay," but still, it's hard for her to say whether that constitutes abuse. She maintains that following orders isn't an excuse but "maybe a little bit. It wasn't just his free will. It's not like he was doing it because he thought it was funny. It didn't come from malice, but from a pressure to follow orders." In war, people will do things they would never otherwise consider. But she also contradictorily says that no matter what the situation, you can't treat people like that.

Part of the confusion is that war isn't only something she sees on television. Andy gives her an intimate understanding of what the abuse does to the perpetrators. She says that Andy was too young and should never have had to see what he did. The more Andy falls apart, the more adamant she becomes against the war. She began to feel that it wasn't enough merely to tell people she was against it or throw a bumper sticker up, in part because she saw that Andy felt exactly the same way.

The image on the news was startling: half a dozen American soldiers, in full battle gear, terrorizing the streets of Washington, D.C. Watching the television, Andy saw them arresting citizens, throwing them to the ground, zip-tying them, and leading them away. It was all part of a mock combat patrol run by the protest group called Iraq Veterans Against the War.

These guys are actually doing something, Andy thought as he watched. "It might be a little crazy, but at least crazy gets some attention."

Andy had never been involved in any type of activism before. If he had had to label himself, he would call himself a Republican, on the right side of moderate, but before going to Iraq he hadn't even been old enough to vote. He'd been concerned with his Camaro and crotch rocket, not politics. Yet he had also never been involved in an international political crisis before. As a soldier who didn't believe in the war, he felt that he fell into a chasm: the Cindy Sheehans and Michael Moores were too out there, but his military buddies who disapproved of the war just wanted to shut up and move on. Andy couldn't get over all of the injustices he'd witnessed and experienced in Iraq. He had tried to go through the proper channels with his complaints about the abuse, and nothing had happened. "The law says you have these channels to report things," Andy says. "But the official channels do nothing but sweep it under the rug." Maybe this would be an outlet that could actually get some response.

Looking up the group on the Internet, he learned that it was mostly composed of young soldiers and veterans who were not so much antiwar as they were against the Iraq war. Scrolling through the member profiles on the organization's Web site, he saw that the majority of IVAW soldiers weren't longhaired hippies or activist types. Many still had high-and-tight haircuts, and some were even enlisted. The group was founded in July 2004 by a handful of soldiers back from Iraq at a Veterans for Peace conference. By the time Andy joined, the group had grown to eight hundred members, from all branches of the military, both active duty and veterans, who had served in any capacity since 9/11. Some members joined in name only, signing a petition here and there. Others volunteered behind the scenes but were too scared to have their names or faces associated with the group, for fear of repercussions. Yet there were also core members who made IVAW and antiwar protests the focus of their postwar lives. Andy figured that as veterans, this group had a more legitimate platform and greater authority than the average peace group. It was exactly what he had been looking for. He filled out the online application and mailed in his proof of service.

In the spring of 2008, the IVAW invited Andy to speak at a Winter Soldier testimonial event, in Silver Spring, Maryland, that was modeled after those held by Vietnam vets in the 1970s. He decided to go for it. In front of the microphone, he was eloquent, yet scripted, and clearly nervous. He had never told his friends these stories, and here he was sharing them in an auditorium with microphones and cameras everywhere. He discussed the prevalence of the term *hajji*, the detainee who had died of diabetic shock, and the man who had been thrown off the back of the truck. On an overhead projector, he showed photos illegally taken inside the prison.

On the advice of the IVAW's lawyers, he steered away from self-incriminating anecdotes, and although he omitted the names of lower-ranking soldiers, he made sure that his commanding officers' names were included. The Winter Soldier testimony didn't attract the mainstream press coverage he had expected. Everyone says they support the troops, but no one wants to listen.

Since then, Andy has spoken at a handful of small university and peace group events and has managed to get some interviews with the local press. He has tried to reach out to larger media outlets, but his stories don't seem to be outrageous enough to compete with the reports of waterboarding.

When Andy gives these speeches, he always sticks to the same few anecdotes. In part, it is because people want to hear those stories, perhaps because stories of graphic violence are sexier than the systemic problems, such as lack of body armor. But I also wonder whether it is emotionally easier for him to stick to the same anecdotal examples, instead of dredging up other memories each time. Public speaking, he says, is difficult but therapeutic. Mostly, it is the simple act of getting the stories off his chest, but he says he also does it with the hope that it might help put an end to the abuse. If he can help fix it, maybe that will eradicate all of the evil he has done. Yet, like many soldiers who testify, Andy talks about what others did and doesn't own up to his own culpability. Part of what motivates him is revenge. Speaking out is a way to get back at his superiors, who had put him in that position in the first place.

Andy has always wanted to get a forestry degree so that he can be a park ranger. In high school he got good grades, but now during lectures about grasses and rocks, he can't concentrate and finds it hard to stay awake in class when he can't sleep at night. His short-term memory is shot, and he's often hung over. He could give the school a doctor's note to qualify for being allowed to take more time on tests, but he's afraid he'll be judged or ostracized. He keeps dropping out of school midsemester, and each time, he has to pay the $2,500 loan back to the military. Sarah tells me she doubts that he will ever graduate.

The agreement is supposed to be that Sarah will finish school while Andy works. Then she can support him, while he returns to college. Although he resents the setup, he knows they have to be practical. But Andy can't hold down a job. The week before I showed up, he had walked off his job as a physician's assistant at a plasma center. He found out that his boss, who always boasted about her father's military service, paid Andy's coworkers more than she did him on the basis that their civilian medical training was superior to his. It was just more of the hypocritical "Support the Troops" bullshit, he complained, which in reality was nothing more than talk. When I asked him what he did before that job, he told me he was just "chilling." A while back he had had a summer job working for an armored car company, transporting money between the Federal Reserve, banks, and ATMs. He had qualified because it was basically like doing military convoys. But jobs that draw on his military experience also feel too much like being back in Iraq. Sarah encourages him to apply to the local outdoors sporting goods store, which specializes in hunting and fishing gear, but with the recession, the store isn't hiring. Andy has put in applications for security guard jobs and a parking meter reader position with the city. When

I checked in with him four months later, he still hadn't found any-thing. Eventually, he landed a medical assistant job at a VA hospital, but when he lashed out at another staff member, they decided that with his PTSD condition, he should be demoted to janitor.

He gets a $750 a month disability check from the Army, and once he completes the daunting pile of paperwork that verifies his marriage to Sarah, it will be a little more than $800 a month. In an incredible stroke of luck, they won $30,000 on a scratch-off lottery ticket, which helps with the mortgage, but they still can take only $10 out of the bank at a time, and their cell phones get cut off while I'm visiting. As the bank account dwindles, their fighting increases.

Andy's bad days are just as intense as when he first came home, but now they happen only once a month or so, not every day. He is still on antidepressants, Buspar for anxiety, and sleeping pills, which he concedes he probably shouldn't be mixing with so much booze. But even after a few pitchers of beer, he often still needs several pills to sleep. He has learned coping mechanisms like sit-ting with his back against the wall to lessen his hypervigilance. He has memorized where the potholes are on his usual routes, so his driving is less erratic. Large crowds still freak him out, his angry aggression is hard to control, and panic attacks can occur at any time. He has nightmares about soldiers and detainees who are dying in front of him. Sometimes during violent nightmares, he will whack Sarah in his sleep, leaving bruises. One time he even bit her, screaming, "We have to fight them tooth and nail."

All of this wears on Sarah. Living with Andy isn't easy. His vio-lent outbursts and erratic driving are scary. She has bruises from where he punches her in his sleep. She doesn't like how much he drinks, and it's hard to be his main emotional support. She has insomnia and persistent headaches and is still on antidepressants for her own depression problems. At one point, Sarah stopped going out with friends or answering her phone, even when her best friend, whom she had known since she was eleven, would call. Her friends were worried—they had never seen her this depressed, and some of them blamed Andy.

"I think Andy being fucked up is just bringing her down," one of her friends e-mailed to another friend. "She needs to snap the fuck out of it and do what's right for her. I want to be completely blunt and be like get a divorce."

Sarah's friends planned an intervention, scheming to find ways to talk to her when Andy wasn't around. "If she wasn't so dependent on him, she would probably come to us for help," the other girl e-mailed back. "He is so self-centered, he doesn't care about anything but his own mental health problems."

Through the gossip mill, Sarah found out about the e-mails. Those were harsh words coming from a childhood friend, and Sarah only felt more alienated. "It really seems right now that no one really gives a shit," she told me. "I don't know. I wish I could say I was doing better."

The intensity of Andy and Sarah's relationship makes them interdependent and isolated. Even they admit that they have a hard time relating to other people. Their school friends' concerns seem trivial compared to Andy's PTSD and Iraq experiences; their military friends don't support their antiwar stance.

On the first evening that I visit Andy, he takes me to the University of Iowa's antiwar activists' meeting. The peace group had been eager to recruit him for its cause. As a veteran, he adds serious credibility to the group's platform, and the members hold an almost hallowed reverence for him. But there is also a certain disconnect between the group's liberal values and Andy's more conservative worldview. Instead of bearing a PETA bumper sticker on his car, he fishes with a bow and arrow and has a live webcam set up to track deer for hunting. Sarah hates it when Andy tears the sleeves off his T-shirts ("It looks so hick!") but has posted a photo of herself and Andy posing with rifles on her Facebook page. Instead of riding a bicycle like the other members of the peace group, Andy drives an SUV. He's no longer a registered Republican, but he still supports the death penalty and opposes abortion. One antiwar activist looks clearly uncomfortable when later, over beers, Sarah says to Andy, "Admit it, I like gay and black people more than you do." When Andy moderates the meetings, he shuts down the rambling conspiracy theorists, who are usually tolerated by the nonconfrontational group. They seem somewhat scared of Andy, perhaps because they know what he is capable of. He assumes that they must realize that he has done worse things than he is willing to confess to them, but I wonder whether they really do. If they did, would they still be so sympathetic and accepting?

The next night, we meet up with Andy's military buddies at a swanky bar in a strip mall near the sea of condos where he lives. Instead of discussing police violence at protests and sustainable strategies to stop the war, we talk about his friend's new job in law enforcement and his animosity against the Bosnian immigrants who are taking over Iowa's meatpacking plants. Andy's military friends hate the war just as much as Andy does, but it's because of what the war did to their lives, not because of their politics. One of them filled out an IVAW profile but claims it was because she was drunk.

During one of Andy's late nights while I was in town, he started to read the book compendium of the Winter Soldier testimonies, including the transcript of his own testimony. As he flipped through the book, memories began to flood back. It shocked him how many details he had forgotten by pushing them to the back of his mind. He was glad there is a permanent record of what he witnessed, but he told me that he hoped that maybe one day he would forget even more. Maybe everything.

On the fifth day of our interviews, Andy reminds me that it is possible to "over-talk" these things. "A reporter will ask questions, and you'll think about stuff you might not have thought about for months," he explains. "You are reliving it all in your mind, and it's exhausting." On my last day in Iowa City with Andy, he says,

"No more questions. It's too much." Maybe he'll try e-mailing me down the road, during one of the many late nights when he can't sleep and has all of this on his mind. But for now, that's it.

At the airport on my way home, I read a blog post by a reporter, Joshua E. S. Phillips, who interviewed tankers from Battalion 1-68, of the 4th Infantry Division, who had engaged in detainee abuse in a small Iraqi prison in 2003. One of the soldiers, Jonathan Millantz, told Phillips that the interview brought up horrible memories, and shortly thereafter he nearly overdosed on pills. Another interviewee whom Phillips had been having difficulty reaching for a follow-up sent him a text message: "Can't do it. Can't talk about Iraq any more—too painful. Can't."

Andy wants me to realize how unusual it is that he is speaking to me—not just because it is emotionally difficult. For most military people, speaking with a journalist is a major taboo, officially and unofficially. Sharing certain information is illegal. Andy doubts that any other soldiers will talk. And it is true: most won't. Those willing to violate the rules, including the people in this book, are castigated for not being "real soldiers." One critical soldier told me that most of the soldiers speaking with me represent the bottom 10 percent, the dregs of the unit, who have no pride, loyalty, or respect—which is why they are willing to break the silence. But in reality, it is these soldiers, dissenting against the abuse, who represent our nation's highest ideals—the ideals our troops are sworn to protect.

Even his military friends, who silently oppose the war, can't believe Andy is talking to reporters and crowds. "You're going to get yourself in trouble," is the constant refrain from military and civilian friends alike. When word got out that Andy was testifying, some of his military friends gave him flak for being a traitor; others flat-out ostracized him. His former roommate, who had also gone to Iraq, started to spread negative rumors about him. They had a drunken confrontation one night at a party, and since that incident, the two have cut off all ties.

Andy's father warns him that all of this antiwar stuff might lead to repercussions. As a career cop, his father is beholden to a "blue code of silence," the policemen's version of military loyalty. He knows that betrayal comes at a high cost. He is always giving Andy advice on how not to get himself into trouble: don't stand out and don't share any information about yourself or anyone else without a lawyer.

The military is infamous for trying to silence soldiers who speak out against the war, and in the global war on terror, it was just as bad as ever. Andy knew there would be intimidation attempts even stateside. He had heard of other cases and knew he was breaking the rules. There are more serious consequences for airing the less-than-honorable deeds of war than merely social alienation, especially for soldiers who, like Andy, are still enlisted and under military rule.

When they enlist, soldiers knowingly forfeit some of the freedoms they enjoyed as citizens. The military is required to maintain political neutrality; political activity is allowed only when soldiers are off duty and out of uniform and if they make it clear that they are not speaking on behalf of the military. According to the rules, soldiers can write letters to the editor, but they can't participate in organized letter-writing campaigns; nor can they display political signs larger than bumper stickers on their cars. While on duty or in uniform, they can't use "contemptuous words" like "gangster" or "fascist" when describing high-ranking government officials and can't participate in partisan campaigns. Andy says there is a lot more that he wants to say, particularly about "certain people in charge," but he can't. For the first time, the military was applying the rules to National Guard and Army Reserve soldiers.

As punishment, soldiers can be formally charged and punished internally or even dishonorably discharged. But enforcement of these rules, soldiers say, is haphazard, with charges such as "disloyalty, contempt, and unbecoming behavior" applied disproportionately for antiwar activities. The Uniform Code of Military Justice's Article 134 gives the brass a great deal of leeway, allowing punishment for any activity that threatens "good order and discipline" or brings "discredit upon the armed forces." Such a charge could go as far as resulting in a dishonorable discharge, which means not only a loss of benefits and a humiliating end to one's military career, but even difficulty in getting any kind of job in the future. A permanent mark on one's record can cause no end of trouble.

Fearing reprisal, Andy consulted a fellow IVAW member, Sergeant Selena Coppa, who faced retaliation starting in 2007 after she criticized the war to fellow soldiers and at an IVAW protest. The Army launched an inquiry, but she was never formally charged. "The investigation was seamless and easy," she told me over the phone while stationed in Germany. "It was the informal retaliation that was severe." At their own discretion, commanders can enact "nonjudicial punishments," such as imposing a diet of bread and water, enforcing longer work hours, and requiring intensive physical activity such as hauling sandbags back and forth or running for hours in full gear. Selena said that one superior officer threatened to have her committed to Walter Reed's psych ward and threatened to give her address to her ex-husband, against whom she had a restraining order. As a career Army soldier and a single mom, she said, "It's hard to explain how much the military has control over your entire life." Fearing reprisal, Selena didn't report the threats, which means there is no paper trail of the incidents. But, she said gravely, "It is not unreasonable for a soldier to not want to speak out against the war."

There are few avenues for recourse in disciplinary matters. Under the Military Whistleblower Protection Act, anyone in the armed forces can take their complaints to the Inspector General's office or directly to Congress. But for many, it seems pointless. Of the 2,820 complaints about retaliation against whistleblowers that were filed with the Inspector General's office between October 2002 and 2008, only 187, or 6.6 percent, were decided favorably with the service member who made the complaint. Nearly three-quarters were closed after only a preliminary review was made that didn't even involve interviews. If there is an investigation involving the unit command, it can instigate more harassment. The military relies on the fact that most soldiers just want to quietly resolve the problems and move on, with as few repercussions as possible.

Going to Congress involves risks as well. One soldier, Jonathan Hutto, set up an online petition for soldiers to voice their complaints about the war to Congress, explaining that it is a legal way for them to safely express their opinions. Even so, many were still too scared to sign. Seemingly with good reason: after signing the appeal last year and shortly thereafter voicing her thoughts on the war to the *New York Times*, U.S. Air Force sergeant Tassi McKee was suspended from her work assignment, stripped of her security clearance, and interrogated by her superiors. Her complaint to the IG earned her back her military assignment, but her reputation among her superiors remained tarnished.

All the same, Andy thought everyone was overreacting: "After being in Iraq, I don't care if someone puts me in an awkward situation for an hour or so."

Andy wasn't simply criticizing the war in general, he was talking about specifics. He was making allegations of homicide and was naming names. When some of his commanders found out, they started to harass him and make inflammatory comments about him. One began calling him at odd hours without any real reason, to the point that Andy had to change his phone number. His platoon sergeant, McArtor, held up computer printouts of Andy's online IVAW profile to soldiers at weekend drills, calling him a traitor and warning soldiers never to do what he was doing. McArtor told soldiers in the unit that Andy had PTSD and was a pussy, too weak to handle the military or the war. "You don't want to be treated differently, especially in the military," says Andy. "And with PTSD there are those people who will treat you differently." Particularly among older soldiers, the idea is that you should just man up and learn to handle it.

Andy was no longer going to drills because of his disability, but he was still friends with lots of people in the unit. When they told him what McArtor was doing, Andy decided to get revenge. If McArtor was going to mess with him, he would dish it right back. Andy told McArtor to his face that he was criminally negligent. Andy added information to his IVAW page that made specific allegations about what McArtor had done in Iraq and the fact that he was harassing Andy at drills. Now when McArtor showed soldiers the printout, Andy was getting the last word.

Eventually, the colonel, Gary Freese, had to step in to referee the two men. He brought both of them in separately to discuss the issue. He told McArtor that it wasn't appropriate to be telling other soldiers about Andy's involvement in the IVAW or to speculate about his mental state.

When Freese met with Andy, the conversation quickly turned from the issue of McArtor's harassment to Andy's antiwar activities. Freese, along with a military lawyer, told Andy that he was allowed to be a member of the IVAW, but he couldn't let it interfere with his job as a soldier. The underlying message was that he was in danger of violating military law, which could result in punishment and a dishonorable discharge.

Later Andy received another call to report to the colonel's office. When I spoke with Andy the night before the meeting, he was worried. They refused to give him any details of what it was about. He felt strange to just be sitting there, when tomorrow he might find out that he was being court-martialed. He was bringing a lawyer with him to the meeting. Maybe he was being paranoid, Andy conceded, but he wanted to be prepared.

When he got there the next day, instead of a few soldiers who were one or two ranks above him, as he'd expected, the brigade colonel and the brigade sergeant major were there. It was the equivalent, he says, of having the state senator come down.

It turned out that the military had conducted a formal investigation into Andy's work with the IVAW and his efforts to recruit other members to start a local chapter. The officers acknowledged that Andy was within his legal rights to speak out against the war. He had always been careful to include the obligatory statement that he was not speaking on behalf of the military or the government. But it was highly encouraged, he was told, that he stop naming names, because this could be considered a punishable act of insubordination. They said that maybe he had interpreted events over there differently than everyone else had. Moreover, they warned him that the officers he was accusing could file civil libel suits against him. He was given a formal write-up and was ordered to undergo formal counseling from a brigade commander. When Andy later told other soldiers about the meeting, they couldn't believe it. They had never heard of that happening before. Suddenly, Andy felt like a target.

During the meeting, the officers had asked Andy why he had waited until now to come out with these allegations. Colonel Freese told him that if he had a real complaint, instead of going to the public, he should go to the Inspector General's office. Andy tried to explain to them that he had filed sworn statements in Iraq and had told the Criminal Investigations Division everything he knew about the diabetic detainee's death. According to Andy, the colonel had said that the five-page sworn statement Andy had handed in to the CID at Abu Ghraib wasn't official enough and would be nearly impossible to ever track down. "Good luck ever finding that one," he told Andy.

Standing up against the detainee abuse seemed so pointless. "Everyone in the Iowa National Guard knows each other," Andy says. "A lot are from small towns, and they joined and served together. It is definitely like the good old boy's club mentality." All the same, he continued, filing a congressional complaint about McArtor's harassment, and that September, yet another set of complaints with the Inspector General's office about the detainee's death. Along with accusations of detainee abuse and negligent homicide, Andy included information about McArtor harassing him and showing a printout of his profile from the

IVAW Web site, up at drill, and sharing information about Andy's PTSD diagnosis.

This time, to Andy's surprise, the complaint to the Inspector General's office about the diabetic detainee's death got some attention.

The photos were gruesome. They showed detainee 173379, some depicting him alive, some with tubes coming out of him and sticking down his throat, and then others of his corpse. The CID officers sitting across the desk from Andy made him look at them and asked, "Is this the guy? Is this the guy that died?" "It was totally for shock value," says Andy. "They were just trying to fuck with me."

He was sitting inside an interrogation room at the police station where his father worked. The CID had wanted to hold the meeting at Andy's house, but instead Andy arranged to meet there, in public, where his father could keep an eye from the other side of the two-way mirror. Andy had filed complaints about his superiors, but now here he was in the hot seat. The irony is that by reporting the abuse, Andy and other soldiers put their own hides at risk. Even with the military's reluctance to investigate, Andy could be incriminated for his involvement. "It's illegal to follow illegal orders, but if you don't follow orders, you can be court-martialed," Andy says. "Do I want to come out and say I did this and have them deny their involvement? You never know what they will come back at you with, and I don't want to go to jail."

The photos were part of the inch-thick pile of documents about the detainee and his death. Included were the in-processing file, the medical reports, and even Andy's complaints, which for so long the military had told him were missing. The CID officers questioned Andy for six and a half hours. But instead of listening to his explanations of the commanders' culpability, they kept turning the questions back on Andy, downplaying his superiors' roles. For about forty-five minutes, they honed in on their theory that Andy was responsible for the death and simply lied about it after the fact to cover his ass. "Why would I make complaints and give you copies of the medical sheets if I thought that I had done something illegal?" he asked them. They countered by asking him why he hadn't just disregarded his captain's orders and taken the patient in anyway.

Andy was exhausted and hadn't eaten before the interview, but he refused to take any breaks—he wanted to wear them down as well, just as interrogators had done in Iraq. But most of all, he was angry as hell and wanted to get it over with.

The next day the CID officers questioned his partner, Andrew Nissen. They made him admit that yes, there had been two instances when he and Andy had brought detainees to the hospital without first calling in for approval. Nissen tried to explain that they had seemed like exceptional cases, though—one had been badly beaten and the other stabbed eleven times. Nissen called Andy afterward to tell him that he was really worried. He was pursuing a career in law enforcement, and being questioned about his participation as a witness to a crime wouldn't look good on his record. The threat of accusations for being an accessory didn't seem far off, and Nissen couldn't risk a less than honorable discharge.

Although neither Andy nor his partner was charged with anything, the intimidation techniques gave Andy a serious scare and reason to pause. Andy says there are other things he would testify about, if he wasn't so scared of further retribution.

Still, Andy downplays the possibility that he could be held responsible. Instead, it makes him furious and all the more determined to fight back. Each time the military treats him unfairly, he retaliates, hiring lawyers, complaining to Congress, and sending angry e-mails. Each time he encounters a roadblock, his temper is set off, and he's ready to fight back, whether it is against an employer, the military, or simply a dude at a bar. Usually, though, it only backfires, leaving him fired, eighty-sixed from bars, or in the same limbo of being ignored. His anger derails him. He tried to file a Freedom of Information Act request for the documentation that the military was withholding, but it was late one night when he couldn't sleep because of thinking about it all. He had been drinking and so most likely made at least a small mistake, which the military can use to say it could not properly identify the form he was requesting. Nothing changes, and he is still left overwhelmed with rage.

Andy can't wait until March, when his military service finally ends and he can take part in street protests, such as mock combat patrols. For now, it is too risky to do something like that, where he would have to be in uniform. "If I really want to become a nut job, I can do it in March, when my active service is up," he says.

He has applied for a medical discharge, but until that is granted, he is still qualified for deployment should his unit be called. The month before his wedding, Andy received a letter notifying him of the possibility of deployment. He and Sarah had spent months and thousands of dollars planning the wedding, but they quickly made arrangements to get hitched at city hall. Luckily, at the last minute, the deployment was called off, and the ceremony went on as planned. But it gave them a wake-up call. They've decided that if Andy does get called up, they will flee to Canada, even though Canada is no longer assuring asylum for U.S. deserters. Going AWOL means a life on the lam, permanently cutting off all ties with everyone, never being able to apply for a house loan, a legitimate job, or a credit card. If a cop ever pulled Andy over and ran his license, "Military Infraction: detain immediately" would flash up on the cop's computer screen, and Andy would go to jail. Besides, he still needed that college money. Andy has contemplated registering as a conscientious objector, but the process is so tedious, and claims are often ignored or denied. For now, he is banking on the odds.

Even after his service ends, he will technically be in the Individual Ready Reserve (IRR), a nondrilling unpaid status for soldiers who are waiting out their eight-year military obligation. Although soldiers in the IRR are legally civilians, the military has increasingly deployed them and considered them under the jurisdiction of the Uniform Code of Military Justice (UCMJ).

Not long after the mock patrol on television that got Andy so excited, the two participating Marines, both of whom were in the IRR, were notified by their superiors that they were being investigated for possibly violating the UCMJ by wearing their uniforms at a political event. If found guilty, they could receive an other than honorable discharge—one step above a dishonorable discharge, stripping them of their benefits; possibly requiring them to repay any grants, including GI bill assistance; and making even civilian employment all but impossible.

One of the Marines, Adam Kokesh, fought back. He promptly fired off an e-mail to his deputy commander, refusing to cooperate with an investigation he viewed as "political harassment." He wrote, "I am deeply offended by the attempt to keep me under the thumb of the organization to which I pledged my life and served so devotedly." The commander responded that Kokesh was being recommended for discharge; Kokesh, in turn, demanded a public hearing. At the hearing, in June 2007, with throngs of supporters and media standing outside the Marine Corps Mobilization Command in Kansas City, a panel of officers imposed a general discharge—the military equivalent of a C-minus report card but with benefits intact.

Since his hearing, Kokesh has received numerous e-mails from soldiers and veterans thanking him for speaking up. Kokesh said that many told him they were scared of getting in trouble simply for e-mailing him. He responded to them on his blog, saying, "I can only imagine how many more of them would be speaking out if we had a military that respected the rights of service members to exercise their freedom of speech."

PART FOUR

Chris Arendt

10

By the Book

Having never left the Midwest, nineteen-year-old Chris Arendt saw the ocean for the first time when he stepped off the plane in Guantanamo Bay, Cuba. But instead of the sandy beaches he had imagined, Chris saw the turquoise Caribbean waters crash up against a rocky shore overshadowed by a military prison. The ocean was stunningly beautiful, especially at sunset, but the aesthetics slammed up against the harshness of reality.

Days earlier, Chris had been at home, consumed with thoughts about losing his virginity, making new friends at college, and getting high. While reading *On the Road* by Jack Kerouac, Chris had the kind of limitless idealistic expectations that are possible only when you are a teenager on the brink of life. And now here he was, about to begin a job as a concentration camp guard. "From the minute I started, I knew," says Chris. "This was going to change me. Forever."

His friend Jake had been e-mailing him from Iraq, describing how miserable he was. Jake said he spent his downtime thinking about trying to hurt himself and fantasizing different ways to kill "hajjis." Chris and Jake had been like brothers growing up, spending nights at each other's houses so often that their mothers became accustomed to seeing them together at the breakfast table. Now, with each e-mail, Chris could see Jake's downward spiral as his anger made him disturbingly more depressed, violent, and hateful.

Chris was scared for his friend, but, more so, he worried whether the same would to happen to him as well. It set the tone for Chris in terms of what to expect.

Before leaving home, Chris had Googled "Guantanamo Bay" and read about banana rats, scuba diving, hot weather, and iguanas. The military had told him it was a military base whose main purpose was to gather intelligence from the terrorism suspects it housed. Chris imagined the kinds of techniques you see on the TV show *24* being used to get information from the terrorists: tying prisoners to bed frames, attaching electrodes to their bodies, pulling out their fingernails. This was the military, after all, not the local police squad, and they were dealing with high-value terrorists, not with ordinary U.S. citizens. It seemed that it would be part of the deal—and he wanted nothing to do with it.

When Chris first entered Camp Delta's blocks, he was not quite sure how to make sense of it all. The only word he has found to try to describe it is *surreal*. A constant incomprehensible chatter of various dialects emanated throughout the block, like the sounds of a busy cafeteria. The fluorescent floodlights were always on, and Arabic posters hung on the wall, which Chris later found out said things like "Confess now and see your family" and "Come clean and get out soon." The smell of prayer oil wafted over the unfathomable stench of men who rarely showered, were often sick, and subsisted on MREs (Meals Ready to Eat). There were rows and rows of bedraggled, sickly men, each in his own seven-by-eight cell. They slept on steel floors or steel beds, each with a single prayer mat and a plastic blanket. Sometimes the cells smelled of cheap cleaning solvents, but other times they had a bitter, ammonialike smell, akin to hot sauce, because of the military-strength pepper spray that was used on detainees. Chris said it smelled like "your face burning off" and that if you walked by, even a while after it was used, your face and eyes would sting.

Having grown up in the middle of nowhere, Chris had never met a Muslim person before, and now here were hundreds. And they weren't only Muslims. For all he knew, these were the worst of the worst, terrorists bent on causing death and misery to Americans like him.

Like most jobs that pay minimum wage, the work was both grueling and boring. Guards spent their ten- to twelve-hour shifts pacing the blocks, manning sally-ports, escorting shackled detainees throughout the camp, or delivering food and other amenities. Every time a detainee was moved, guards had to go through the twenty-minute process of shackling him, even if it was only to transport the man a few yards. The shackles were complicated three-piece suits—hand and leg irons connected by a waist chain—that had to be put on through the bean hole in the cage door, and some of the detainees struggled against them. A trip to the five-minute shower and fifteen minutes of recreation meant six rounds of shackling and unshackling.

Soldiers were ordered to cover their nametags with green electrical tape and were punished if the detainees knew their names. It worked both ways: guards weren't allowed to call detainees by anything other than their ISN numbers. Guards couldn't talk to the detainees at all, except for the absolute basics. Guards were punished if they slipped up and called them *prisoners* even in informal settings, so instead the guards used '*tainer*, *package*, or simply *it*. The detainees in their jumpsuits and the soldiers in their military gear became anonymous masses that the military pitted against each other.

The anonymity made it easier not to have any personal interactions with the detainees as individuals. Chris was grateful for that aspect of it. He figured that the prisoners hated his uniform, not him. But on the other hand, Chris worried that the anonymity of his military uniform meant that the detainees had no way to differentiate him from the others. Did they understand that he didn't want to be there? Did they get that as a National Guard member, he hadn't signed up for this kind of thing?

The soldiers had been warned during predeployment training that the detainees would try to attack them using weapons, mainly shanks, made out of anything, even toilet paper hardened with toothpaste. During bayonet and knife training, the soldiers were made to yell, "I will get stabbed, but I will not die."

Chris never encountered any real weapons, but the detainees regularly hit guards in their faces, threatened them, and called them names like *ibn sharmoota*, which is Arabic for "son of a whore." The prisoners threw "cocktails," concoctions of feces, urine, and other bodily fluids, in the guards' faces and urinated and defecated on the walls. In the one-year period ending in August 2006, the Joint Task Force at Guantanamo had recorded "3,232 incidents of detainee misconduct, including 432 assaults with bodily fluids, 227 physical assaults, and 99 efforts to incite a disturbance or a riot."

The detainees routinely resisted through foot dragging. They refused to obey trivial orders, such as being weighed, returning paper plates, and moving when told. They banged on their metal cells for hours at a time, the sound echoing throughout the prison. They encouraged one another to rebel. When one prisoner disobeyed or hurled a cocktail at a guard, the others cheered him on, usually chanting in unison, "Allahu Akbar" ("God is great").

There were also some detainees, hungry for human contact, who would stick their thin fingers out through the steel mesh walls to try to touch whoever passed their cages. It seemed as though they tried to come up with any excuse they could to talk to a guard. They were constantly begging, like homeless people, for more toilet paper or another toothbrush. If you gave in and brought them what they wanted, they only continued to harass you for more. They pleaded with the guards, professing their innocence, but Chris figured they were lying and resented that they were trying to put one over on him.

On one of his first shifts, Chris was assigned guard duty on the notorious Oscar Block, where detainees who have misbehaved are kept in solitary isolation and are forbidden to talk. Each time Chris reached the end of the block, a one-armed detainee in cell number twelve hassled him for toilet paper. Chris had already given the man the allotted eight sheets, but the detainee continued with, "MP, MP, more toilet paper," until Chris lost his temper.

Chris opened the bean hole and shoved a huge bundle of toilet paper inside. Suddenly, the detainee grabbed his arm and yanked it back. Chris was scared and shocked, but mostly he was angry: the man could have broken his arm. The warnings about the detainees wanting to hurt the guards were real. Chris pulled back and just stood there staring at the guy, thinking of all the things he could do in retaliation to this man. He saw the look of deep hatred in the man's eyes. It was no longer prisoner and guard. They were enemies, and this was war.

"I could have given a fuck whether or not they spent their lives sitting in a cell in there," says Chris. The detainees' very presence made Chris mad; without them, he wouldn't even have to be there.

One of Chris's jobs was transporting detainees to the metal trailers on the outskirts of the camp for interrogations. Whenever he opened the door, he would be hit with the icy blast of the air-conditioners. Often he was ordered to short-shackle the prisoners' ankles and wrists to the metal eyehole ring on the floor, so that they were left squatting down on their haunches in a sort of standing fetal position. Sometimes the detainees tried to rock back to ease the pain on their backs and legs, but that would only cut off the blood flow to their arms. After delivering the detainees, Chris and the other guards had to leave immediately. Just as at Abu Ghraib, what happened in those rooms was none of their business.

According to Chris, there were video monitors inside, but they were usually broken—and according to Chris there was one room in particular where they were always broken. One interrogator, "a monster of a dude," as Chris puts it, said he played the bad cop in the good cop/bad cop routine with detainees. But mostly, the interrogators, a mix of FBI, CIA, and private contractors, kept to themselves and shared no details.

The soldiers had a weird kind of reverence for the interrogators, who emanated a powerful mystique. They were the ones on the front line, saving America from another 9/11-style attack. Unlike the soldiers, they could dress however they wanted, which often meant beards and ridiculous-looking Hawaiian shirts. Occasionally, Chris saw a female interrogator—"a total cougar," says Chris—blond, attractive, and busty. The ghost in the miniskirt, as he calls her. The interrogators were allowed access to all areas of the camp and seemed to operate by their own set of rules, completely outside the chain of command.

Speculations about the interrogations were bolstered by rumors that circulated through the camps and passed down from one unit to the next. Some soldiers gossiped that the female interrogators were having sex with detainees and that interrogators were beating the prisoners. When Chris first heard the loud, jarring music coming from the interrogation rooms, an all-American mixed tape of hip hop, country, and pop, he thought it must be soldiers fooling around. But the songs were played over one another, out of sync, like two dueling nightclubs. What was that about?

Like most soldiers, he had a morbid curiosity about the sessions, but frankly, he says, he didn't want to know. "I knew that some could get pretty rough," he says. "But I didn't know how rough 'rough' was."

Some of what Chris didn't know has since been revealed through endless documents obtained by organizations such as the ACLU and testimonies from soldiers detailing the torture and abuse conducted inside the interrogation rooms. The abuse was a horrific mixture of the physical, psychological, sexual, and religious. Detainees were beaten and their limbs dislocated. One interrogator threw a mini-fridge and a chair at a detainee. Women have performed lap dances and grabbed detainees' genitalia. Army interrogator Jeanette Arocho-Burkart, dressed in skimpy clothing, smeared fake menstrual blood on a detainee, which is one of the most degrading things you can do to a Muslim man. The interrogators have thrown the Koran on the floor and prevented detainees from bathing before prayer or praying at all.

During months of interrogation, Mohammed al-Qahtani had to be hospitalized twice when his heart rate dropped to 35 beats per minute. Interrogators performed a puppet show that made fun of his work with al Qaeda, made him bark like a dog, and taped a photo of a 9/11 victim on his pants and hung another of partially clad women around his neck. At one point, interrogators put a party hat on him, brought him a birthday cake, and sang "God Bless America."

The Standard Operation Procedures (SOP) manual offers detailed instructions for an array of "debilitation tactics" to be used in and out of the interrogation rooms. Military working dogs were to be used for "physical security and as a psychological deterrence." There were the various stress positions, including the Worship-the-Gods position, in which "the detainee is placed on knees with head and torso arched back, with arms either folded across the chest or extended to the side or front." These instructions cover how to "manhandle" a detainee by "pushing or pulling" a handcuffed detainee around the room and tips on how to avoid bruising detainees. But perhaps most egregious are the "degradation tactics" that cover various slapping techniques and instructions to strip detainees, by "tear[ing] clothing from detainees by firmly pulling downward against buttons and seams."

The SOP forbade some detainees access to the Red Cross. All were denied access when they first arrived. Instead, they were put

in isolation for a month, and sometimes longer, at the discretion
of the interrogators.

Guantanamo was run by the book—the problem being that
the rules in that book ordered abuse.

When I first contacted Chris, he told me that he would talk to
me only if I met with him in person. He said that this stuff was
too difficult to talk about over the phone. Even when I got to
Portland, he seemed unsure of how much he was willing to tell
me. It seemed as if he was sizing me up.

He was staying in a punk rock house on the southeast side of
Portland, home to a rotating eight or ten kids, who ranged in age
from eighteen to twenty-eight. The house is filled with secondhand furniture, musical equipment, and ongoing craft projects.
Out in the back, torn-up couches are jammed onto a cement
patio, alongside a plywood bar that someone built from a broken skateboard ramp and a shed filled with a dozen or so bikes.
When I visited, a British student named Danny, who was passing
through on a bike trip, was sitting on a futon, tattooing a giant
fairy down a girl's side.

Chris had claimed a corner of the living room with a single
bare mattress and a few pictures on the wall. The "emo den,"
as he calls it, is scattered with all of his belongings—zines and
stencils he's made, stacks of books, piles of clothes, a sleeping
bag, all of which can be easily crammed into his giant traveling
backpack.

With a gangly beanpole frame and a goofy grin, Chris looks
like an overgrown kid. His arms are covered with colorful car-
toon-like tattoos of a brontosaurus, a rabbit, stars, and spiraling
waves. A self-proclaimed hipster, he rolls up his too-tight pants to
reveal striped knee socks or leg warmers, which match his finger-
less gloves. His mishmash of scarves, layered long underwear, and
thrift store T-shirts looks haphazard, but it's all carefully thought
out. He usually carries a military-issue camel-pak backpack,

which perfectly compartmentalizes his small drawing notebooks and pens, a pouch of rolling tobacco, and a water bottle. At times he coyly pivots one leg, feigning a level of shyness for being the center of attention, a place he truthfully covets. He keeps his head shaved except for a fauxhawk that slides asymmetrically down his forehead in a long curl of bangs, which he twirls sometimes when he gets nervous, like while talking to girls on the phone.

"Specialist Arendt, for lack of a better word, is a unique individual," Mike Ross, another guy in Chris's unit, later told me. "He is soft, the kind of guy someone might beat up. Artillery is a rough game filled with rough, manly men. How he ended up in field artillery I will never know."

The name of the game in the military is to try not to stand out, but Chris's whole shtick is nonconformity. In his senior year of high school, he carried a briefcase instead of a backpack and started to wear fake glasses. At drill, he showed up with blue hair. He was an anarchist punk who read poetry, among a tough conservative bunch. Instead of bringing a NASCAR video game to Cuba for entertainment, he brought the book *Aesthetic Theory* by Theodor Adorno. A lot of the soldiers simply felt sorry for Chris. He was clearly not cut out for the job. At the unit's going-away party, his grandmother looked around and said, "I bet you are the only soldier here who is a vegetarian."

"Grandma," he said, "I'm probably the only one here who can even spell it."

National Guard soldiers, or weekend warriors, as they are demeaningly called, are considered, even by themselves, to be a lesser branch of the military than full-time servicemen. They are less trained, less regimented, and generally less enthusiastic. Yet even out of this second-rate group, Chris was at the bottom of the bunch. Not only was Chris one of the youngest in the unit and the last to enlist before they deployed, he was also the biggest slacker and the least interested. His uniform hung off his skinny preadolescent-looking frame. He complained when exercises were physically painful and was a smart-aleck to other soldiers.

It seems a wonder that Chris ever signed up in the first place. According to him, it wasn't a spur-of-the-moment decision. He says that from as early as he can remember, he figured he would end up in the military. His grandfather, whom he idolized, was a Navy vet from World War II, perhaps the most noble and justified war the United States has ever taken part in. In Chris's eyes, his grandfather epitomized the hero, fighting against the embodiment of evil.

The military had always been presented to Chris as a realistic and practical option toward jump-starting one's life—Chris's mom had been in the Air Force and now had a successful career as a property manager. As Chris repeatedly points out, for kids like him living in a trailer in Charlotte, Michigan, it was the only ticket out and a way to go to college like the rich kids. The way he saw it, it was either join the military, sell meth, or gamble on whether he could land a factory job.

Now, Chris blames his mom for not telling him about the student loans, scholarships, and grants that could have helped pay for college. But the college counselors in his high school hadn't told him, either. Chris wasn't on top of the application process, and the military offered the kind of money a high schooler can barely imagine. To Chris, it just seemed so easy. "Honestly," he says, "I was ready to bank. I was going to ride that cash crop all the way."

Joining the military was a chance for Chris to finally prove that he was a man. It's a common reason for many high school boys to enlist, but for Chris it was more pronounced. He had repeatedly been called a faggot and a pussy, not only by classmates, but by his stepfather. Chris didn't share his stepfather's love of hunting, mechanics, and sports; instead, he was a sensitive mama's boy who wanted to read and play video games. His stepdad was physically abusive and constantly picked on him. His grandmother and his mother tried to protect Chris, which only made things worse. "Man up!" his stepdad often yelled at Chris. So, to prove them all wrong, Chris took the ultimate step in manning up and learned just what some people think it means to be a real man.

. . .

At first, Chris wanted to go all out and join the Marines. But after 9/11, all that changed. Surprisingly, for Chris and lots of other kids his age, the terror attacks hadn't personally resonated with them as a big deal. As a teenager, he found the world of international politics less relevant than the daily goings-on of his own life. There were always stories of explosions and mass deaths around the world. It was the nationalistic fervor that raged in response to the events of 9/11 that jarred Chris. Signs that read "God Bless America," "Let's Roll," and "These Colors Don't Run" appeared in windows and along highways. Flag lapel pins became mandatory for politicians. As Bush said, there was "the unfurling of flags, the lighting of candles, the giving of blood, the saying of prayers" across the country. It was as though everyone suddenly forgot all of their criticisms about the country. Race relations between whites and the few blacks in his town were already tense, but here were Muslims, a whole new group and what some saw as a legitimate justification to hate them. One day at soccer practice, a screaming match broke out when a girl argued for the "nuking of all the ragheads." Chris lost patience with this type of intolerance.

Chris was embarrassed that he might be associated with the nationalistic fervor and the new converts who were signing up to kick some Muslim ass. He was also scared by the reality of actually having to fight a war. His friend's dad, who was his recruiter, suggested that Chris join the National Guard instead of the Marines. The man made a big deal out of the fact that the Guard never deployed—it was called "National," after all. Chris did the math and figured that even if his friend's dad was wrong, there was no way that the military would send a raggedy National Guard unit whose members had spent most of their training learning to shoot cannons. His mom met with the commander at the armory, who reassured her that Chris would never get deployed. There weren't even enough people in his unit to make that a possibility, he explained. The commander didn't mention the possibility that this small unit could combine with another nearby unit to become large enough to send to war.

It was a gritty brown October day in 2003 when Chris got the call. "Raging Bull! Raging Bull!" It was the code for deployment, the call from his commander that Chris had been dreading. He just sat there in his car, stunned. Then he drove home, cried, went to his friend's house, and got high. Really high. "How do you go about saying good-bye for this?" he asks me. "'Bye. I'll be back in a year. I'll be all fucked up. I hope you guys are ready for my new drug addictions."

With the possibility of deployment a harsh reality, Chris panicked and tried to get out of having to go. It seemed pointless to try to declare that he was a conscientious objector. Filing is lengthy, difficult, and rarely successful. "It's not as if you can just jump on the conscientious objector train at the last minute," he explains. In retrospect, because Guantanamo is billed as a cake assignment outside the war zone, it was likely that even if he was granted conscientious objector status, the military could have sent him there all the same. Going AWOL seemed impossible, especially at his age.

Instead, he told his company commander that he was not the right man for the job. He tried to sound as ill-equipped and crazy as possible, playing every card he could think of. He told them that he was a drug addict. He said he didn't believe in war. He said the deployment would break him. If he didn't kill himself, he'd kill someone else.

Despite this, the military, desperate to maintain its numbers, had been increasingly overlooking such factors, even during recruitment. Between 2000 and 2005, there was a 42 percent increase in the number of waivers issued to accept new recruits despite criminal records, a history of drug abuse, and medical problems.

For the next month, Chris made more than a dozen trips to the psychiatrist's office for mental evaluations. During the whole process, Chris thought he was putting one over on the military. But these days, he wonders whether what he was saying was closer to reality than he realized. Now he wishes he had just been honest with them. Instead of hamming it up and exaggerating, he wishes that he had simply told them that war was a wretched thing, he didn't believe in it, and if he went, he would lose his mind forever.

By the time of Chris's predeployment training in Fort Dix, New Jersey, he still hadn't received word on whether he would have to go. But during the final teleconference call with a colonel and a psychiatrist, despite everything that Chris told them, they announced that Chris was deemed psychologically fit for deployment.

When Chris's grandmother found out that he was trying to shirk his responsibilities, she was upset. "He can't just give up," she said. "He can't just up and quit the service. What would people think?" How was she supposed to explain to her friends that in the wake of the national emergency, instead of leaping at the chance to exact revenge and protect America, her grandson was dodging his patriotic responsibilities? If there was ever proof that Chris wasn't a real man, this was it.

A week before the unit's deployment date, Saddam Hussein was captured. Wasn't this mission accomplished? Chris thought, This could be the end of the war. Maybe the unit won't go, or even if it does, it will only be for a couple of months. I can do two months. Shortly after that, he was on the plane heading for Cuba.

Within the unit, a group of guys decided to take Chris in. They were the "fuck-around quotient," Chris explains, the loafers who worried more about getting beers after training than a promotion and didn't mind that Chris wasn't a bloodthirsty soldier. They gave Chris a hard time, teasing him about his overly sentimental and emotional side, but they also watched his back and defended him against the others. When soldiers railed on him, these guys told them to shut up, pointing out that Chris was probably smarter than all of them combined. Whenever Chris taunted a soldier who was twice his size, he relied on his new crew to back him up in a fight.

Chris's friends weren't so much antiwar as they were anti-being-sent-to-war. They hated the mission and resented being at Guantanamo. Being the lower-ranking soldiers, they were stuck with all of the dirty grunt work, while the commanders were pushing papers and living the good life, oblivious to all of the problems in the camp. "I got pissed off," says Chris. "Obnoxiously pissed off. I was so angry, so frustrated, on a continual basis." Growing up poor, resentment against the rich was par for the course. In Cuba, here it was all over again. "Everyone knew what the score was, from the stupidest soldier on down," he says. "They sold us out. All of us. That's an obnoxious use of humans and an aces way to ruin people's trust in you." So Chris and his friends did what they could to mess with the brass, implementing a serious foot-dragging campaign. "We tried to just gum up the whole thing by being totally bullshit about everything, because everything was totally bullshit."

At Guantanamo, detainees occasionally begged not to be brought to the interrogation room. But, as Chris points out, they would still be taken an hour later, only they would be beaten up and smelling like mace. Any time a detainee refuses to be transferred, disobeys an order, or breaks any number of the SOP's rules—exercising without preapproval, harassing a guard, masturbating—soldiers can call in a five-man Initial Reaction Force (IRF) team. The IRF members are dressed in full riot gear, with heavy plastic shields, leather restraints, leather gloves, a garden hose, and bottles of oleoresin capsicum spray, a military-grade mace. The team would storm the cell, throw the detainee to the ground, hold him down, and pummel him. Afterward, the detainee would be escorted to the barber, who would shave his hair, which many detainees found humiliating. The medics who had been standing by during the attacks would then irrigate the mace victim's eyes. The pepper spray was so thick that detainees in nearby cells, coughing, would ask to be transferred to other cells. It takes only one violent punishment for a prisoner to learn the consequences of resisting.

IRF (pronounced "erf") teams were drawn on a rotating basis from whoever was on duty, but gung ho glory hounds, frustrated about missing out on the chance to fire their weapons in the war zone, would often volunteer. IRFs were the one sanctioned opportunity for soldiers to kick some terrorist ass. Some soldiers added a notch to their helmets for each of their IRFs. Over time, some of the helmets became seriously marked up. The SOP said that soldiers should use only the minimum amount of force necessary, but it also added a useful loophole: "Nothing limits your right to use all necessary means available and take all appropriate actions in defense of yourself and US Forces against a hostile act or hostile intent."

The norm during IRF attacks was excessive brutal force, and at times the cells were left covered in blood. In one instance, a soldier kicked a detainee in the head repeatedly for several minutes as Chris and the others watched. Chris figured that someone else would report it, but no one did.

Seeing grown men act this way sickened Chris. "They were just wolves," he says. "Their only response to the situation was to hurt everything around them. The military is the only place where that isn't only accepted but perpetuated." The soldiers bragged about how they were going to kick some towel-head ass. It was typical macho bravado. If they were examples of what it meant to be a man, Chris wanted no part of it. And yet, Chris was side by side with these guys.

When I ask Chris why he didn't report the abuse or refuse orders, he asks me what he was supposed to say or do. The camp's operations were by the book. Even if he was concerned, he explains, what could he as a low-ranking soldier do? Was he supposed to go to his chief commander and argue that the entire concept of the suspension of the Geneva Conventions in an offshore military detention center, without granting detainees the right of habeas corpus, was illegal? How could an E-4 question the decisions that went up the chain of command to the president? One of the first things Chris can remember being told in basic is that you can't sue the military. A whole different set of rules applies—the Uniform Code of Military Justice—and it was nothing like the civilian laws. The rules at Abu Ghraib may have been confusing at times, but at Guantanamo, the military spelled out for the soldiers, in detail, that what they were doing was legal and crossed no lines.

Chris explains that it's not as easy to say no as people imagine. It's No, Team Chief. No, Section Chief. No, Platoon Sergeant. No, First Sergeant. No, Platoon Leader. No, Battalion Commander. No, Brigade Command. No, Division Commander. No, Commander of the Army. "That's a lot of no's to issue to people who you don't want to confront," Chris says. "You can say no all you want, and then you can go to jail. Unless you go by the book, and then you have to say, 'No, Chaplain.' 'No, Psychiatrist.' And not just no, but you have to dress it all up. 'No, because I don't think that Jesus wants me to.' 'No, because I'm too crazy. But not so crazy that I should go to an insane asylum.'" And if you take it further, it is, No, Donald Rumsfeld, No, Dick Cheney. No, President Bush. It's against the law to follow illegal orders, but there was a team of White House lawyers and officials arguing that these techniques, which violated the Geneva Conventions, were authorized and legal. Chris's fear of disobeying far outweighed his remorse.

Even if he had stepped aside, Chris argues, there was a whole line of other soldiers ready to step up to the task. "Taking one cog out of the machine doesn't change anything, doesn't make the issue just slip away." Orders were thrown down randomly to soldiers, like chips in a plinko machine, because these were simple jobs that anyone, even the least competent, could do. "You won't spare that detainee. You will only invite the wrath of your superiors and other soldiers. It would achieve nothing besides getting yourself fucked with."

Refusing orders, Chris tells me, or saying no never crossed his mind. He wouldn't even have known how. "Following orders is just what soldiers do," he says. Soldiers feel impotent in the face of their superiors, and that's exactly how the military wants them to feel. At home during training and drill, this dynamic is firmly in place, but stranded overseas, it is inescapable.

The military is supposed to be a well-oiled machine where commanders can rely on soldiers to quickly carry out their orders to complete the larger mission's strategy. They don't pay privates to think. Stopping to question directions can mean tactical disasters and even deaths. Opposing orders in other situations could lead to a court-martial.

Even with so many officially mandated tactics of mistreatment, soldiers showed creativity when it came to turning ordinary daily operations into small acts of abuse. They took away prisoners' food as soon as the allotted meal time was up, even if the detainees hadn't yet finished eating. They turned off the showers while the prisoners were still covered with soap. The soldiers were perpetually late when picking up detainees chained up inside interrogation rooms and manhandled prisoners during escorts. One day Chris and three other guys were escorting a detainee to the interrogation rooms. Chris had just watched the detainee being IRFed, and now the prisoner was unable to walk and lacked the will even to try. Chris and three other guards dragged him across the gravel, but when that didn't work, they picked him up and carried him like a board. One of the soldiers, who wore a Kevlar helmet etched with trophy grooves, was raving about how awesome their job was, getting to do this kind of stuff to the detainees. It made Chris feel uncomfortable, but he just laughed, not wanting them to see him as the wimp he knew he was.

Chris can't remember exactly how the next part went down, but as they carried the detainee through the final sally-port to the interrogation room, they smashed the prisoner's head into a metal pole. He wasn't knocked unconscious or even bleeding, but it was a sickening blow.

What Chris did that day may not sound so bad, especially compared to the large-scale atrocities of war. What was the damage of one man's head being bashed into a pole in the grand scheme of things? Yet attacking someone who is so defenseless, so utterly without any control, crosses a line.

Soldiers operating in combat zones have the understandable excuse that they have to make rash decisions to save lives and survive. Even killing innocent civilians when these people drive too close to checkpoints can be understood when soldiers are being blown up by car bombs. Trigger-happy soldiers who make mistakes are acting on hypervigilance, which is often necessary when sniper fire is imminent. But Chris and those other soldiers didn't even have the justification that they were softening up the detainee to make him talk. They had no defense for hurting prisoners, but they had no other channel for their anger or enthusiasm. Just like other soldiers, they were trained to be killing machines but were robbed of sanctioned opportunities to act out.

When Chris tells the story, it's in the passive tense. Another guy sort of initiated it, he says, but still, he went along with it. He can remember vividly what it all looked like but says he can't remember how it felt or what was going through his head. Yet talking about it now, three years after his coming home, or even just mentioning it makes him sick to his stomach. He thinks about that day a lot. He realizes that he should have said something, but because he was the same rank as the others, he didn't feel that it was his place to reprimand them.

Compared to other incidents of detainee abuse that have been reported, this incident was trivial. But it revealed something to Chris about who he is and what he is capable of. "Over the past two weeks," he tells me on my last night in town, "I've come to realize some very ugly and very American things about myself. I've realized the level of ignorance in my actions that caused me to feel very sick."

Chris apologizes for the days when he didn't call me back. He wants to tell me his story, he says, but he just can't do it all at once. "It's too much to answer right now," he says of some of my questions. "I'm going to need a couple more years to figure that out." When I offer to extend my stay to two weeks, he is grateful, because it means he can have days off in between our talks.

Chris is only just now figuring out how to channel his emotional chaos into phrases. He likens it to unpacking moving boxes or a military-issue duffle bag. While he was at Guantanamo, he shoved some stuff down to the bottom, not wanting to deal with it. Now, he's unpacking it, bit by bit, but there is still a lot crammed away that he hasn't—and maybe can't—yet address.

Few would see Chris as a torturer—his worst offense was slamming someone's head into a wall. But for Chris it isn't the individual acts that make a man a torturer, but his role in the larger machine and his mentality toward the detainees. When Chris learned that he was capable of not caring what happened to the detainee, he saw a dark side of himself.

Chris thinks people make too big a deal about the abuse that occurred during interrogations. As Chris explains, "No interrogator hit a detainee any harder than the guards did." In fact, he was surprised that interrogators didn't push things further.

But unlike most people—both soldiers and those at home—Chris was bothered more not by the individual acts of abuse, but by the very existence of the camp and the policy of indeterminate detention without trial. Chris says that detainees often returned from interrogations looking dejected, angry, or forlorn. But the sleep deprivation, isolation, and routine humiliation being used throughout the camp were just as debilitating as the interrogation techniques. "People are perpetually fucked up in

Guantanamo," he says. "One more interrogation doesn't break a man more than he's already broken."

Detainees themselves have said that it is the perpetual tactics of isolation, sleep deprivation, and having all senses cut off that are harder to endure than the soldiers' violent outbursts, which at least come to an end.

Chris preferred working the night shifts, when the prison was quiet and most of the detainees were asleep. Sometimes he would sneak in a book—*The Letters of Vincent van Gogh*, *The Tale of Genji*, *A Moveable Feast*—to pass the time. The fluorescent lighting bounced off the mint-green mesh of the cells, creating an eerie, almost sci-fi ambience. From miles away, you could see the light emanating from the glowing bubble of the camp. The light, almost the color of night vision, was both nauseating and disarmingly beautiful.

One night, while Chris was manning sally-port three, the wailing began. It was coming from a prisoner in the psych ward on Delta Block, about twenty-five yards away. All night the howling continued, a lone voice in the still night. Even though the man was howling in Arabic, Chris knew exactly what he was trying to say. He was screaming about desperation, misery, and defeat. "Guantanamo drives strong men to their knees and weaker men beyond the brink," Chris says. "It isn't about physical injury; it is about emotional, mental, and intellectual exhaustion. It attacks people's minds." Sleep deprivation, light and sound manipulation, exposure to extreme temperatures, and solitary confinement are used on detainees because they have been proven to induce psychological disintegration, regression, and even hallucinations. And with this man, the tactics had clearly been successful.

It was the animalistic moan of a psychologically deranged man, but in some ways it was the most rational response to being at Guantanamo. It was the sound that Chris himself wanted to make.

Chris spent a lot of time imagining what it must be like to be trapped in a seven-by-eight cell for perpetuity. "Having them sit there in a cell of solitude, watching an American flag waved in front of them for years—it was just like some kind of weird horror film," he explains. "We defeated them with time, impossibility, and frustration." Chris still has nightmares in which he's a detainee in one of the cells. Every time he imagines it, he always comes to the same conclusion: he would do whatever he could to kill himself. Which is what many of the detainees did.

The suicide attempts usually came in spurts: two or three for a few days, and then a couple of weeks without any. According to the Department of Defense, in 2003 alone there were 350 acts of "self-harm," including 120 "hanging gestures." The August before Chris arrived, there was a mass attempt by 23 detainees. Most of the time, though, a prisoner would try to hang himself by tying up his sheet a few feet above the floor and slumping into it. It's a slow, difficult way to kill yourself, one that requires determination. The soldiers were told to confiscate any item that a detainee could possibly use to kill himself. But that was useless. In December 2007, the *New York Times* reported that a detainee had tried to slit his throat with his fingernail. As Chris walked the blocks every ten minutes during the night, he could see little purpose for the job other than providing suicide watch.

The military classified the suicide attempts not as acts of desperation but as "asymmetric warfare" and punished detainees who tried to take their own lives, often by placing them in solitary. "This was not an act of desperation," said Harry Harris Jr., the commander of Guantanamo's Joint Task Force about the subsequent suicides of three detainees. "We have men here who are committed jihadists. They are dangerous men and they will do anything they can to advance their cause."

"Because of the dangerous nature of the men in our custody," he added, "we train for the possibility that a suicide attempt may be used by detainees to create an opportunity to conduct an assault, take a hostage, or kill the guards."

Colleen Graffy, a State Department official, called the suicides a "PR move" and "a tactic to further the jihadi cause." SouthCom commander General Bantz J. Craddock told the press that the suicides "may be an attempt to influence the judicial proceedings." Harris explained that the suicides proved only that the detainees were "dangerous men and committed jihadists willing to die and order others to commit suicide." Suicide attempts were punishable offenses, acts of war, and were to be treated as such.

After Chris spent a month or so on the blocks, the detainees' brown faces began to take on individual personalities. He found himself occasionally referring to a prisoner as *him* instead of *it* and using nicknames. Instead of ISN number 239, the mean, angry detainee being kept in isolation in Oscar Block was called "the Professor." His aggressiveness scared Chris, but Chris also saw the reverence that other detainees had for the man and admired his determination to fight back against being detained.

Chris started to understand the complex social hierarchies among the detainees and their strategies for organizing mass protests. There were detainees within each cellblock who took on leadership roles. Other served as counselors, teachers, or translators and liaisons with the guards. They figured out communication systems to pass information from one cellblock to the next, spreading news about guards' mistreatment and plans for protests, such as hunger strikes. The officials schemed about ways to disrupt the prisoners' organizing, to no avail. It was far more impressive to Chris than any antiwar protest back home.

A few years before Chris arrived, the hunger strikes had been even more dramatic and widespread. On February 27, 2002, trays of uneaten food piled up: 159 meals from lunchtime were returned untouched, 109 at dinner. The next day, 107 breakfasts and 194 dinners. The total number of hunger strikers was probably higher than 200, although it was difficult to determine, because some prisoners, explaining that they feared they'd be punished if they didn't eat, disposed of the food but didn't eat it. The strike would end up lasting two months and became the first publicly known mass hunger strike at Guantanamo.

Chris admired the relative patience, grace, and endurance that some of the detainees displayed in the face of utter horror. Every morning as the sun rose over the oceanside cliff, the men would get up off their concrete slabs, kneel down on their mats, and, in unison, break into morning prayer. Chris couldn't understand their words, but the beauty of their voices, the spirit of their unity, and their devotion to their faith moved him.

ISN number 555 became Triple Nickel. As a Christian, Triple Nickel was tormented and threatened by the fundamentalist Muslim detainee. But Triple Nickel was flamboyant and had a wild sense of humor, making himself a sort of camp icon. When guards walked by, he would jokingly catcall to them. During transports to the interrogation rooms, Triple Nickel bragged that the interrogators gave him porn magazines, knowing full well that such items were officially off-limits to soldiers.

Triple Nickel's real name was Abdul Majid Muhammed. He was a twenty-eight-year-old drug runner, with no connection to any terrorist groups, who had been captured by the Northern Alliance in Afghanistan while transporting drugs. Before he was released, the military diagnosed him with severe borderline personality disorder. He was returned to Iran, although he was wanted in that country for having deserted the army years ago. He found out that while he had been at Guantanamo, a drug dealer had killed one of his two children. During his tribunal, he kept apologizing for dealing drugs and promised never to do it again.

In fact, in 2009 it was revealed that out of the eight hundred men who have been held at Guantanamo, only two dozen have been declared to be terrorists. Most of the detainees around Chris were simply people who had been picked up for associating with certain types of people or for simply being in the wrong place at the wrong time. Even military commanders themselves admit that many of the detainees were innocent.

Chris worried incessantly about what the detainees thought of him. The prisoners, with an obvious moral high ground and a better education, cut him down with their condescension. Every look of hatred from a detainee merely reaffirmed Chris's own self-abhorrence. He began to compulsively apologize to detainees, but no matter how he tried to phrase his remorse, it sounded pathetic and meager. He tried to be respectful when escorting the detainees—not tying their handcuffs too tight, walking slowly enough so that they could walk and not be dragged. He uses the word *polite*, but he wonders how polite you can be when you are short-shackling someone. He tried to get the detainees whatever extra comfort items he could, even though he risked getting in trouble with the interrogators, who purposely withheld these items as punishment for the prisoners' not talking. But despite this, he only felt anxious, self-conscious, and hated. Chris volunteered to be the one videotape the IRF attacks to try to document what was going on. He disobeyed orders to swing the camera around while videotaping, in order to miss a lot of the action. While the other soldiers tried to elbow him out of the way or block him with their bodies, Chris tried to shove himself inside the cell and record what he could.

During a night shift in mid-March 2004, Chris struck up a conversation with one of the detainees, who was younger than most and spoke fluent English. The prisoner never confirmed or denied the charges that he was a terrorist bomb builder, but as he lay back in the corner of his cell, his mat up against the wall, he started to explain how he had been arrested at a university protest. He and Chris began to discuss the efficacy of student activism and the limitations of peaceful protests. Chris was more educated than most of the country bumpkins in his unit, and he felt relieved to have someone whom he perceived as his intellectual equal to talk to. No other soldiers were interested in having a dialogue about any kind of activism, let alone antiwar activism. Chris was hungry for this kind of interaction. Knowing that there was a conversation to come back to made the guard shift that much more bearable. Chris figured that the detainee must have thought he was being patronizing. For one, the detainee lived in a place where a military takeover was actually a reality.

Chris told him that if America were invaded, by some "fascist power telling him how to live his life, he'd be right there, as part of some pretty radical ventures to kick them the fuck out," even building bombs if it came to that.

Chris had to be careful. Not only would what he was saying offend most soldiers—or even Americans—on a deeply personal level, it was also treasonous. If he were overheard, it would mean trouble. The SOP states that "Personnel will not fraternize with detainees. This includes idle chatter and small talk conducted with the detainee." During the ten-minute intervals between Chris's patrols down the block, he would kneel down on the floor near the detainee's cell, where he was partly hidden by the metal door to the stairs. He had to keep an eye out in case anyone saw him, and Chris knew the hallway was miked, but he figured that the likelihood of someone listening to every minute of every tape was slim.

A few days after his conversation with the detainee, Chris was taken off the blocks.

11

An Origami Bird's Eye View

The Detention Operation Center (DOC) seemed like a better place than the blocks for a scrawny, brainy, know-it-all kid like Chris, who not only couldn't intimidate detainees, but seemed to sympathize with them. The DOC is the central office where all of the detention and security operations are coordinated and accounted for. The SOP describes it as the "nerve center of the facility." All of the orders from military intelligence and the other interrogators from various agencies were sent to the office, and then the DOC dispatched them out to soldiers. Every report and form about any camp operation was sent there and was entered into the central computer system. Because the DOC personnel had access to the computerized version of the always changing SOP, they had to deal with endless calls from guards who were confused about which rules applied. The DOC handled the radio communication between Camp Echo and Camp Delta and with other military bases. There was equipment to account for, as well as the hundreds of keys to the shackles, the cages, and the sally-ports that guards seemed to keep misplacing, putting the DOC guys' asses on the line. To this day, Chris refuses to carry any keys besides the small black key to his bike lock. He can't hold "those small, sand-colored, little pieces of shit" without being overcome with anxiety.

Chris saw his transfer to the DOC as a punishment: the shifts were longer, there were fewer days off, and the pace was frantic. By the end of his tour, he was working seven days a week with no breaks.

On busy days, even taking a bathroom break meant creating a backlog that he'd have to scramble all day to fix. He still has chronic bladder problems from holding his urine in so long. Some days, he couldn't even take lunch, so he snuck peanut butter and jelly sandwiches in, until his commander put them on the long list of contraband, along with personal reading material, cell phones, and extra clothing. "It was just one more indicator that the top brass didn't care about us," Chris says.

The chain of command was out of whack. As an E-4, Chris should not have been giving orders to most of the soldiers who reported to him, and he definitely shouldn't have been answering to interrogators, who operated outside the chain of command and didn't seem to have to answer to anyone.

There was a long list of numbers representing the detainees who needed to be moved throughout the camp, whether to other cells, to rec and showers, or to the interrogation rooms. A line of soldiers, of all ranks, snaked down the hallway, waiting for their orders. CIA interrogators called the office, asking where the hell their detainees were. Sometimes, the Tetris-style coordination of which detainee could move to which cell was too confusing, and Chris would fall behind on the schedules.

While working on the blocks, Chris had never understood why so many detainees had to be moved from one cell to another, often on the same block, for no apparent reason. But now, looking at the massive grid and the lists, he saw the larger scheme behind it all. On the blocks, Chris had never moved the same guy twice in a row, but now he saw that certain detainees, called the "frequent fliers," were being moved from one cell to another every few hours, as part of the sleep-deprivation program. He also realized that some detainees were left in interrogation rooms for entire days, in stress positions, without food or water, with the freezing temperatures and the raucous noise, to piss and shit on themselves, without ever being visited by an interrogator.

From his position in the DOC office, Chris was able to see the larger picture of the detainee operations at Guantanamo. He understood how each individual, seemingly small act was part of a larger machine that had been created to destroy the prisoners.

It was something that is purposely hidden not only from the public at large but even from the soldiers working there. As a noncommissioned officer from Chris's unit explained, "When war is written in history, it is in broad terms, but for soldiers there, your scope is three feet in front of you, and that is what you understand." Although Chris was still barred from the interrogation rooms, from his vantage point he saw that what was happening at the camp was torture. Modern-day warfare isn't just about bombs blowing off limbs, but minds breaking down.

When Chris realized the magnitude of the larger system of abuse and torture, he tried to use his position at the DOC to make things easier for the detainees. He gave priority to orders to transfer prisoners out of interrogation rooms as soon as the session was over, versus bringing people to the interrogation rooms. If detainees complained that the lingering OC spray of an IRF attack was bothering them, he moved them to a different block.

Eventually, though, the sheer volume of work translated into a level of banality. It was awful, but consistently awful. And with time, the sense of what is normal loses its meaning when there is nothing normal to compare it to. As the job wore on Chris, there were days when it just seemed like too much of a hassle to justify the extra work. He was tired from too many back-to-back shifts and not enough sleep, and the coffee pot couldn't hold enough to keep him going. It was tough to get any vegetarian food. He tried snagging the Muslim-appropriate vegetarian MREs that were meant for the detainees, until someone freaked him out by saying that there might be drugs in those meals. Soldiers were repeatedly getting sick from the detainees who were in ill health, but they didn't always have the days off they needed to recuperate.

"My brain was barely working," Chris explains. "I had such a long backlog of stuff that I couldn't deal with because it was just happening so repetitively that I couldn't even take it all in. You just shut off." Moving one detainee because his toilet was blocked up, sparing that one detainee from momentary suffering, came to seem so futile, he explains, when you consider that regardless, the man is still in a concentration camp.

"Let me tell you a big secret," Chris says late one night. "Most of us didn't really care about the detainees." Every once in a while, Chris would let himself imagine what happened to the shackled men behind the closed doors of the interrogation rooms, but most of the time he was concerned about his own survival. "For the most part, my schedule was pretty booked," he says. "There wasn't a lot of time for existential and ethical dilemmas."

Chris was worried more about how the soldiers would react when he ordered them to do menial work, like picking garbage out of the razor wire around the perimeter of the camp, than he was about how the detainees were coping. Sending someone to the interrogation rooms or ordering sleep deprivation didn't feel like a big deal. "I wasn't even sending people," he explains, "I was sending numbers. It was not Moazzam Begg, it was 558." Detainee 555 had to go to the gold room for an interrogation. Package number 1002 had to be transferred to a different cell-block every four hours. It wasn't so hard.

On the blocks there was flesh involved. You had your hands on a detainee's arms, and you could smell his body. "But even still," says Chris, "you can find a way not to care." It takes, what, twenty minutes? And then the guards get to chill, have a smoke, and shoot the shit. From the distance of the office, it was even easier not to care.

"Stage two of deployment psychosis: extreme detachment," wrote Chris in an e-mail to his friend Jake, who was in Iraq. "It's the same bizarre scenes, the same brown walls, all day, it never changes. I stare at the stapler, willing it to staple my face. I can't wait until the word *detainee* is a distant memory again. I'm so sick of everything we fight about. This is so fucked up."

Morbidly unsympathetic, Jake e-mailed back, "Haha, you've only been gone not that long. Wait for the 10 month mark to roll around, and you'll be ready to shoot the back of your head off with pleasure." This was not exactly the reassurance Chris needed. But at least Jake was somewhere Chris could almost imagine, unlike the people back home who seemed so distant. Jake might have been in the war zone of Iraq, not on an island in the Caribbean, but just like Chris, he was being yelled at by commanders, was forced to do things against his will, and was slowly being broken down mentally.

To cope with the anger, boredom, and wretchedness, Chris created an internal fantasy world into which he could retreat. He had always been a bookworm, so it made sense to lose himself in books, but this was an all-consuming constant narrative. On the blocks, he hummed songs like "You Are My Sunshine." He daydreamed about the utopian life that he would live after Guantanamo, bucking the dull mainstream existence of minimum-wage jobs and trailer parks that his family and friends fell into. Before he'd left for Cuba, he had discovered Jack Kerouac, and he and a group of friends from college had concocted a vision of living the beatnik lifestyle together as great writers, traveling from one adventure to the next. Chris daydreamed about his possibilities. It was teenage romanticism magnified by a fierce determination to block out his surroundings. As his fictional mental landscape grew, his physical surroundings became inert and his job easier.

He became obsessed with a girl whom he had met online, through CampusMatch, a precursor to Facebook. Even though he knew deep down that there wasn't anything between them, he concocted a full-blown relationship and wrote her endless e-mails, waxing poetic about their love and making promises for the future. He just needed some connection to normal life.

Every time anything of perceived significance happened in the camp—a soldier was reprimanded, a detainee requested to see a chaplain, an interpreter, or a doctor or even just showed "extreme emotion"—a soldier filled out a regulation form and handed it in to the DOC. Chris was supposed to take the forms, enter the jargon, the numbers, and the dates into the computer system, and then discard them. But one day, instead of throwing the paper away, Chris folded a report into a small origami crane.

It had all started with the lyrics from a song called "My Favourite Chords" by the Weakerthans, a Canadian indie folk band, which he played incessantly on his Walkman: "And me and my anger sits, folding a paper bird, letting the curtains turn to beating wings."

Chris looked up how to do origami online and started folding. Every time a detainee was brought in for interrogation, put in isolation, or had his prayer beads confiscated, a report was filed, and Chris folded it into an origami bird. For every suicide attempt, IRF attack, and hunger strike, there was a paper crane. Eventually, the delicate creatures filled the surfaces of the DOC office. They lined up along Chris's desk, piled up next to the computer, and floated onto the floor. Soon there were so many that his commander ordered the cessation of the creation of any more paper birds by all detentions operations personnel. But Chris kept folding anyway.

Some of the detainees passed their time by carving poems or intricate patterns of flowers with their fingernails on their Styrofoam cups. The detainees occasionally handed these "cup poems," as they called them, from cell to cell when they could. Shaikh Abdurraheem Muslim Dost, a Pakistani poet and essayist, journalist, religious scholar, and the author of nearly twenty books, was one such detainee, whose time overlapped with Chris's service. On one of his cups, he wrote in Pashto:

Handcuffs befit brave young men,
Bangles are for spinsters or pretty young ladies.

On another:

What kind of spring is this,
Where there are no flowers and
The air is filled with a miserable smell?

Soldiers confiscated the cups and handed them in to the DOC in trash bags to be handed over to military intelligence department, supposedly to analyze for secret codes. Each cup came with a form reporting the event, which Chris would take and fold into a paper bird. The detainees would be issued other cups and start drawing once again.

Chris found something inspiring about the prisoners' determination and patience in how they passed their time. Even in the camp, there were small moments of beauty: the song of the morning prayers, the sunsets behind the prison, and the intricate drawings on the Styrofoam cups. The juxtapositions twisted Chris up inside, exaggerating the horrors around him. When he came home, Chris wrote about the birds in a zine. It was the best way he could think of to try to explain life in Guantanamo.

Everyday I twisted these wretched forms into something new and contemplated the beauty of this little bit of freedom the detained and the detainer had found here in that place without freedom and I hoped that when history wipes, finally, the dust from these cages, they would find my birds and they would know that no concentration camp can contain that which will always exist: beauty.

For weeks, Chris had been hiding out in his room in between shifts at the prison, contemplating suicide. He would lock his door and not talk to anyone. He made little ghost missions down to the kitchen to grab some peanut butter and jelly sandwiches, but, for the most part, when he wasn't on the blocks, he was in bed. He didn't want to do anything. On his days off, instead of scuba diving or playing golf like the others, he spent hours drifting in and out of sleep in a kind of half-conscious dream state. He didn't want to get drunk. Didn't want to socialize. Didn't want to play video games or watch a movie. The last time he had hung out with friends, they were playing Risk, and he had thrown the board game full of pieces across the room when he started to lose.

When I ask Chris what he thought about during those hours of staring at his wall, he can only describe what it looked like. He describes the stacks of books, which he had ordered from Amazon, that spilled out from under his bed, covered his dresser, and filled the duffle bags in the closet alongside his uniforms and gear. He maps the layout of the apartment: the microwave and the cupboards in the kitchen, adjacent to the living room, his shared bedroom upstairs, where two single beds were divided by the TV and a PlayStation.

He says that smelling incense brings him mentally back to his room in Cuba, where he used to burn it to hide the chemical smell from the air-conditioners. So does the indie music he used to listen to there—Neutral Milk Hotel, Smog, the Shins, Bright Eyes. Sometimes, he purposely listens to those songs, but mostly he tries to avoid them. Yet really it can be anything, at any random time, that can transport him back to Guantanamo without warning.

· · ·

Basic wasn't the only time that brass assigned extra duties that were meant to break soldiers down. One day, Chris's commander issued a new order: after ten-hour shifts, soldiers had to do an hour of physical training.

One day, instead of joining the rest, Chris ran—and ran and ran—until he made himself sick. Back home in his bed, nauseated and reeling, something in him just cracked. There are stress positions for detainees and stress positions for soldiers, and Chris had hit his breaking point.

He grabbed some military regulation 550 cord and looped it around one of the blades of the rickety overhead fan in his room. He climbed up on his bed, put his head into the noose, and jumped. But the fan cracked, his feet hit the floor a foot beneath him, and the blade fell, hitting him on the head. He says it was a lame attempt, and he didn't really think it would work, but he also says he had never been so happy about shoddy hardware. He went to the store, got some new screws, reattached the blade, and never told anyone what had happened.

"That was the place that I was making decisions from, so, what do you expect? Do you always get everything right? Are you always the hero?" he asks. "Under certain circumstances, there are almost no opportunities for you to be the hero. At best, you can crawl your way up to be an acceptable enemy."

12

Not the Country We Thought We Were

In many ways, Chris is a textbook case of post-traumatic stress disorder. When he first came home, he had severe panic attacks—one time he even asked his roommate to help him check into a VA hospital. (His friend told him that the VA was bullshit, and all he had to do was chill out, smoke some pot, and talk about what was going on.) Chris acted severely paranoid, freaking out that narcs or men in suits were following him.

Even three years later, Chris has intrusive thoughts and a hard time concentrating. He has panic attacks, periods of depression, and sleepless nights. He wakes up sweating from nightmares about Cuba. Sometimes he dreams he is back in his room, lying in his bed at the barracks. Other times he is a detainee, pacing inside the seven-by-eight cell late at night, feeling trapped and angry. Sometimes the dream is as simple as Chris merely being back in the military, knowing he is about to be redeployed.

On those nights, he knows that the next few ones will be just as restless and haunted. He will toss and turn and eventually wake up in an anxious panic or lie there half asleep, thinking about all of the soldiers still on the island.

Yet Chris thinks the categorization of PTSD as a disease is bogus. He's not sick, he says. He is having what he sees as a rational, healthy reaction to being at Guantanamo. He is vehemently against psychiatric medications. He doesn't want to blunt his reactions or feel okay with what happened. It isn't a mental illness but "a buildup of disenchantment with the world," he explains. War showed him the dark side of people, and now that he is home, he can't stop seeing it everywhere he looks. Hearing Chris describe it, it almost makes sense. His description of the VA overmedicating troubled soldiers sounds like some kind of sci-fi dystopia straight out of Aldous Huxley's *Brave New World*, where citizens are given soma pills to placate them and keep them from questioning things. Instead of PTSD, Chris prefers terms like "anger," "resentment," and "betrayal." I ask him whether the word *guilt* should be added to the list, but he trails off and goes inside to get his pot. "I'm a chemical fiend," he apologizes. And the conversation is over.

When Chris first came home, people say he was always pacing around, or, as Chris explains, it was as if he had drunk five cups of coffee, even though he was usually stoned on pot. Neuroticism, his friends say, was almost a shtick. He seems awkward and uncomfortable in his own skin but at the same time disarmingly extroverted.

Chris would ramble incessantly about everything, often going in circles and saying whatever popped into his mind. But when it came to Guantanamo, he hardly talked at all. He shrugged it off like a piece of trivia, an odd but interesting thing that he had done last semester. It was either that, or, "I was there, it sucked, and the war sucks." He complained about the boredom, the long hours, the alienation, and what jerks most of the guys in the unit were. He described working in an office, going to the beach, and reading in the barracks—hardly noteworthy stuff. His close friend Ben figured that nothing traumatic could have happened; otherwise Chris, the continuous talker, would have mentioned it. If there were something to talk about, he would have.

Part of Chris wanted to talk about it but felt that he couldn't. It seemed like people back home didn't want to hear about it. At a welcome-home dinner of sorts, Chris could barely get a word in edgewise while everyone filled him in on what he had missed: who was sleeping with whom and how drunk everyone was last weekend. Chris thought that they would have tons of questions about his time overseas, but none of them seemed interested in what he had done and seen. His friends admit that they didn't think much about his deployment. When he was deployed, they were just relieved that he wasn't going to be in Iraq, so although they had missed him while he was gone, they shrugged it off. Cuba was filled with sunny beaches; it sounded like a vacation.

Chris was scared that he would sound like the Vietnam vet Walter from the movie *The Big Lebowski*, who related everything to the war and never shut up about his military service. Chris was afraid to burden his friends and didn't want them to see him as "broken and twisted, when all I want is to just be normal."

It also seemed pointless, because he realized that no matter how hard he tried, he didn't know which words could ever really express what it was like. Soldiers often say that people who have never gone to war have no way to comprehend what it is like. When it came to Guantanamo, few people really even understood what it was. At least with combat, people have a vague, albeit highly romanticized and mythical, idea, but Chris had absolutely no starting point to begin to explain. "I tried and I choked on it and had no idea how," he tells me. "It is impossible, and it's impossible for everybody. I think a lot of people just get sick of trying to explain it." What is the value in dragging it all up, if no one will even understand?

Mostly, the topic of his service came up when Chris bitched about still having to go to drill. The nights before he had to report, he would ingest ridiculous amounts of different drugs, hoping to fail a drug test and get kicked out. For many of his friends, Chris was simply the crazy druggie who would show up and get blitzed. Chris wanted to walk away from his experience in Cuba and be done with it, but each month he had to put his uniform back on and report to drill. "I could've burned my uniform off my body when I got back," says Chris. "I didn't want to be in it a minute longer." That uniform represented the entrapment of authority, the anonymity of his nothingness status, and the shell of bravado that he has to wear in the military.

His friend Jake, who came back from Iraq around the same time as Chris did, was the only one who seemed to understand. Guantanamo and Iraq were worlds apart, but they saw each other going through similar problems readjusting. The two acknowledged it, yet anytime Chris tried to broach his politics of being against the war, Jake didn't want to hear about it.

Once again, Jake reflected for Chris an ominous prediction of whom he might become—or maybe who he already was. Jake was trying to fuck his way through his depression and anger. "He had a Pokemon concept of women," trying to collect as many conquests as possible. Yet clearly it wasn't working.

Chris also looked to escape into the world of women. Instead of seeking the physical escape of one-night stands as Jake did, he is on an endless quest for love, approval, and someone to take care of him and calm him. If these women can love him, maybe he can convince himself that he's not a monster. Chris wants to "capture them and snare them in this web of romance," as he puts it. He is always chasing or running away from girls, often simultaneously. He falls hard for women, calling friends in the middle of the night to tell them how he has finally found true love. Yet his relationships tend to be as brief as they are intense, ending when he loses interest, becomes too self-occupied, or as often happens, starts cheating. He is always moving on to the next one.

He'll swear off women, but, like a true addict, he can't last a day. He worries that his baggage is too much to unburden on anyone. He describes himself as toxic, almost contagious, as if he should be quarantined.

For a while Chris dated a vegan feminist named Katie. It seems an odd match: a former Guantanamo guard and a radical liberal activist. Chris was always trying to impress her with his anarchist ideals but at the same time defend his military service. He boasted to her and his other friends that he had been taken off the blocks because, unlike the other guards, he actually talked to the detainees and treated them like real people. He said he identified more with the prisoners than with the other guards. Katie criticized him for signing up in the first place but then also felt sorry for him. Chris assumed that she tried to keep his past a secret from her activist friends. Dating a soldier associated with torture doesn't exactly gain you any cred in that scene. Chris, in turn, was ashamed and "constantly felt like the enemy."

Mainly, Chris felt detached and alone. He was taking classes at the local college in Lansing, but he tended to hang out an hour and a half away in Kalamazoo with his friends Ben and Tony, who, like Chris, preferred debating to playing video games. He moved in with Scott, whom he used to drive around with in high school, going to punk-rock shows. They had both grown up poor, with similar family dramas, so Scott knew him well and looked out for him. But all the same, Chris wasn't sure where he fit in or who he was supposed to be.

While at Guantanamo, Chris had fanaticized about an idealistic life that he would return to when he finally got home. He was ready to embark on the plan to live like the Beat writers in *On the Road*, a romantic notion that he had clung to so fiercely in Guantanamo. But when Chris got back, Ben, whom they had decided was more like Kerouac, while Chris was Cassady, had abandoned the dream. Ben, the supposed torchbearer, had come to realize that *On the Road* was a work of fiction, an unrealistic fantasy. The Beats were sexist, self-indulgent. Ben realized that he'd rather become a university professor than live in an endless search for a mythical party. Their conversation shattered Chris, and he got angry. There seemed to be some truth in what Ben was saying, but Chris couldn't let go of the talisman that had gotten him through Cuba. The harsh reality of home, and his future, came crashing down.

Among the soldiers in his unit, the topic of Guantanamo was barely acknowledged. It was as if they had never even gone. They simply went back to being a regular artillery unit in the National Guard, attending monthly drill and going through the motions.

Half of Chris's unit had deployed to Iraq to work at Abu Ghraib. By contrast, they bragged about the pellet guns and the gas canisters they had shot at detainees. But among soldiers from Guantanamo, there was an eerie silence.

Part of it was the issue of treason: when they left the camp, like Brandon and everyone else who has worked at Guantanamo, they were made to sign a nondisclosure statement. Revealing information about the camp was considered treason. While there, they had been told not to discuss operations when calling home. Rumor was, the phones were tapped, and even using words like *detention*, *camp*, or *prisoner* could result in trouble.

Occasionally during downtimes at drill, some of the soldiers from Guantanamo apologized to one another for some of the stuff they had done—nothing detainee-related, but minor things, like brawls at the Tiki Bar and harsh words during off hours. It felt to Chris like a subtle message hinting at a larger guilt.

Three years after the unit had come home from Guantanamo, on the dawn of Chris's last day of annual training, he and one of his sergeants, a particularly surly guy, were sitting around the campfire, drinking coffee and smoking cigarettes. Maybe there was something about staring into the fire or the early dawn hours, which can feel like stolen time, or perhaps it was just because the sergeant knew that Chris wore his PTSD on his sleeve. The sergeant, who normally always shouted orders at Chris, told Chris about a dream he had had that night, a recurring dream he'd been having since he'd left Cuba. He described being in a long, narrow corridor between two fences of razor wire that stretched on forever. He said that detainees—or sometimes armed men—would charge after him. So, in the dream, he would start digging to try to escape under the wire, only to find himself in yet another cage. No matter how many cages he dug through, barely escaping, there was always another one, and the men kept gaining ground.

"It seemed like man code for 'This has destroyed my life, too,'" says Chris. "Like he was saying, 'I can't escape the haunting thoughts, and maybe what we did wasn't right.'"

Usually, soldiers rush through their post-deployment psychological assessment forms, checking whatever boxes will send them home. But not Chris. Filling out the mental assessments, he answered the questions truthfully. "Have you had any experience that was so frightening, horrible, or upsetting that you have had nightmares or thought about it when you didn't want to?" Check. "Have you felt numb or detached from others?" When had he not? Thoughts of suicide? Hell, yeah. All day, every day.

These answers earned him a meeting with a group of the top brass. Chris was seriously intimidated by sitting across the table from the uniformed officers, but all the same he confessed his suicidal tendencies, surprising the officers with his candor. Even with the increased awareness about PTSD, the taboo is still stiflingly acute. To Chris's surprise, instead of mocking him and telling him to man up, they were fatherly and sympathetic. They told him they were seeing similar problems with other soldiers: alcoholism, divorces, DUIs, and domestic abuse. The soldiers weren't admitting to having PTSD and certainly weren't going to the military mental health clinic. In fact, the clinic in Lansing complained that no one was using its services. Instead, there were violent outbursts, addictions, arrests, divorces, losses of child custody and jobs. Returning soldiers all over the country were falling apart. Suicide rates of returning soldiers are at record highs. In January 2008, the *New York Times* reported there had been 121 cases of recently returned soldiers from Iraq and Afghanistan who had "committed a killing in this country, or were charged with one." The Pentagon doesn't keep track of returnees' records, so the *Times* conducted interviews and scoured local newspapers and police, court, and military records, so the true number was probably much higher. A third of the victims were spouses, girlfriends, children, or other relatives. Thirteen of the soldiers committed suicide shortly after the killing. Few had received anything more than the cursory postdeployment psychiatric evaluation.

The brass sent Chris to a psychiatrist, who deemed him officially unfit for duty. Instead of discharging him, his commander let him stay on and drill, so he could draw benefits. They told him that even if the unit was recalled, he wouldn't deploy, and when his time was up, he'd get an honorable discharge. In return, he had to see the psychiatrist on a regular basis.

Chris worried that if he made any real therapeutic progress, they could rediagnose him as being fit for duty and send him back. It wasn't a risk he was willing to take. When he had seen a psychiatrist for his predeployment assessment, he felt as if he was being judged and evaluated, not helped. There is pressure on the doctors by the military, which they work for, to put the military's wishes ahead of the patient's well-being. It was a common situation, which could lead to unethical practices and questionable diagnoses. So Chris kept telling his commanders that he was working on setting up an appointment, and he kept putting it off.

That August, Chris moved up to Chicago with his girlfriend, for what seemed like a new start. He still had to make the trek to

Lansing for the monthly drill, but even so, living in Chicago felt worlds away. He was enamored of the hipsters, bought himself a fixed-gear bike, and cruised around Logan Square. He tried to work a series of jobs where he didn't have to interact too much with people: taking down party sets with an all-Spanish-speaking crew, doing receiving at a bookstore, busing at a vegan café.

With time, he changed his narrative about Guantanamo. He told his friends about how many good books he'd had time to read over there and how he was lucky to be one of the few Americans to ever get to visit Cuba. He said that maybe he had been overly dramatic about how hard it was. Yet, in some ways, the switch just made it seem as if maybe he was trying too hard to convince himself that it had all been okay.

Then there was nothing. No talk about it whatsoever. Chris tried to fully distance himself from being a soldier or a vet. Everyone expected him to simply move on and put Guantanamo behind him.

Chris may have stopped talking about Guantanamo, but mentally he could never escape it. Trying to put on a front of normalcy only made him feel even more isolated and depressed. He saw himself spiraling downward, and he knew that just getting high every day was not the solution.

Chris couldn't talk to his girlfriend about what he was going through. After waking up from nightmares, he'd spend the rest of the night on the couch, without explaining to her why, which often led to fights. One day she told him about a veterans' group in the area that she had heard about from a cute guy she had been hanging out with. Chris had vaguely heard about group therapy organizations like Vets for Vets, and although the idea of a bunch of old guys sitting around rehashing war stories, AA-style, didn't appeal to him, he figured that he had to try something. Feeling jealous, territorial, and competitive with his girlfriend's new friend—not to mention desperate—Chris decided to check it out.

When he got to the group's office, he was stunned to find a bunch of young counterculture guys, who were more punk or hippie than military. They were tough guys but activists, channeling their militaristic sides into fighting for veterans' rights through demonstrations and outreach. It was the Chicago chapter of the Iraq Veterans Against the War, the largest and most active group within the nationwide grassroots organization, which Andy had also joined. They were there to offer one another emotional help and, even more important, to let others know that it's okay to speak out against the war. Chris immediately signed up and began to volunteer that day.

Hanging out with IVAW members, Chris realized that he wasn't alone. It wasn't just that they were having the same problems that he was with maintaining relationships and holding down jobs, but unlike the other veterans he knew, including Jake, they were also angry with the politicians who had sent them overseas. Within the IVAW, it was not only accepted but expected that he would be antiwar and antitorture. Anger with the system was almost a requirement for group eligibility. None of the members had been to Cuba, but Chris felt that even without his explaining anything, they understood who he was and where he was coming from.

In January 2008, the IVAW heard about an upcoming anti-Guantanamo street protest and floated the idea by Chris that maybe he might consider speaking. Putting himself out there in public was a risk. Hell, talking about it at all made him feel vulnerable. But the public protest aspect appealed to his activist anti-authoritarian side. To everyone's surprise, Chris said, "What the hell. Let's do it."

It was a cold winter day when Chris took the podium before crowds of protesters holding signs that denounced the military, torture, and Guantanamo. He was terrified. He imagined the hatred they must have for him, the torturer. So, in his speech he told the audience that not all of the guards there were bad people, that many, like himself, had been put in a moral conundrum with no easy way out.

As promised, the IVAW members made a human barrier to protect him as he left the stage. Chris was scared that angry mobs of antiwar protesters would lash out at him, but the IVAW guys knew that the real onslaught would come from journalists seeking interviews and liberals wanting to recruit him for their causes. Those were the types, after all, who would be in the audience. IVAW members in the past had had trouble with being overwhelmed by such requests. At times, they felt as if they were being used. The left, just like the right, only wants to hear certain things. They want examples of the worst kinds of abuse, complete castigation of the military, told by soldiers who have heroically stood up and said no. It can be just as stifling in ways as others' denial of any wrongdoing. After the journalists and activists had gathered a few gruesome anecdotes about the war, they would usually move on, leaving the soldiers alone with their pain.

But Chris didn't know that. He saw, for the first time, that there were people besides soldiers who actually wanted to hear what he had to say. Instead of seeing him as damaged goods, they thanked him for being brave enough to testify. He wasn't a torturer, but a whistleblower helping to put a stop to the abuses. Instead of a war criminal, he could be a war hero.

These days, when it comes to the IVAW, Chris describes himself as an addict. He has pursued the group with the same enthusiasm he normally reserves for girls. He has gone with the group to protests at both the Republican and the Democratic National Conventions. It is how he identifies himself, how he spends his time, who his friends are, what his life's mission is. Using a permanent marker, he has boldly written "Iraq Veterans Against the War" on all of his clothes, which makes some people he meets feel a little put off, intimidated, or confused as to whether or not to thank him for his service.

Some of his nonmilitary friends weren't exactly sure what to make of all this. Most of all, it seemed odd that Chris had gone from trying to have nothing to do with the military to making his status as a vet his primary identity. Some people didn't really understand the point of the group. The group members were saying that they were activists, but they didn't seem to actually be accomplishing anything. Other friends admitted to feeling a little jealous: Why was Chris opening up only to these new friends when his old friends had been there for him for so long? Some of his friends think his work with the IVAW holds him back from moving on. One of his housemates, Danny, the British student passing through town on a biking tour, tells me that he worries about how intense Chris's work with the IVAW is. He is sweetly protective of Chris and wishes Chris could see all of the other things life can offer.

Even Chris wonders whether it is healthy to be so all consumed with the IVAW and to have his identity so firmly based on it. It's almost become a career and a life's mission. He has traded in the keys to the cells, but is mentally still a prisoner of his own guilt and resentment.

In March 2008, Chris attended the three-day IVAW Winter Soldier event in Silver Spring, Maryland. It was modeled on the Vietnam War testimonies, which had led to congressional hearings and helped turn public opinion against that war. It was the same event, by happenstance, that Andy Duffy attended. Over two hundred and fifty veterans from around the country came together in the huge auditorium.

Outside, angry crowds were protesting the event, calling the soldiers traitorous for airing the military's dirty laundry. They accused the soldiers of making up stories about the horrors of war, not realizing that if anything, soldiers were downplaying whatever aspects of their stories could possibly put a comrade, or themselves, in trouble. Many of the soldiers spoke in generalities. Part of this is pure self-preservation. Talking is hard and wears soldiers down. Onstage, some soldiers breakdown at certain points and simply have to stop talking.

When Chris took the microphone, he described the IRF attacks, the endless "numbers, shackles, and keys" at the operations center, and the boredom on the blocks. He posed the question of whether the indefinite detention at the camp was itself torture and pointed out the difference in semantics between *detainee* and *prisoner of war*, as well as between *detention facility* and *concentration camp*.

Chris opened his speech with "I would like to share with you how one goes about becoming a concentration camp guard without ever having really made many decisions." Chris knows the shock value of comparing himself to a Nazi guard. He knows Americans don't want to equate themselves with Hitler's regime. By conjuring up that one image, he can explain that we are on the wrong side and that we have become the ultimate evil. But as self-damning as he might be, that opening also shows how much he tries to skirt any sense of agency. It was a decision someone else made on Chris's behalf.

Like so many other soldiers who had been in similar situations, Chris has a hard time coming to grips with his own personal responsibility for what he did—which is understandable, particularly for someone so young. Chris often shifts the blame onto those who outranked him. "I could no more easily get off that island than the detainees could," he tells me. "I was a prisoner in a looser sense, but we were all oppressed into our roles in these scenarios. There was a gun to my head. I couldn't just not do it. I had no choice, and everyone understands that."

Not everyone does understand that, however. The excuse that following orders could justify your actions was tossed out during the Nuremberg trials. Yet according to the Uniform Code of Military Justice, disobeying legal orders—which, at the time, Chris's duties technically were, according to the White House lawyers—is an illegal offense. "I am who I am, and I've done what I've done, and I've seen what I've seen," Chris says. "I was asked to do an absurd job, an evil job, and I did it." He acknowledges his role, even in the DOC office where he was one step removed. But, he argues, he did his best to get out of the situation, and compared to other guards he was hardly abusive.

Unleashing the stories and feelings at Winter Soldier which he had been suppressing cracked open a fissure for the rest to pour out. It may have been empowering to speak in front of crowds of antiwar soldiers and activists, but it came with a psychological price.

Chris sat through several panels hearing story after story about the horrors of war. He heard about American soldiers being raped by men in their unit and a detainee getting kicked as water was poured over his face, and saw "trophy photos" of mutilated dead bodies of Iraqi civilians. But after he spoke, he went outside and chain-smoked for the rest of the evening. "It was a tidal wave of vile shit coming out of people's mouths for three days," he says. He had brought his girlfriend with him, and it was helpful to have her there for support. But that night they got into a huge blowout. She felt ignored and isolated there among the IVAW members. Other girlfriends and wives have expressed the same alienation among that tight-knit clique that shares with one another the most private things. They seemed to know how to reach Chris in a way she never could. Chris was acting understandably selfish—it was the "all-Chris show that weekend," as Chris puts it, and her emotions took a backseat. She accused him of being on a quest to get the whole world to fall in love with him and never being satisfied with what he had. He agrees. If enough people like him, maybe he can convince himself to do the same. But he tells me that he never got enough people to jump on the bandwagon.

Months later, a German girl challenged Chris and a group of IVAW members. "So you think being a part of IVAW buys you out of your actions and what you've done in the world?" she asked them. Chris tried to argue that he can't take back what he has done, so he is just trying to do his best to counter some of those wrongs. More pointedly, though, he told her that, of course, it can never alleviate his guilt. "If anything, IVAW makes us feel more guilty," he explains, "because you are broadcasting it to the world."

• • •

When some of Chris's friends watched the event later on YouTube, they were shocked. They had never heard the stories that he told that day at the Winter Soldier event—about the IRF attacks, the shackling, the torture inside interrogation rooms. In his speech, he clarified the fact that he had enlisted after 9/11, even though he had told his friends otherwise because he'd been afraid that he would seem like one of the gung ho soldiers who were out for revenge. One friend, Tony, who watched the event online, took that as a signal that things were going to be different. Chris was coming clean. They were going to hear a lot of things about Chris that he hadn't told them before, things that they might not want to hear. Now that Chris was testifying, it was paramount that he tell the truth.

Four months later, Chris showed a few of his friends a short article that appeared in *Esquire* magazine, which quoted him admitting for the first time that he had tried to commit suicide. Chris also sent his mother a copy. It was the only way he could tell them about what had happened, because he couldn't articulate it to their faces. It was a jarring way for them to find out, and they felt hurt that Chris had been able to bare all to a journalist—a stranger—and not to them.

When Chris got home from Silver Spring, he fell apart. In part, he was terrified that there would be consequences for his publicly sharing classified information. He imagined that every van or car that drove past his apartment was filled with special agents. Unleashing his secrets and hearing about other soldiers' horrors had unhinged him. He walked out of French class one day, frustrated by how juvenile other students were acting. Eventually, he just stopped going to classes altogether. He began to hole up inside his apartment. He fiercely wanted to be out doing something, being with people. But instead, he just watched the winter through his window.

Now when he sees the weather turning gray again, he feels the depression creeping back and knows what to anticipate. "I've seen its type again and again and again, and I know that it is going to mostly be a time of continuously thinking about suicide," he says. "I know this isn't going to change. This is going to be difficult." He tries to console himself with the romantic notion that maybe it simply means that he is an artist, not a broken, wounded vet. But that sounds better than it feels.

That summer, some wealthy donors lent their house in Martha's Vineyard to a group of twenty-seven IVAW members to hold a retreat. The veterans spent the summer days and nights making art, playing music, writing poetry, and drinking beer. One guy showed them how to shred their uniforms and mulch them into paper. No one had a job or a cell phone. It was a big hippie fest. Being inside this IVAW bubble was safe, inspiring, and freeing—almost like being one of the Lost Boys in Peter Pan's Never-Never Land. Although they knew the reason that had drawn them all together, they didn't talk about the war. But on the last day, they shared testimonies with locals about the horrors of war. Hearing the stories from this now tight-knit group was too much for Chris. After he spoke, he went outside on the porch, started to cry, and then just zoned out, staring off into the woods for almost two hours. He had begun to remember and face things he didn't want to—things about Cuba, but also deeper things about himself, his past, and even his childhood.

After returning to Chicago, one day while riding his bike to work, he started to cry and knew he had to get out of there. He gave two weeks' notice that he was quitting his job, but then every day when he came to work, he'd cry or get really anxious and uncomfortable, so he stopped showing up. His tumultuous relationship with his girlfriend was finally over for good. He ditched his apartment and hit the road.

It's not that uncommon for soldiers to take off and go off the grid for a while after being deployed. Many travel overseas, take a road trip around the country, or simply use their savings for hedonistic escapism. One of Chris's friends just up and went to India on the spur of the moment. Soldiers are so outside the normal societal experience that sometimes it is the only thing that makes sense to them.

When Chris did it, he made the excuse that it was a political research project to see what life was like for homeless vets. He was going to spend fifteen months—the length of his deployment—traveling around the country interviewing veterans about the problems they faced. He imagined himself a sort of Studs Terkel, collecting the stories of everyday Americans who were carrying the country's burden. But he ended up conducting only a handful of interviews and admits that more than anything it was a personal venture. He and another IVAW member hit the road and hitch-hiked their way to Portland, going wherever the road seemed to take them along the way. They stayed in a tent in an IVAW friend's parents' backyard, slept at truck stops, and crashed on people's couches. They shoplifted, panhandled, Dumpster dove, and accepted handouts from people in the IVAW network to get by.

Wandering gives Chris an excuse not to get too attached. Never having his name on a lease or on credit cards or bills means that Chris is further off the grid. Half of that is a political "fuck you" to the system, not wanting to "support the war machine" in the slightest degree, but it's also a way to escape and keep people at arm's length. It is hard to be back in a situation where anyone has control over his life, whether it be a girlfriend, a boss, or a landlord. "I have seen the wretched shit that authority can make people do," he explains, and anything even slightly resembling that puts a sour taste back in his mouth.

Chris's mother, Kari, worries about Chris wandering from place to place without a job and getting his clothes at the Salvation

Army. She tries to get him to come home and offers to buy him new sneakers and jeans at Walmart, but he turns her down. She wishes he would call home and e-mail more often so that she would know he is okay. She doesn't understand his notions of a punk rock lifestyle and sees only the inner turmoil that is behind it all. She hates how Chris tells everyone that he is homeless. She figures they must think she's a bad mom, neglecting him, when in reality she is a doting parent who has dedicated her life to her kids. She sacrificed to provide for them, and now here was Chris, choosing to eat out of Dumpsters.

Kari hates that Chris starts off so many of his speeches saying that he grew up in a trailer park in the middle of a cornfield with a bunch of rednecks, in nowhere Michigan. She understands that he is making a valid point. Military recruiters do target poor kids, and Chris sees himself as a victim of a class war. "I'm a victim, in that my family has been economically repressed and I was never given any opportunities. The victim of a culture that has pushed us, our whole lives, to join the military," says Chris. Sons of the elite and Harvard graduates enlist, but when they do, they join as officers, not as National Guardsmen. People like Chris sign up for the military because they lack options; teenagers with New England pedigrees go to West Point as a step toward becoming senators. Their connections and résumés mean they will be fighting a war on a tactical level, not emptying waste buckets inside prisons. And if they have reservations about the war's tactics, they can raise their objections with other officers or even with politicians and the media. It is a two-track system, with people in the working class being trapped from the time before they even sign up until long after they retire.

But still, it drives Kari crazy, because she worked so hard to be the best mom she could to Chris and his sister. When the kids were young, Kari had spent her days working at the office of an Air-Way factory and weekends running volunteer youth programs at a community theater and a church. Chris and his sister may have been jealous of their cousins who had new Nikes, thanks to their dad's job at GM, but Chris had the newest Nintendo.

Kari points out that it wasn't a trailer but a double-wide, with three bedrooms and a full basement. Their home had several acres of lawn, with a rock garden and a porch. She and her husband joke that they should get pink flamingos for their yard and a muumuu for Kari, to fulfill Chris's stereotype.

I visited Kari in rural Michigan. Chris was supposed to be in town, but because of his normal unpredictable wandering, he had ended up elsewhere. Chris always cites his mother as a major influence in his life, so I was interested in talking with her, seeing the area where Chris had grown up, and meeting some other members of his unit.

Kari lives with her husband, Tim, in Charlotte, twelve miles away from where she raised Chris. She, her daughter, Jessica, and her mother, Nedra, all live in the same manufactured-home community, which means they can visit one another often without wasting gas. The area is a brown landscape of factories, cornfields, and strip malls. An hour and a half from Detroit, it is dependent on Ford, GM, and Chrysler and has been hit hard by the recession. There's 12 percent unemployment, a statistic that doesn't include those working part-time who are unable to make ends meet. Kari says it feels like going down on the *Titanic* without a lifeboat in sight.

Kari was recently laid off from her job managing a series of apartment complexes. After working there for six years, it was more than work; it was her identity. The job she had after that one resulted in on-the-job harassment and a lawsuit against the employer for wrongful termination. She now has a job at a motel that pays only ten dollars an hour, instead of the fifteen she'd been getting by on before—but, she says, at least she has a job.

Tim is a Vietnam vet. He joined the Navy to avoid being drafted into fighting in the jungle. He says that shooting anonymous enemies on the distant shore might have made his job easier than the one Chris had working face-to-face with detainees.

All the same, he can relate. Though never part of the antiwar movement, he is just as adamantly against war as Chris is. He has seen what it has done to people. When Tim was on his way to Vietnam, two men jumped off the ship rather than go fight; they were shredded by the vessel's propellers and killed. It's too hard for Tim to watch many of the Winter Soldier testimonies, but he and Chris talk about the IVAW a lot. Tim drives a Ryder truck delivering car parts to warehouses. For a while he worked long, grueling double shifts, but ever since one of the factories shut down, there are times when there's no work for him. He's lucky, though, not to be one of the nine hundred workers the factory laid off. He has looked for other jobs, but openings are few and far between. When a small company announced that it was hiring two snow plowers, it received twelve hundred applicants. He and Kari doubt that they will ever be able to retire.

Jessica, Chris's younger sister, used to work as a "factory rat," making RVs and military trucks at Spartan. She had little pride in the work. Having seen the quality of work on the line, she says she would never buy a Spartan RV. As one of the few women employees, she had to put up with all kinds of sexual harassment. She filed a complaint against one man, but he confronted her alone in a hallway one morning, asking her why she had gone to the boss. After that, she tried to just sling it back to the guys. When RV sales declined and the military contract ended, Jessica was one of the three hundred who were laid off. It was good timing, though, she says, because she was pregnant and now has time to take care of her baby. But her boyfriend's unemployment checks have already run out, and his occasional odd jobs are hardly enough to cover the car payments and the mortgage on their home. She doesn't know the first thing about Chris's work with the IVAW or what he testifies about, but she wears the IVAW T-shirt he bought for her. She has never left Charlotte and seems a little jealous that Chris's antiwar work has taken him to so many places.

Kari's mother, Nedra, is comfortably retired, having worked for decades for the state. While the other family members are scrambling financially, she donates hundreds to her church. According to Kari and Tim, her relative wealth makes her out of touch with everything that is going on. Kari says her mother "just doesn't get any of this stuff—the economy, the war, Guantanamo. She has everything paid for, lives in her own little world." She spends her days visiting her tight-knit group of friends, whom she has known since high school, or home making elaborately decorated Fabergé-like eggs.

While I was visiting, Kari drove me out to see this much-contested trailer, five miles outside of Olivet. Five miles doesn't sound far, but in the small town, population 1,800, people rarely ventured past Main Street. The community is isolated to the point that Kari felt like an outsider moving there from Lansing, which is an hour away. Going to Olivet these days, she's guaranteed to see kids from Chris's high school who still live there.

Having to drive down the dusty road through the cornfields to their house made Kari and the kids feel cut off. When I see the house, it is a far cry from the ramshackle trailer that Chris's description had conjured up. It is the size of a small one-story house, with a pleasant porch, on a large tract of land. Kari explains that when she lived there, it was even more spruced up. Yet all the same, it is a trailer, in a cornfield, in the middle of nowhere. It doesn't stand out in the area, though, because the neighborhood is filled with raised ranches, dilapidated barns, and other mobile homes. All the same, Kari's mother, Nedra, who had lived next door at the time, told me that when the trailer was delivered, the next-door neighbor called up, irate. He wasn't going to live next to no trailer, he told her. Kari had permission from the county, however, and there was nothing he could do.

What Kari doesn't understand is that Chris stresses his working-class roots partly because they make him proud. When asked at a speech whether he was still proud of America, he explained that he was definitely not proud of the torture policy or the leaders or of the fact that Americans didn't stand up to them. But he said that he is proud of the working class, their ethics, labor, and culture, all of which have produced things like the assembly line, car manufacturing, American literature, and rock and roll, which make America great. The blue-collar are what hold up this country, the good and the bad. They carry its burdens and do its dirty work, but they also are the driving force that keeps it going.

One evening after dinner, while we are sitting on the overstuffed couches in her living room, Kari shows me home videos of Chris growing up. In chronological order, we watch Chris go through birthdays and Christmases, unwrapping boxes of plastic trucks, dinosaurs, and LEGO bricks. There is his first birthday, at the apartment where Kari lived alone with him. Chris had been a test-tube baby, a rarity back in the eighties. Even though his parents put so much effort into conceiving him, his dad split when Kari was eight months pregnant, leaving her for another woman. As a result, Kari became a single mom. She had to get a doctor's permission slip to return to work right after Chris was born so that she could make the rent. But in the videos, her parents and sister-in-law all coo over Chris, not just on that birthday, but for his first haircut, and on Christmases. We see him splashing in a plastic kiddy pool outside in his grandma's yard and playing with other kids at preschool, and later in middle school plays.

At one point, Tim, Kari's second husband, joins the picture. First, he is a young man in a trucker's hat and a plaid flannel shirt, still her boyfriend, playing with Chris. Next, Tim is sitting by the tree, shirtless, at their new single-wide trailer with their new baby, Jessica. Then there is the Christmas where Kari and Tim are in the same frame, handing the kids gifts without speaking to each other. They look sullen as Chris and his younger sister grab at the presents. It's the only hint we see of what Tim was like off-camera, abusive to both Kari and Chris.

Kari was extremely protective of Chris, and Tim knew that hurting the boy was a good way to get at her. Tim hated her coddling and always yelled, "Cut the cord, Kari," and "Stop being such a pussy, Chris." The worse he was to Chris, the more protective she became, creating a cycle. Chris and his younger sister also fought bitterly. She was daddy's girl, and the house was divided. Even though she was younger, she used to beat Chris up and once even chased him around the house with a knife.

The last video we watch is a commemorative tape of Chris's time at basic. It starts with stock footage of random soldiers performing exercises on obstacle courses, but then focuses on Chris's unit's own training. We see them arriving, duffel bags in tow, and then learning how to do a proper pushup. There are shots of them snaking along in mud under wires, jumping through barrels, climbing through rope courses, shooting guns and cannons, and rolling tanks down roads. There are boys who get stuck on top of the plywood walls, too scared to rappel down, and others who fall while leaping over walls. The commanders yell at those kids, telling them not to be babies. The tougher and stronger-trainees yell out, "War Dawgs!" and pump their fists.

Chris's only cameo appears when they were made to enter a small room filled with tear gas wearing gas masks. Inside, orders were to take off the masks, so that they can appreciate the difference between breathing with and without protection. The boys stumble out of the room, blinded, some with their hands on whoever is in front of them to lead the way. Some vomit, others have long strands of drool hanging from their mouths. When Chris stumbles out of the gas-filled room, he is crying. The camera zooms in as he kneels down, buckled over in pain, and vomits, while the command sergeant looms over him screaming. Chris is even more reticent to discuss training than he is to talk about his time at Guantanamo. He tells me that it was humiliating, physically grueling, and basically just "sucked." He complained the whole way through. While other soldiers were bonding, he was being taunted. It's later from his grandmother that I find out that Chris failed one of the tests and had to be held back. She also tells me that he was assigned to keep an eye on his bunkmate, who was on suicide watch.

Kari gets upset every time she watches the film, but she also laughs, saying she cannot even imagine Chris doing any of this. She had kept waiting to get an official call from the National Guard telling her to come take him home. The mission of basic training is to break down a boy and build him back up as a soldier. If there was ever a boy who needed to be rebuilt to be able to serve in the army, it was Chris. At graduation, his commander told Kari that out of all the people he had ever trained, Chris had progressed the furthest. He was the most improved player. Kari was shocked that he had graduated and sent the newspaper announcement to her exes to show them that they were wrong about Chris.

Chris's biological father showed up unannounced at Chris's military graduation. He hadn't seen his son since Chris was a toddler. Unlike any other event or achievement in Chris's life, this had warranted a visit. Chris's dad wanted to take them all out for dinner, and Kari worried that Chris would be seduced by this newfound approval from his dad.

Kari saw Chris gain confidence at basic, but when he came home, she also saw a haze of inner turmoil—almost as if he had been partially brainwashed into the "Sir, yes, sir!" military mentality and had to battle to fully regain who he was. Or, as Chris puts it, he was suffering from having been "relegated to a nothingness status."

When I ask Kari why Chris ever signed up for the military in the first place, she bursts into tears. She says it was a particularly rough patch in their lives. She had left Tim because he was increasingly abusive, and she was hiding out with her daughter in a motel a few towns over. Chris, a senior in high school, had opted to stay at a friend's house instead. Things were chaotic. Kari was driving hours to get to work. Then Jessica got pregnant and had to get an abortion. The final bombshell was the news that Chris had enlisted.

Despite everything he has been through, Chris still maintains that being in the military was valuable, and he is glad he served. He now knows he can withstand more pain and walk greater distances than most people. He defends the military as a good choice for kids who don't have a lot of other options.

Kari agrees—after all, she was in the Air Force herself and credits that for getting her to where she is today. All the same, it came with a risk. "I don't even know what I would have done if he'd joined for college money and then come home in a body bag," Chris's mom tells me. "I would have felt like the worst mother in the whole world for not being able to scrape up enough money to keep him out of that predicament."

When Chris first came home from Guantanamo, he sometimes stopped by Kari's house but was jittery and unable to sit still. His mother could see in his eyes how sad he was, how part of him had shut down. He never wanted to talk about what was in his head. She never saw him cry anymore, but he had also lost his ability to laugh. He used to have a light, funny side, and now he was just in this "dark, murky place." She worried about him and tried to listen to what he had to say, but it was hard for her—and for him.

The day that Kari saw Chris testify at Winter Soldier, though, things clicked into place, and she understood better what he and the other soldiers were going through. She realized that Chris now had a mission in setting the story straight.

Chris had told his mom that he was going to a veterans' testimonial event and to check it out on FreeSpeech TV. At the time that it aired, she was vacuuming and had it turned on in the background. By happenstance, she looked up at the screen right before Chris stepped up to the microphone to testify. She had no idea that he was there to talk himself. She called her daughter and her mom: "Oh, my God! Chris is on TV!" And then she sat down to hear, for the first time, what Chris had really gone through at Guantanamo Bay.

Chris woke her up, and it was a rude awakening. As she puts it, she wasn't thrilled about it. "I was all about the red, white, and blue," she says. "Like everyone else I knew, I bought into all the propaganda and just wanted to go get those bastards."

If Kari was to believe what Chris was saying, it would mean that America, in which she had so much faith and pride, and for which she had served, was not the country she thought it was. Kari's son was everything to her, but now he was asking her to question her entire worldview. She was a mother, but also an American.

She started to search for more information, listen to other soldiers testify, and watch documentaries about the war. It was clear that Chris wasn't the only one who had seen these things.

Listening to Kari talk about documentaries about the sham of the Iraq war and the horrors of Guantanamo, the way the hard-working people in Michigan are being tossed aside, and how she tries to wake people up about how the troops are being mistreated, you would never suspect that she was once an über-Republican. She says it isn't she who has changed but her country. She still cries when flags go by in parades and gets weepy when she passes a military cemetery or when people sing the national anthem.

"But after I saw what they tried to shove up our asses and tell us what was what, I started to say, 'Really? Why am I buying into all this when all you do is lie to people?'"

Each time Kari watched something on FreeSpeech TV about detainee abuse or read about it on the Internet, she would ask Chris whether this was really the way it was. In the back of her mind, she kept thinking, Why didn't you tell me all this before?

I asked Kari whether she agrees that Chris seems to shirk his personal responsibility for what he did, and whether she agrees that he was in fact responsible. Kari agrees but doesn't think it was intentional. "Maybe he just hasn't come to terms with the fact that he needs to own up," she says, "or maybe he hasn't felt that he is responsible."

She says she can understand how he could think it isn't his fault and might simply be mad that the military made him do those things. But really, Kari points out, what was he going to do? Say no and end up in prison? Not to mention the abuse he would have faced from the other soldiers. "Perhaps he felt it was better to just be oblivious to it and block it all out. I think a lot of times when you are doing something that you hate, you sort of do."

At her old job where she faced daily harassment, she said, it was horrible, but you just go in, do your job as best you can, make your money, and go home. For most Americans, doing the best you can means putting up with a lot.

Tim perhaps most of all, understands what goes through Chris's mind. "The military is a form of brainwashing," he explains. "You are there and you are stuck and you have to do what they say or else." Tim mentions that he didn't say no in Vietnam. He was just shooting from offshore, but still, he knew that each time he pulled the trigger, it was to kill someone. "You can spend your whole life trying to discount what you did, argue that you had to, that you did it for your country, but you always have that ghost deep down inside you, haunting you. There is no way you can make it go away." Maybe Chris doesn't have to voice the fact that he feels guilty or responsible. Mainly, Kari and Tim credit Chris for quickly getting himself out of the blocks so that he wouldn't have to directly do morally reprehensible things.

Kari is insanely proud of Chris and sees all of the opportunities that have opened up for him through the IVAW—the travel, the friends, the experiences. But, ultimately, she is scared that people will hurt him for speaking out and worries when she sees him looking so sad. She compares him to John Lennon—someone who, in her mind, was ultimately sacrificed for having a message that was too much ahead of its time. She just wants Chris to move on, get therapy, live somewhere stable, or even come home. Why can't someone else's son be a martyr for this cause?

13

Seeking Redemption

One fall day in 2008, Chris checked his e-mail, and there in his in-box was a message from a former detainee. It was Moazzam Begg, who had been imprisoned while Chris was there, even though the two had never directly interacted. When Moazzam was released and returned to Britain, he began testifying publicly, and even wrote a book, called *Enemy Combatant,* about his time at Guantanamo. He had seen the Winter Soldier testimony online and was impressed with Chris. Now Moazzam was inviting Chris to accompany him on a speaking tour in the United Kingdom.

Chris knew it was too good an opportunity to pass up. Internationally touring with a former detainee upped the ante for Chris, in terms of potential treason charges. While that made him nervous, it was also an ultimate "fuck you" to the state, and a way to elevate his activist platform. It was radical, it would get attention, and it was right up Chris's alley. Not to mention, it would take his wandering adventures all the way overseas.

He had to admit, though, that he was nervous about meeting a former detainee. He read Moazzam's book and was fascinated to hear his perspective of the same events. But Chris also read that, as he had feared, the detainees felt morally superior to and judgmental of the guards. Moazzam wrote a lot about his perception of the guards in his book. He was condescending and disparaging, not so much about how they treated the detainees, but about how uneducated, materialistic, and self-consumed they were. He called them ignorant whiny rednecks. He recognized that many didn't want to be at Guantanamo, or even in the military, but that just made him critical of how little conviction they had.

But Chris figured this could be his chance to show Moazzam that some of the guards were more than that. Maybe confessing and apologizing to a detainee, instead of to a crowd of Americans, could actually be redemptive.

Right before Chris left for London, he was interviewed by a newspaper reporter from his hometown in Michigan. The reporter quoted Chris calling the deployment "an awful waste of time" and "terrifying" and announced his upcoming tour speaking out against Guantanamo in the UK with former detainees. In the article, Chris explained that there was no way for guards to know whether the detainees were guilty or not. He said the work was a mixture of mundane and horrifying. "If they need a toothbrush, you give it to them. If they need toilet paper, you give it to them," he said. "If they're hanging, you cut them down." The article was surprisingly vague, making no specific allegations of abuse, no accusations of torture. But the headline alone was enough: "Ex-Guardsman Denounces Gitmo." By denouncing Guantanamo, Chris was denouncing the unit's entire deployment, their sacrifices, and everything they had fought for. When Chris said he was anti-Guantanamo, everyone understood that he was accusing the soldiers of torture. He told the reporter that the IVAW is "not anti-troops, we are the troops and we're doing this for our brothers and sisters." The guys in his unit thought differently.

It was drill weekend when the article hit the stands, and one of the soldiers in the 119th battalion brought a copy to the armory, where it got passed around. Soldiers who had served with Chris were shocked that the local paper had printed the story. Some of them had seen the YouTube video of Chris testifying, and a few had even heard about the *Esquire* piece, but this was different. This was the newspaper that their families, friends, colleagues, and parishioners read. To say they were mad was an understatement. "It caused an uproar," says Shawn McBride, who oversaw a team of guards while serving at Guantanamo with Chris. He reminds me that since he is still on active duty, he has to watch what he says and does publicly. He tells me that he would never hunt down Chris personally, "but there are over two hundred people here who went down there with him and know where he is from."

"More than anything, we just felt betrayed by Chris," says Mike Ross, who was a sergeant first class in Chris's unit at Guantanamo. "To think that someone would sensationalize things they never saw and by default make his own unit, a proud unit, look like we were some kind of degenerates. He was selling us out and selling out his entire country." At the urging of a group of soldiers who felt the same way, Mike wrote a letter that was published in the *Lansing State Journal*, calling Chris's comments misleading and insulting.

Chris's former roommate at Guantanamo told his friends that Chris was lying about the suicide attempt. He and Chris had worked opposite shifts and fought bitterly. But still, he says, if Chris was so depressed as to be suicidal, he'd have known. Chris was just playing the sympathy card.

In response to the article, readers, including soldiers from his unit, posted comments on the paper's Web site calling for Chris's prosecution or at least a dishonorable discharge. They called him a "whiny, liberal wussy," a paid Obama supporter, and a poor soldier.

As with so many who retaliate against antiwar soldiers, they tried to discredit Chris. They had ample fodder: the reporter had inaccurately reported that Chris had guarded Moazzam, when in fact they had only been there at the same time, something Chris had always been clear about. Moreover, they pointed out, as is true, that Chris had only worked on the blocks a short while.

Even though it is easy to confirm Chris's story—he has his official paperwork, after all, and much of what he testifies about is heavily documented by the Defense Department—the reporter was scared that what he had written was wrong. When he called, the National Guard office refused to comment. When I followed up for months afterward, I was met with the same silence.

I meet up with Mike during his downtime between contract jobs building trenches, which are less frequent due to the recession. Mike is a dedicated soldier who has served more than twenty years in the Army. "I went in just to do it," he says of joining the military, "and I stayed because I liked it." He takes pride in his job, in his unit, and in his country. He runs the flag up outside his house every morning. At Guantanamo, he had been offered a job doing mechanical work, but he opted to stay on the blocks guarding detainees.

Mike has no problems with techniques such as sleep deprivation, stress positions, or indefinite detention, so he balks at the accusation of torture. To Mike, what they did at Guantanamo was not wrong. "Forty thousand red-blooded Americans—good soldiers, good, patriotic, even-minded, middle-class Americans have gone through there," he points out. "I don't believe that if something wrong was going on, they all would have turned a blind eye." He points out that the treatment couldn't be wrong if the Red Cross was there, brushing aside its report calling the detainee treatment "tantamount to torture." By the time the unit had arrived at the prison, it was being run like a tight ship. Everything from IRFs to solitary confinement was clearly delineated in the Standard Operating Procedures manual, with the blessings of those highest up in the DOD. The legal and moral lines were laid out for the soldiers in print. Now, after the fact, people were redrawing those lines.

Even an anonymous supporter, who considered himself Chris's friend, disagreed with his legal and moral assessment. He applauded Chris for speaking his mind and also questioned indeterminate detention but maintained that he "did not witness or take part in anything that violated my own morals. Chris simply has a different set of morals than me."

Mike worries that I am going to paint him as some kind of "warmonger." He had tried to do small things to help out the detainees—give them back their comfort items whenever possible, make sure the cuffs weren't on too tight. Chris didn't realize that even soldiers who acted like hardasses around one another could be just as sympathetic as he was.

Mike tells me that it was a cake deployment. If anything, it was just boring and tedious. The worst part of the IRF attacks, he says, was all of the paperwork involved. The soldiers would rather have been in on the action in Iraq, but regardless of what was asked of them, they did their job, and did it with pride.

People Mike works with asked him what was up with the article, whether that stuff was true. These were questions that he had heard before, when allegations about Guantanamo had first arisen. "It is disheartening to think American people would think bad of a soldier who is willing to pack up and go halfway across the world," says Mike. They had made sacrifices for their country, done what had been asked of them, shown honor and restraint. When cocktails of feces and urine were thrown at guards, "we just wiped it off, wrote it down, and accepted it as part of the job," he tells me. "Does that sound like the work of torturers?" Now some skinny-assed punk kid was running around telling everyone that they were no better than the guys at Abu Ghraib. Mike feels just as forsaken and betrayed by his country, not because of what was asked of him, but because his country was now turning its back on him and labeling him a torturer.

While at Guantanamo, Mike says, he and others had felt bad for Chris because he was obviously having such a hard time. They tried to defend him from the other MPs, who liked to push him around. Even if Chris was a poor soldier, he was one of them. "Honestly," says Mike, "I'm sorry that I was ever nice to him."

According to Mike, what Chris was doing was treasonous. Not only was he sharing classified information, but he was also touring with alleged terrorists, our enemies, with whom we were still at war—the equivalent in Mike's mind of doing a book tour with Charles Manson. "If he had disagreed with what was happening, why didn't he say something then instead of years later on an anti-American propaganda tour?" asks Mike. Besides, he says, as a soldier it's not your job to question orders but only to carry them out.

"It is not the business of specialist so-and-so, in some obscure battery in the National Guard, to straighten the world out," explains Mike. "He might really think it was wrong, but a lot of people think it is wrong and that we shouldn't even be detaining them. But we are, and those decisions are well above you. They are decisions for the president, the Congress, and the DOD."

According to Mike, if Chris were to try to come back to Lansing or any other "God-fearing part of the country," he'd be hard up to find a job, friends, or a wife. Mike certainly wouldn't hire the guy who had "toured with al Qaeda." Chris could have had a great life living in Lansing, he says, what with his military experience, "but he has put a black mark against himself forever."

Chris's grandma, Nedra, also worried about the repercussions and what people would think. Kari, so proud and excited about Chris's IVAW work and his trip to the UK, had helped set up the newspaper interview, assuming that readers would be as supportive of her son as she was. Nedra thought it was a mistake. People wouldn't like what he is doing, and it could simply backfire and cause him problems. When Nedra first saw the article, the only thing she said to Kari was that she hoped none of her friends would get mad at her. To Nedra's amazement, few people did. She is disappointed that her minister, who is highly involved in his parishioners' lives, merely sloughed it off when she told

him about Chris's testifying. At church, she overheard a woman
whose son had also served at Guantanamo say that the detainees
deserved the treatment they got: they were terrorists who threw
feces at guards. "But if you throw people in a cage, how do you
think they will respond?" asks Nedra during our conversation.
Out of her close circle of friends, only one person objected. "But
maybe," Nedra concedes, "they just don't say their criticisms
to me."

As with Kari, the video of Chris at the Winter Soldier event
was the first time Nedra had heard anything negative about
Guantanamo. "It was amazing to me," she says. "We had no idea
that was happening. We were supposed to be so wonderful, and
here we were treating people that way."

However, she doesn't share any of these criticisms about the
detainee abuse with Kari, Chris, or any of the family. She also has
a way of filtering Chris's message and hears only what she wants
from his testimonies. She didn't like Chris's comment in the article that he thought Guantanamo was a waste of time. She thought
the reporter had mischaracterized Chris when he described him
as anti-Guantanamo, even though Chris so clearly is.

Chris's stepdad, Tim, who is a friend of some of the people
in Chris's unit, tried to avoid the topic of the article and Chris's
antiwar work altogether. After I made five phone calls to him,
it was only at his daughter Jessica's urging that he would finally
speak to me. He said curtly, "Chris knows what I think of all that.
I don't need you writing down anything I have to say." When I ask
Jessica, who of all the family members knows Tim the best,
what Tim meant by that, she says she assumes that he thinks
that what Chris is doing is wrong. Once again, Chris is being a
wimp. The biggest thing for Tim, she guesses, is the embarrass-
ment he'll feel in front of his friends. But she's not sure whether
Chris knows how his stepdad feels. Perhaps she merely hopes that
Chris doesn't.

It's hard for Chris's family to see all of the hateful online comments. When Kari first offered to call news outlets to garner press

for Chris, he had been excited. But after the *Lansing State Journal* article came out, he told her to stop calling the local stations. He had promised that he would never get the soldiers from his unit involved in all of this. Even if people in places like Lansing are the ones who needed to hear the message the most, Chris just told his mom that they didn't get it and never would. It simply wasn't worth it.

In a blog entry that Chris wrote before leaving for the UK, he swore to be completely honest. "I am going there as a messenger of change, but to do that I will have to be honest. And there are some things that it is easier to idealize than to tell the truth about. I have done some things and thought in certain ways that do make me guilty of being what they hope I am not." He had been playing the role of the whistleblower, but he had to own up to his role as a torturer. And on the blog, for the first time he publicly shared the story of smashing the detainee's head into the pole. "I am not going there an innocent man," he wrote. "War turned us all into cowards and hypocrites, and none of us have much room to stand morally. I am going there as a bearer of honesty. So that they can see my face and know that even this is corruptible. And I hope they understand. If they don't, I will not know what to do with myself."

A few weeks later in London, in front of a large crowd, including former detainees, Chris told the full story. He described the pole incident, he explained how at times he had left detainees in interrogation rooms for longer than he needed to and admitted that he didn't report any of the abuse. During downtimes in the car, while driving from one speaking engagement to the next, Chris owned up to Moazzam and the other detainees about his own guilt and complicity. Moazzam, who has been testifying about the torture at the prison, is understandably extremely damning, but toward lower-level guards like Chris who are trying to make amends he is shockingly forgiving. He advocates truth as the only path to reconciliation and is grateful to the soldiers who are willing to help shed light on what happened. Yet when he saw how difficult it was for Chris to admit to what he himself had done, he told Chris that for his own self-preservation, it was better to stick to generalities in public.

It would be understandable if out of all the audiences, Chris would want to sugarcoat his story the most to the victims themselves. But in an odd way, speaking with the detainees, much like speaking with IVAW members, was freeing for Chris, because they were also among the few people who truly understood the horrors. Even if they were on opposite sides of the wire, there is a strangely intimate relationship between the two groups. As Moazzam explains, an odd bond is built between guards and detainees through the one-on-one interactions, especially in the privacy of solitary confinement. Moazzam understood that the soldiers, particularly the younger members of the National Guard, were there against their will. When they told him that they also felt imprisoned by Guantanamo, Moazzam pitied them.

Chris oscillates between wanting to be as politically active and outspoken as possible and despondently wishing he could push it all behind him. At times Chris e-mails his mom saying that he is so glad when certain speaking engagements are over and explains that he needs to lie low and recuperate. Yet then the next e-mail she receives is full of Chris's enthusiasm about plans for a whole slew of protests and lectures that he has set up. On the tour to the UK in January 2009, Chris wrote, "I am very tired and I know that this trip will be really difficult. I am looking forward very much to coming home. This place is nice, [but] it is too hard to tell this story over and over again. I am already sick of my own voice. But people want to know these things and I feel like I have a responsibility to tell them."

Conclusion: A Nation That Tortures

None of us likes to think that we could ever be capable of the acts that occurred in these prisons—and perhaps many of us would not do what those soldiers did. The men who were capable of abusing the prisoners, whether at Abu Ghraib, Guantanamo, or small forward operating bases, whose names most Americans have never even heard of, were not evil rogue soldiers or bad apples. But neither were they heroes: many set out with the highest of ideals but were robbed of those. They were merely average Americans, regular people—often just teenagers—who were being used by the government like any tool of war, whether it be guns, tanks, or handcuffs.

The war waged within the detention centers and the damage it does to both soldiers and detainees is far subtler than what happens in combat. When compared to soldiers who have had their faces melted and limbs blown off by IEDs, it is difficult to see the soldiers who worked in prisons as true victims of war. Yet these soldiers have injuries that may be just as permanent. Likewise, horrendous death tolls have robbed us of sons, daughters, husbands, and wives, but all Americans also suffer a different kind of loss—that of our moral standing and our innocence.

This book is not only about the journeys of soldiers who were assigned the task of carrying out our nation's torture policy, it is about the journey of America as a whole. Just as these soldiers struggle with the question of what kind of monsters they have become, we have to collectively ask ourselves: What kind of country have we become?

We entered this war in a fury of patriotism, vowing not only to protect citizens' lives but to defend the freedoms that the United States stands for. In fighting this war, we have betrayed those ideals. America likes to think of itself as a moral leader, but with our torture program, we have reached new depths in our violations of human rights. Perhaps it's because we envision ourselves as the beacon of freedom that we are blind to the level to which we have fallen.

The soldiers are not the only victims here—nor are the thousands of innocent men who were accidentally detained. Americans have all been betrayed, and we should all be angry.

Veterans in Cumberland described a lost generation of soldiers who had a black mark against them for working at Abu Ghraib; they didn't realize that this applies to a generation of Americans at large. Most of us may be many steps removed from what happened in those prisons, but we all suffer the repercussions. America is adrift, stuck in a moral limbo.

This is a story of homecomings. But in many ways, these soldiers have never truly been able to come home, because the country that they left is not the same as the one that they returned to.

Even people who have no problems with the use of torture—whether civilians or soldiers—are still affected. As Brandon Neely said, soldiers who are the most ardent supporters of U.S. military policy did and saw things that will damage them forever. Those who believe that the United States did what it had to do in response to the 9/11 attacks still have to come to terms with whether we as a country want to abandon the original tenets that made America great. What price are we willing to pay for domestic security?

When Chris Arendt's mother heard him testifying on television about the untold horrors of Guantanamo, even she did not want to believe it. It wasn't so much that she doubted her son, but that she trusted her country. As she put it, she was all about the red, white, and blue, but she had to come to grips with the fact that the flag no longer represented what she thought it had. There is a desperate need for most of us to hold on to the myth of America. Soldiers have been robbed of that luxury, and before long, the rest of us will be left empty-handed and disillusioned as well.

It's not the soldiers in this book whom we should be angry with, but the people at the highest levels who engineered the torture program in the first place. The ones who really should be held accountable for leading our country this far astray are people such as then vice president Dick Cheney, who laid the groundwork; former secretary of defense Donald Rumsfeld, who authorized the techniques; and lawyer John Yoo, who concocted legal loopholes to condone the abuse.

People without a direct connection to torture, who have never held a detainee by a leash, have a much easier time justifying it. This is a new kind of war, they argue, against a new kind of enemy. If the terrorists are willing to commit war crimes, we should do the same. Lawyers, academics, and politicians get caught up in the thorny debate of the efficacy of torture techniques. They point to the hypothetical ticking-time-bomb theory. War is war, and in the larger scheme of things, of what importance is one individual being nearly drowned compared to the bombing of villages? It is shocking to hear Americans even debating the issue of whether to institute an official torture regime.

The arguments in favor of the United States' use of torture aren't limited to the bar stools of Appalachia or the barracks in Iraq. They are happening in the classrooms of Ivy League universities and among politicians and talking heads on the nightly news. Using vague rhetoric such as *environmental manipulation, stress positions*, and even *waterboarding*, the discussions hardly conjure up the realities of what was happening in prison. But by making torture, or "harsh interrogations," officially sanctioned programs, the Bush administration has hidden the truth in plain sight.

For many of the soldiers who did the actual softening up of the prisoners and who lived with the prisoners who had been tortured, efficacy is a moot point. The soldiers who were directly involved in carrying out these seemingly innocuous tasks, such as keeping men awake, hooded, or naked, eventually realized that they were part of a larger torture regime. What value is there in fighting for your country if the way in which you fight means losing yourself and that which you are trying to defend? When this reality hit the soldiers, it was a tough blow. Likewise, when the country as a whole recognizes the reality of the direction our leaders have steered us in, we will face a rude awakening. If we truly want to support the U.S. troops, we need to back them in placing that burden where it really should lie.

Sergeant Andrew Duffy attached a yellow-ribbon decal with the words "Support the Truth" to his car. It was a simple gesture that spoke volumes. While many Americans continue to deny soldiers' stories, men such as Andy are left to feel the guilt, simmer in rage, and live in hell. Their country asked them to commit war crimes yet now refuses to acknowledge their complaints. These soldiers have seen firsthand that yes, America is a country that tortures, a country that has instituted war crimes as its official policy. Now it is our turn to admit these truths.

Unfortunately, as a country we are only now coming to terms with what happened in these prisons, and the likelihood of the true culprits ever being held accountable seems eons away.

There are many things that the soldiers can teach us—not only about what happened in the prisons, but about how we as a country are supposed to move on. These soldiers are all in various stages of reconciliation: anger, shame, disbelief, and despair. Some are just now taking the first steps toward coming to terms with what they did. For many, there are things that they have not yet admitted and perhaps never will, even to themselves. But we should take a cue from the soldiers who are trying to make amends, whether by reaching out to former detainees or by attempting to hold their government accountable.

As a country, we are at a crossroads. Do we want to follow suit and own up to what we have done, hold those directly at the helm accountable, and try to make amends? Or, like some of the soldiers, do we want to simply sit with our sense of betrayal, disillusionment, and anger at who we have become?

In May 2002, President Bush withdrew the country's signature from the treaty that binds it to the jurisdiction of the International Criminal Court, for fear that Americans could be held accountable for war crimes. In 2006, he amended the 1996 War Crimes Act, in hopes that he could retroactively protect policy makers from charges of war crimes. Arguments have been brought forth in Washington that the Obama administration should seek truth hearings instead of convictions, for fear that it could become a politically divisive issue, pitting one party against the other. But even if officials are able to protect themselves and their cronies from officially paying the price and from being hauled in front of the world to answer for their crimes, the United States will still pay a price. Just as the soldiers are unable to protect themselves from their self-recrimination and disillusionment, our country is not protected by these official safeguards. Our moral selves have been forever tarnished.

Speaking with these soldiers, at times I saw a far-off look in their eyes as their speech slowed down, and they were clearly back in those prisons, grappling with what they had done. But there were also moments when I forgot that they were soldiers capable of abuse—soldiers who were, in fact, torturers. I hoped that maybe they had moments, too, where they could forget. Unfortunately, it didn't seem that simple.

One night, Chris Arendt and his roommate, Danny, and I rode rickety bikes across Portland on our way to a bar. We were in search of a girl whom Chris had a crush on, as was often the case when hanging out with Chris. I had promised to play wingman in helping to reel her in, although it didn't seem like he would need much help. We had met the girl earlier that week at the independent press shop where Chris hung out. He had showed her the zine he was working on about his time at Guantanamo. In her fifties-style black-framed glasses and stylish vintage clothes, she was exactly the kind of girl whom Chris sought out, for acceptance, escape, and redemption. She told Chris how much she was impressed with his antiwar activism, and he was hooked. But later that night at the bar, she told me that if she were a business owner looking to hire someone, she would never hire a veteran. They would simply be too damaged to be trusted to hold down a job. Chris, in his Iraq Veterans Against the War T-shirt, must have looked like an intriguing anomaly, but it was clear that the real burdens of war and the world inside Guantanamo were nothing she wanted to shoulder. She didn't want to hear his stories about Guantanamo, nor about his guilt, shame, anger, and betrayal.

Chris seemed so happy that night—coyly flirtatious and somewhat shy, talking about bands and ordering beer. When he asked me whether I thought he had a good chance with the girl, I didn't have the heart to tell him that like so many others, she probably wouldn't be willing to really listen to his story for long. She knew on a theoretical level about what had happened at those prisons, but facing it head on, and dealing with the con-sequences, is something that no one wants to do.

Notes

It is astounding that there are still people who deny how widespread the use of ordered torture was in U.S. military prisons, given the reams of documentation. There are stacks of information, including memos from the CIA, the FBI, and the Department of Defense; military investigations and assessment reports; Standard Operating Procedure manuals; interrogation logs; sworn statements; leaked Red Cross reports; court depositions; and even press releases. In researching this book, I relied on such official documentation, as well as on the testimonies of scores of soldiers, to piece together the larger story. As I wrote this book, additional memos kept coming out, providing even more evidence to support stories that I was hearing from the soldiers themselves.

The soldiers included in this book represent a small sample of those who shared their stories. Although I wasn't able to include all of them in this book, each soldier's perspective helped not only substantiate the facts about what happened inside the prisons, but also proved that the experiences of the soldiers depicted here are by no means isolated examples.

Likewise, the detainees' testimonies offered an extra layer of corroboration of life inside the prison. Their accounts paralleled those of the soldiers, only from the exact opposite side of the fence. As prisoners have been released, we have heard their stories directly, but others' voices have been revealed through the testimonies collected by lawyers and human rights advocates, as well as in official military and FBI reports, including *Summaries of Evidence for Combatant Status Review Tribunal* by the Combatant Status Review Board and FBI interviews with detainees that the ACLU gained access to through FOIA requests. Particularly key testimonies for this book were those from Rhuhel Ahmed, Asif Iqbal, Shafiq Rasul, David Hicks, Jumah Mohammed Abdul Latif al Dossari, Isa Ali Abdulla al Murbati, Abdullah al Noaimi, Adel Kamel Abdulla Haji, and Moazzam Begg.

Because much of this book is an examination of how the torture debate evolved here at home, I looked at instances where these soldiers' stories appeared in the public sphere. The ways in which their personal sagas played out in the print media, on radio and television, and online not only dictated how we understand the narrative of U.S. policies of torture, but also directly affected the experiences of those soldiers and influenced how they made sense of what they had done. The publicity in Cumberland, Maryland, and the news of the Abu Ghraib scandal were especially integral to this reporting. Even those involved, from Joe Darby to the soldiers' families back home, learned about and experienced so much of the scandal through television. The media's scrutiny of the town and the soldiers exposed views and opinions that are usually left unspoken. Whenever the mainstream media revisited the topic, the experience was relived again. In some ways, the media became an additional character of this book. Following is a list of that media coverage.

Alderton, Jeff. "372nd MP Company Relocating." *Cumberland Times-News*, February 16, 2007.

———. "372nd MP Unit Staying in Cresaptown." *Cumberland Times-News*, January 11, 2008.

Arendt, Chris. "What It Feels Like . . . to Be a Prison Guard at Guantanamo Bay." *Esquire*, August 2008.

Cooper, Anderson. "Exposing the Truth." *60 Minutes*. December 10, 2006.

Edwards, Travis. "Military Police Company Returns Home." *DefendAmerica News*. Fort Lee Public Affairs Office, August 5, 2004.

Harper, Tim. "A Reversal of Soldiers' Fortunes." *Toronto Star*, May 20, 2004.

Hume, Brit. "Cheney on Guantanamo Detainees." Fox News, January 27, 2002.

Hylton, Wil S. "The Conscience of Joe Darby." *GQ*, August 2004.

———. "Prisoner of Conscience." *GQ*, September 2006.

Loew, Ryan. "Ex-Guardsman Denounces Gitmo." *Lansing State Journal*, January 11, 2009.

McCormick, Gavin. "Family: GI in Iraq Photos Followed Orders." Associated Press, May 8, 2004.

The Rachel Maddow Show. MSNBC. February 18, 2009.

Reed, Charlie. "Ex-Guard, Prisoner Speak Out against Gitmo." *Stars and Stripes*, February 9, 2009.

Rosin, Hanna. "When Joseph Comes Marching Home." *Washington Post*, May 17, 2004.

Rumsfeld, Donald. Testimony before the Senate and House Armed Services Committees. CNN, May 7, 2004.

Sabar, Ariel. "Accused of Abuse, Soldier Goes from Patriot to Pariah." *Baltimore Sun*, May 9, 2004.

Sawyer, Diane. "Specialist Joseph Darby Family of Prison Hero Inter-
  viewed." *Good Morning America*, August 16, 2004.
Shadrick, Tai. "60 Minutes Story on Whistleblower Triggers
  Backlash." *Cumberland Times-News*, December 16, 2006.
Vincent, Glyn. "In the Sand Box." *Paris Review*, Spring 2006.
Williamson, Elizabeth. "In W.Md., Resentment over Iraq
  Prison Scandal; Unit's Home Unfairly Tarnished, Some Say."
  Washington Post, May 9, 2004.
———. "Prisoner Abuse Scandal Brings 27 Seconds of Fame to
  Soldier's Relatives." *Washington Post*, May 9, 2004.

Other works referenced in this book include:

Arendt, Chris. Blog posts. WarriorWriters.org.
———. *Paper Birds: Styrofoam Flowers.* Self-published, November
  2008.
Basoglu, Metin, Maria Livanou, and Cvetana Crnobaric. "Torture
  vs. Other Cruel, Inhuman and Degrading Treatment." *Archives
  of General Psychiatry*, March 2007.
Begg, Moazzam. *Enemy Combatant: My Imprisonment at Guant-
  anamo, Bagram and Kandahar.* London: The Free Press, 2006.
Bianco, Anthony, Stephanie Anderson Forest, Stan Crock, and
  Thomas F. Armistead. "Outsourcing War." *BusinessWeek*,
  September 15, 2003.
Blass, Thomas. *The Man Who Shocked the World: The Life and
  Legacy of Stanley Milgram.* New York: Basic Books, 2004.
DeBatto, David. "Whitewashing Torture?" Salon.com, December 8,
  2004.
Falkoff, Marc, ed. *Poems from Guantanamo: The Detainees Speak.*
  Iowa City: University of Iowa Press, 2007.
Friedman, Matthew J. "Posttraumatic Stress Disorder among
  Military Returnees from Afghanistan and Iraq." *American
  Journal of Psychiatry*, April 2006.
Glaberson, William. "Guantanamo Prisoner Cuts His Throat
  with Fingernail." *New York Times*, December 5, 2007.

Haney, Craig, Curtis Banks, and Philip Zimbardo. "Interpersonal Dynamics in a Simulated Prison." *International Journal of Criminology and Penology* 1 (1973).

Hodge, Charles W., Jennifer Auchterlonie, and Charles Milliken. "Mental Health Problems, Use of Mental Health Services and Attrition from Military Service after Returning from Deployment to Iraq or Afghanistan." *Journal of the American Medical Association* 295, no. 9 (March 2006).

Johnson, David Read, Hadar Lubin, Robert Rosenheck, Alan Fontana, Steven Southwick, and Dennis Charney. "The Impact of the Homecoming Reception on the Development of Posttraumatic Stress Disorder: The West Haven Homecoming Stress Scale (WHHSS)." *Journal of Traumatic Stress* 10, no. 2 (April 1997).

Miles, Steven H. "Abu Ghraib: Its Legacy for Military Medicine." *Lancet* (August 21, 2004).

————. *Oath Betrayed: America's Torture Doctors.* Berkeley: University of California Press, 2009.

Milgram, Stanley. "Issues in the Study of Obedience: A Reply to Baumrind." *International Journal of Criminology and Penology* (1973): 69–97.

————. *Obedience to Authority, An Experimental View.* New York: Harper & Row, 1974.

Milliken, Charles S., Jennifer L. Auchterlonie, and Charles W. Hodge. "Longitudinal Assessment of Mental Health Problems among Active and Reserve Component Soldiers Returning from the Iraq War." *Journal of the American Medical Association* 298, no. 18 (November 14, 2007).

Ozbay, Faith, Douglas C. Johnson, Eleni Dimoulas, C. A. Morgan III, Dennis Charney, and Steven Southwick. "Social Support and Resilience to Stress: From Neurobiology to Clinical Practice." *Psychiatry* 4, no. 5 (2007): 35–40.

Phillips, Joshua E. S. "What Killed Sergeant Gray? Reporters Notebook." *American Radio Works*, October 2008.

Sontag, Deborah, and Lizette Alvarez. "War Torn." *New York Times*, January 2008.

Zarembo, Alan. "A Theater of Inquiry and Evil." *Los Angeles Times*, July 15, 2004.

Zimbardo, Philip. *The Lucifer Effect: Understanding How Good People Turn Evil.* New York: Random House, 2007.

Zimbardo, Philip G., Craig Haney, Curtis Banks, and David Jaffe. "A Pirandellian Prison: The Mind Is a Formidable Jailer." *New York Times Magazine*, April 8, 1973.

Index